CHELSEA HOUSE PUBLISHERS
Modern Critical Views

HENRY ADAMS
EDWARD ALBEE
A. R. AMMONS
MATTHEW ARNOLD
JOHN ASHBERY
W. H. AUDEN
JANE AUSTEN
JAMES BALDWIN
CHARLES BAUDELAIRE
SAMUEL BECKETT
SAUL BELLOW
THE BIBLE
ELIZABETH BISHOP
WILLIAM BLAKE
JORGE LUIS BORGES
ELIZABETH BOWEN
BERTOLT BRECHT
THE BRONTËS
ROBERT BROWNING
ANTHONY BURGESS
GEORGE GORDON, LORD BYRON
THOMAS CARLYLE
LEWIS CARROLL
WILLA CATHER
CERVANTES
GEOFFREY CHAUCER
KATE CHOPIN
SAMUEL TAYLOR COLERIDGE
JOSEPH CONRAD
CONTEMPORARY POETS
HART CRANE
STEPHEN CRANE
DANTE
CHARLES DICKENS
EMILY DICKINSON
JOHN DONNE & THE
   17th-CENTURY POETS
ELIZABETHAN DRAMATISTS
THEODORE DREISER
JOHN DRYDEN
GEORGE ELIOT
T. S. ELIOT
RALPH ELLISON
RALPH WALDO EMERSON
WILLIAM FAULKNER
HENRY FIELDING
F. SCOTT FITZGERALD
GUSTAVE FLAUBERT
E. M. FORSTER
SIGMUND FREUD
ROBERT FROST

ROBERT GRAVES
GRAHAM GREENE
THOMAS HARDY
NATHANIEL HAWTHORNE
WILLIAM HAZLITT
SEAMUS HEANEY
ERNEST HEMINGWAY
GEOFFREY HILL
FRIEDRICH HÖLDERLIN
HOMER
GERARD MANLEY HOPKINS
WILLIAM DEAN HOWELLS
ZORA NEALE HURSTON
HENRY JAMES
SAMUEL JOHNSON
BEN JONSON
JAMES JOYCE
FRANZ KAFKA
JOHN KEATS
RUDYARD KIPLING
D. H. LAWRENCE
JOHN LE CARRÉ
URSULA K. LE GUIN
DORIS LESSING
SINCLAIR LEWIS
ROBERT LOWELL
NORMAN MAILER
BERNARD MALAMUD
THOMAS MANN
CHRISTOPHER MARLOWE
CARSON MCCULLERS
HERMAN MELVILLE
JAMES MERRILL
ARTHUR MILLER
JOHN MILTON
EUGENIO MONTALE
MARIANNE MOORE
IRIS MURDOCH
VLADIMIR NABOKOV
JOYCE CAROL OATES
SEAN O'CASEY
FLANNERY O'CONNOR
EUGENE O'NEILL
GEORGE ORWELL
CYNTHIA OZICK
WALTER PATER
WALKER PERCY
HAROLD PINTER
PLATO
EDGAR ALLAN POE

POETS OF SENSIBILITY &
   THE SUBLIME
ALEXANDER POPE
KATHERINE ANNE PORTER
EZRA POUND
PRE-RAPHAELITE POETS
MARCEL PROUST
THOMAS PYNCHON
ARTHUR RIMBAUD
THEODORE ROETHKE
PHILIP ROTH
JOHN RUSKIN
J. D. SALINGER
GERSHOM SCHOLEM
WILLIAM SHAKESPEARE (3 vols.)
   HISTORIES & POEMS
   COMEDIES
   TRAGEDIES
GEORGE BERNARD SHAW
MARY WOLLSTONECRAFT SHELLEY
PERCY BYSSHE SHELLEY
EDMUND SPENSER
GERTRUDE STEIN
JOHN STEINBECK
LAURENCE STERNE
WALLACE STEVENS
TOM STOPPARD
JONATHAN SWIFT
ALFRED LORD TENNYSON
WILLIAM MAKEPEACE THACKERAY
HENRY DAVID THOREAU
LEO TOLSTOI
ANTHONY TROLLOPE
MARK TWAIN
JOHN UPDIKE
GORE VIDAL
VIRGIL
ROBERT PENN WARREN
EVELYN WAUGH
EUDORA WELTY
NATHANAEL WEST
EDITH WHARTON
WALT WHITMAN
OSCAR WILDE
TENNESSEE WILLIAMS
WILLIAM CARLOS WILLIAMS
THOMAS WOLFE
VIRGINIA WOOLF
WILLIAM WORDSWORTH
RICHARD WRIGHT
WILLIAM BUTLER YEATS

Further titles in preparation.

Modern Critical Views

A. R. AMMONS

Modern Critical Views

A. R. AMMONS

Edited with an introduction by

Harold Bloom

Sterling Professor of the Humanities
Yale University

1986
CHELSEA HOUSE PUBLISHERS
New York
New Haven   Philadelphia

THE COVER:

The poet Ammons is seen against the context of his great poem, *Corsons Inlet*, in a cosmos of sand dunes and ocean, thus renewing the Whitmanian genre of the Sea-Drift Vision, of the solitary self confronting the waste places at the water's edge.—H.B.

PROJECT EDITORS: Emily Bestler, James Uebbing
ASSOCIATE EDITOR: Maria Behan
EDITORIAL COORDINATOR: Karyn Gullen Browne
EDITORIAL STAFF: Laura Ludwig, Joy Johannessen, Linda Grossman, Peter Childers
DESIGN: Susan Lusk

Cover illustration by Jennifer Caldwell

Printed and bound in the United States of America

Library of Congress Cataloging in Publication Data

A. R. Ammons.
    (Modern critical views)
    Bibliography: p.
    Includes index.
    1. Ammons, A. R., 1926–   —Criticism and interpre-
tation—Addresses, essays, lectures.   I. Bloom, Harold.
II. Series.
PS3501.M6Z53   1986   811'.54   85–6673
ISBN 0–87754–620–7

Chelsea House Publishers
Harold Steinberg, Chairman and Publisher
Susan Lusk, Vice President
A Division of Chelsea House Educational Communications, Inc.
133 Christopher Street, New York, NY 10014

Contents

Editor's Note

This volume gathers together a representative selection of the best criticism that has been devoted to the poetry of A. R. Ammons during the last fifteen years. It begins with the editor's general survey of Ammons's work through 1970, and with Richard Howard's pioneering essay on the same body of poetry, first published in 1969, supplemented by some of Howard's later reviews of Ammons. These two essays map the fundamental contours of Ammons's cosmos, and chronicle his early transcendentalism and its crises. The review by John Ashbery, one of Ammons's most distinguished poetic contemporaries, helps to place the poet of saliences and peripheries in the American grain, a placement articulated in a wider perspective by the reflections of the scholar Hyatt H. Waggoner and by the reviews of Helen Vendler.

A fuller account of the relation between form and subjectivity in Ammons is provided by the essays of Patricia A. Parker, David Kalstone, Jerome Mazzaro and Linda Orr, all of which first appeared in an important but now hard to locate Ammons issue of the magazine *Diacritics*. The second essay by the editor, though by no means a palinode in regard to the first, attempts to correct widespread misapprehensions concerning his earlier overview of Ammons. It is followed by two illuminating reviews by the critics Denis Donoghue and R. W. Flint, and by the poet Robert Pinsky's analysis of the discursive element in Ammons's work, as well as the poet Frederick Buell's tribute to what is most subtle in his precursor's stance.

An interview with Ammons himself begins the final phase of this book, which goes on to a retrospective essay by Hugh Luke and a deeply informed review by the poet David Lehman. John Hollander's advanced reading of "I Went to the Summit," the Sublime dedicatory poem to *Sphere*, serves as the prelude to Helen Regueiro Elam's concluding essay, which sums up many of the insights achieved by the earlier criticism, while moving on to a fresh understanding of the intricate balancing of radiances and dark consolations in Ammons. At fifty-eight, Ammons is in his poetic prime, and no final estimates of his eminence are now possible. But, as this book demonstrates, Ammons is one of the legitimate heirs of the great American sequence that includes Emerson, Thoreau, Whitman, Dickinson, Frost, Stevens, Hart Crane, Theodore Roethke and Robert Penn Warren: the tradition of the American Sublime. The central place of Ammons in that vital line of seers and artists is beyond dispute.

Introduction

Nature centres into balls,
And her proud ephemerals,
Fast to surface and outside,
Scan the profile of the sphere;
Knew they what that signified,
A new genesis were here.
— EMERSON, *Circles*

In 1955, A. R. Ammons, in his thirtieth year, published his first book of poems, *Ommateum, with Doxology*. *Ommateum* consists of thirty Whitmanian chants, strongly influenced by the metric of Ezra Pound (though by nothing else in Pound). *Doxology* is an intricate religious hymn, in three parts, more ironic in tone than in direction. In the lengthening perspective of American poetry, the year 1955 will be remembered as the end of Wallace Stevens's career, and the beginning of Ammons's, himself not Stevens's heir but like Stevens a descendant of the great originals of American Romantic tradition, Emerson and Whitman. Beyond its experimentation with Poundian cadences, *Ommateum* shows no trace of the verse fashions of the fifties; I cannot detect in it the voice of William Carlos Williams, which indeed I do not hear anywhere in Ammons's work, despite the judgments of several reviewers. The line of descent from Emerson and Whitman to the early poetry of Ammons is direct, and even the Poundian elements in *Ommateum* derive from that part of Pound that is itself Whitmanian.

Ommateum's subject is poetic incarnation, in the mode of Whitman's *Sea-Drift* pieces, Emerson's *Seashore*, and Pound's *Canto II*. The Whitman of *As I Ebb'd with the Ocean of Life* is closest, suggesting that poetic disincarnation is Ammons's true subject, his vitalizing fear. In the "Foreword" to *Ommateum* he begins his list of themes with "the fear of the loss of identity." The first poem of the volume, the chosen beginning of this poet's outrageously and wonderfully prolific canon, is an assumption of another's identity. This other, "Ezra," is neither Pound nor the biblical scribe of the Return, but a suddenly remembered hunchback playmate from childhood, brought back to the poet's consciousness by a report of his death in war. The whole of Ammons is in this first poem, but half a lifetime's imaginings will be necessary to transfigure this shore-burst into the radiance already implicit here:

> So I said I am Ezra
> and the wind whipped my throat
> gaming for the sounds of my voice
>   I listened to the wind
> go over my head and up into the night
> Turning to the sea I said
>   I am Ezra
> but there were no echoes from the waves
> The words were swallowed up
>   in the voice of the surf
> or leaping over swells
> lost themselves oceanward
>   Over the bleached and broken fields
> I moved my feet and turning from the wind
>   that ripped sheets of sand
>   from the beach and threw them
>   like seamists across the dunes
> swayed as if the wind were taking me away
> and said
>   I am Ezra
> As a word too much repeated
> falls out of being
> so I Ezra went out into the night
> like a drift of sand
> and splashed among the windy oats
> that clutch the dunes
> of unremembered seas

As in the *Ode to the West Wind* and *As I Ebb'd with the Ocean of Life*, so here the poet's consciousness is assaulted by the elements he seeks to address, reproved by what he hopes to meet in a relationship that will make him or keep him a poet. The motto of Ammons's first poem might be Whitman's:

> Nature here in sight of the sea taking advantage of me to dart upon
>   me and sting me,
> Because I have dared to open my mouth to sing at all.

Later in *Ommateum*, Ammons echoes *As I Ebb'd* more directly, recalling its terrifying contraction of the self:

> Me and mine, loose windrows, little corpses,
> Froth, snowy white, and bubbles,
> (See, from my dead lips the ooze exuding at last,
> See, the prismatic colors glistening and rolling,)
> Tufts of straw, sands, fragments . . .

This becomes, in his ninth chant, Ammons's emblem of the last stage of "peeling off my being":

> but went on deeper
> till darkness snuffed the shafts of light
> against the well's side
> night kissing
> the last bubbles from my lips

The Emersonian ambition to be possessed fully by the Transcendental Self is Ammons's early theme as it was Whitman's, and is still pervasive in Ammons's latest lyrics, but turned now in a direction avoided by his precursors:

> When you consider the radiance, that it does not withhold
> itself but pours its abundance without selection into every
> nook and cranny not overhung or hidden; when you consider
>
> that birds' bones make no awful noise against the light but
> lie low in the light as in a high testimony; when you consider
> the radiance, that it will look into the guiltiest
>
> swervings of the weaving heart and bear itself upon them,
> not flinching into disguise or darkening; when you consider
> the abundance of such resource as illuminates the glow-blue
>
> bodies and gold-skeined wings of flies swarming the dumped
> guts of a natural slaughter or the coil of shit and in no
> way winces from its storms of generosity; when you consider
>
> that air or vacuum, snow or shale, squid or wolf, rose or lichen,
> each is accepted into as much light as it will take, then
> the heart moves roomier, the man stands and looks about, the
>
> leaf does not increase itself above the grass, and the dark
> work of the deepest cells is of a tune with May bushes
> and fear lit by the breadth of such calmly turns to praise.

This extraordinary poem, *The City Limits*, marks one of the limits of Ammons's art, and almost releases him from the burden of his main tradition. "The guiltiest swervings of the weaving heart," for a poet as poet, are those that swerve him away from his poetic fathers into an angle of fall that is also his angle of vision. For an Emersonian poet, an

American Romantic, the angle of vision becomes the whole of life, and measures him as man. Sherman Paul, acutely measuring Emerson's own angle, provides the necessary gloss for this Emersonian poem, *The City Limits*:

> The eye brought him two perceptions of nature—nature ensphered and nature atomized—which corresponded to the distant and proximate visual powers of the eye. These powers, in turn, he could have called the reasoning and understanding modes of the eye. And to each he could have assigned its appropriate field of performance: the country and the city.

We can surmise that the sorrow of all Emersonian poets, from Whitman to Ammons and beyond, comes from the great central declaration: "I become a transparent eyeball; I am nothing; I see all; the currents of the Universal Being circulate through me; I am part or particle of God." But if "Thought is nothing but the circulations made luminous," then what happens when the circulations are darkening? The currents of the Universal Being do not cease to circulate, ever, and the "mathematic ebb and flow" of Emerson's *Seashore* is no consolation to temperaments less rocky than Emerson's own (one thinks not only of Whitman, but of middle Stevens, and late Roethke). To a grim consciousness like Frost's in *Directive*, the wisdom of the Emerson of *The Conduct of Life* is acceptable, admirable, even inevitable, and this late Emersonian strain may never be so worked out in our poetry as to vanish. But Ammons has none of it, and the toughness of his own consolations and celebrations comes out of another tradition, one that I do not understand, for everything that is Southern in American culture is necessarily a darkness to me. Ammons is a poet of the Carolina as well as the Jersey shore, and his relation to Whitman is severely modified by rival spirits of place. The Ezra-poet is as obsessed with sandstorms as any Near Easterner; for him the wind makes sheets of sand into sea mists. In *The City Limits* the radiance, despite its generosity, cannot reach what is overhung or hidden, and what is wholly hidden cannot be accepted into the light it will not take. There is for Ammons a recalcitrance or unwilling dross in everything given, and this "loneliness" (to use one of his words for it) marks his verse from *Ommateum* on as more than a little distinct from its great precursors.

I am writing of Ammons as though he had rounded his first circle in the eye of his readers, and there is no other way to write about him, even if my essay actually introduces him to some of its readers. The fundamental postulates for reading Ammons have been set down well before me, by Richard Howard and Marius Bewley in particular, but every critic of a still emergent poet has his own obsessions to work through, and makes his own confession of the radiance. Ammons's poetry does for me what Stevens's did earlier, and the High Romantics before that: it helps me to live my life. If Ammons is, as I think, the central poet of my generation, because he alone has made a heterocosm, a second nature in his poetry, I deprecate no other poet by this naming. It is, surprisingly, a rich generation, with ten or a dozen poets who seem at least capable of making a major canon, granting fortune and persistence. Ammons, much more than the others, has made such a canon already. A solitary artist, nurtured by the strength available for him only in extreme isolation, carrying on the Emersonian tradition with a quietness directly contrary to nearly all its other current avatars, he has emerged in his most recent poems as an extraordinary master, comparable to the Stevens of *Ideas of Order* and *The Man With the Blue Guitar*. To track him persistently, from his origins in *Ommateum* through his maturing in *Corsons Inlet* and its companion volumes on to his new phase in *Uplands* and *Briefings* is to be found by not only a complete possibility of imaginative experience, but by a renewed sense of the whole line of Emerson, the vitalizing and much maligned tradition that has accounted for most that matters in American poetry.

Emerson, like Stevens and Ammons after him, had a fondness for talking mountains. One thinks of Wordsworth's old men, perhaps of the Virgilian Mount Atlas, of Blake's Los at the opening of Night V, *The Four Zoas*, of Shelley's Mont Blanc, which obstinately refuses however to take on human form, and affronts the humane revolutionary with its hard, its menacing otherness. Emerson's Monadnoc is genial and gnomic:

> "Monadnoc is a mountain strong,
> Tall and good my kind among;
> But well I know, no mountain can,
> Zion or Meru, measure with man.
> For it is on zodiacs writ,
> Adamant is soft to wit:
> And when the greater comes again
> With my secret in his brain,
> I shall pass, as glides my shadow
> Daily over hill and meadow.
>
> Anchored fast for many an age,
> I await the bard and sage,
> Who, in large thoughts, like fair pearl-seed,
> Shall string Monadnoc like a bead."

Emerson is not providing the golden string to be wound into a ball, but one of a series of golden entities to be beaded on a string. Monadnoc awaits the Central Man, the redemptive poet of *Bacchus*. Thoreau, in his fine poem on the mountains, characteristically avoids Emerson's humanizing of an otherness, and more forcefully mountainizes himself:

> But special I remember thee,
> Wachusett, who like me
> Standest alone without society.
> Thy far blue eye,
> A remnant of the sky,
> Seen through the clearing or the gorge,
> Or from the windows of the forge,
> Doth leaven all it passes by.
>
> Upholding heaven, holding down earth,
> Thy pastime from thy birth;
> Not steadied by the one, nor leaning on the other,
> May I approve myself thy worthy brother!

Wachusett is not to be strung like a bead, however strong the bard and sage. Thoreau is a more Wordsworthian poet than Emerson, and so meets a nature ruggedly recalcitrant to visionary transformations. Ammons, who has a relation to both, meets Emerson's kind of mountains, meets a nature that awaits its bard, even if sometimes in ambush. In *Ommateum*, there is not much transformation, and some ambuscade, and so the neglect encountered by the volume can be understood. Yet these chants, setting aside advantages in retrospect, are remarkable poems, alive at every point in movement and in vision. They live in their oddly negative exuberance, as the new poet goes out into his bleak lands as though he marched only into another man's phantasmagoria. One chant, beginning "In the wind my rescue is," to be found but mutilated in the *Selected Poems* (1968), states the poet's task as a gathering of the stones of earth into one place. The wind, by sowing a phantasmagoria in the poet's eyes, draws him "out beyond the land's end," thus saving him "from all those ungathered stones." The shore, Whitman's emblem for the state in which poets are made and unmade, becomes the theater for the first phase of Ammons's poetic maturity, the lyrics written in the decade after *Ommateum*. These are gathered in three volumes: *Expressions of Sea Level* (1964), *Corsons Inlet* (1965), and *Northfield Poems* (1966), which need to be read as a unit, since the inclusion of a poem in one or another volume seems to be a matter of whim. A reader of Ammons is likeliest to be able to read this phase of him in the *Selected Poems*, whose arrangement in chronological order of composition shows how chronologically scrambled the three volumes are.

Ammons's second start as a poet, after the transcendental waste places of *Ommateum*, in in this *Hymn*:

I know if I find you I will have to leave the earth
and go on out
    over the sea marshes and the brant in bays
and over the hills of tall hickory
and over the crater lakes and canyons
and on up through the spheres of diminishing air
past the blackset noctilucent clouds
        where one wants to stop and look
way past all the light diffusions and bombardments
up farther than the loss of sight
        into the unseasonal undifferentiated empty stark

And I know if I find you I will have to stay with the earth
inspecting with thin tools and ground eyes
trusting the microvilli sporangia and simplest
        coelenterates
and praying for a nerve cell
with all the soul of my chemical reactions
and going right on down where the eye sees only traces

You are everywhere partial and entire
You are on the inside of everything and on the outside

I walk down the path down the hill where the sweetgum
has begun to ooze spring sap at the cut
and I see how the bark cracks and winds like no other bark
chasmal to my ant-soul running up and down
and if I find you I must go out deep into your
    far resolutions
and if I find you I must stay here with the separate leaves

The chants of *Ommateum* were composed mostly in a single year, from the Spring of 1951 to the Spring of 1952. In 1956, Ammons fully claims his Transcendental heritage in his *Hymn*, a work of poetic annunciation in which the "you" is Emerson's "Nature," all that is separate from "the Soul." The *Hymn*'s difficult strength depends on a reader's recognition that the found "you" is: "the NOT ME, that is, both nature and art, all other men and my own body." Juxtapose a crucial passage of Emerson, and the *clinamen* that governs the course of Ammons's maturity is determined:

The world proceeds from the same spirit as the body of man. It is a remoter and inferior incarnation of God, a projection of God in the unconscious. But it differs from the body in one important respect. It is not, like that, now subjected to the human will. Its serene order is inviolable by us. It is, therefore, to us, the present expositor of the divine mind. It is a fixed point whereby we may measure our departure.

Emerson's fixed point oscillates dialectically in Ammons's *Hymn*. Where Emerson's mode hovers always around metonymy, parts of a world taken as the whole, Ammons's sense of the universe takes it for a symptom. No American poet, not Whitman or Stevens, shows us so fully something otherwise unknown in the structures of the national consciousness as Ammons does. It cannot be said so far that Ammons has developed as fluent and individual a version of the language of the self as they did, but he has time and persistence enough before he borrows his last authority from death. His first authority is the height touched in this *Hymn*, where everything depends upon a precision of consequences "if I find you." "The unassimilable fact leads us on," a later poem begins, the leading on being Ammons's notion of quest. If all that is separate from him, the "you," is found, the finding will be assimilated at the final cost of going on out "into the unseasonal undifferentiated empty stark," a resolution so far as to annihilate selfhood. One part of the self will be yielded to an apprehension beyond sight, while the other will stay here with the earth, to be yielded to sight's reductiveness, separated with each leaf.

This is the enterprise of a consciousness extreme enough to begin another central poem, *Gravelly Run*, with a quietly terrifying sense of what will suffice:

> I don't know somehow it seems sufficient
> to see and hear whatever coming and going is,
> losing the self to the victory
>   of stones and trees,
> of bending and sandpit lakes, crescent
> round groves of dwarf pine:
>
> for it is not so much to know the self
> as to know it as it is known
>   by galaxy and cedar cone . . .

But as it is known, it is only a "surrendered self among / unwelcoming forms." The true analogue to this surrender is in the curious implicit threat of Emerson's Orphic poet:

> We distrust and deny inwardly our sympathy with nature. We own and disown our relation to it, by turns. We are like Nebuchadnezzer, dethroned, bereft of reason, and eating grass like an ox. But who can set limits to the remedial force of spirit?

The remedial force of spirit, in this sense, is closest to being that terriblest force in the world, of which Stevens's Back-ache complains. Ammons, who knows he cannot set limits to such force, warns himself perpetually "to turn back," before he comes to a unity apparently equal to his whole desire. For his desire is only a metonymy, and unity (if found) compels another self-defeating question:

> You cannot come to unity and remain material:
> in that perception is no perceiver:
>   when you arrive
> you have gone too far:
>   at the Source you are in the mouth of Death:
>
> you cannot
>   turn around in
> the Absolute: there are no entrances or exits
>   no precipitations of forms
> to use like tongs against the formless:
>   no freedom to choose:
>
> to be
>
>   you have to stop not-being and break
> off from *is* to *flowing* and
>   this is the sin you weep and praise:
> origin is your original sin:
>   the return you long for will ease your guilt
> and you will have your longing:
>
>   the wind that is my guide said this: it
> should know having
>   given up everything to eternal being but
> direction:
>
> how I said can I be glad and sad: but a man goes
>   from one foot to the other:
> wisdom wisdom:
>   to be glad and sad at once is also unity
> and death:
>   wisdom wisdom: a peachblossom blooms on a particular
> tree on a particular day:
>   unity cannot do anything in particular:
>
> are these the thoughts you want me to think I said but
>   the wind was gone and there was no more knowledge then.

The wind's origin is its original sin also; were it to give up even direction, it would cease to be *Guide*, as this poem is entitled. If the wind is Ammons's Virgil, an Interior Paramour or Whitmanian Fancy remains his Beatrice, guiding him whenever wind ceases to lead. The poetic strength of *Guide* is in its dialectical renunciation of even this daimonic paramour. For the wind speaks against what is deepest and most self-destructive in Ammons. "Break off from *is* to *flowing*" is a classic phrasing of the terrible dream that incessantly afflicts most of our central poetic imaginations in America. "Unity cannot do anything in particular"; least of all can it write a poem.

The wind, Ammons's way to knowledge, is certainly the most active wind in American poetry. In *Ommateum*, the wind is a desperate whip, doubting its own efficacy in a dry land. It moves "like wisdom," but its poet is not so sure of the likeness. In the mature volumes, it is more a blade than a whip, and its desperation has rendered it apologetic:

> Having split up the chaparral
> blasting my sight
> the wind said
>   You know I'm
>   the result of
> forces beyond my control
> I don't hold it against you
> I said
> It's all right I understand

For the wind "dies and never dies," but the poet goes on:

> consigned to
> form that will not
> let me loose
> except to death
> till some
> syllable's rain
> anoints my tongue
> and makes it sing
> to strangers:

To be released from form into unity one dies or writes a poem; this appalling motive for metaphor is as desperate as any wind. Wind, which is "not air or motion/but the motion of air," speaks to a consciousness that is not spirit or making, but the spirit of making, the Ezra-incarnation in this poet:

> I coughed
>   and the wind said
> Ezra will live
> to see your last
>   sun come up again

I turned (as I will) to weeds and
the wind went off
    carving
monuments through a field of stone
    monuments whose shape
wind cannot arrest but
taking hold on
changes

While Ezra
    listens from terraces of mind
wind cannot reach or
weedroots of my low-feeding shiver

When the poet falls (as he must) from this Ezra-eminence, the
terraces of mind dissolve:

The mind whirls, short of the unifying
reach, short of the heat
    to carry that forging:
    after the visions of these losses, the spent
seer, delivered to wastage, risen
    into ribs, consigns knowledge to
    approximation, order to the vehicle
of change . . .

He is never so spent a seer as he says, even if the price of his ascensions
keeps rising. If from moment to moment the mode of motion is loss, there
is always the privileged *Moment* itself:

He turned and
stood

in the moment's
height,

exhilaration
sucking him up,

shuddering and
lifting

him
jaw and bone

and he said
what

destruction am I
blessed by?

The burden of Ammons's poetry is to answer, to name that enlargement of life that is also a destruction. When the naming came most
complete, in the late summer of 1962, it gave Ammons his two most
ambitious single poems, *Corsons Inlet* and *Saliences*. Though both poems
depend upon the context of Ammons's canon, they show the field of his
enterprise more fully and freely than could have been expected of any
single works. *Corsons Inlet* is likely to be Ammons's most famous poem,
his *Sunday Morning*, a successfully universalizing expression of a personal
thematic conflict and its apparent (or provisional) resolution. But *Saliences*, a harder, less open, more abstract fury of averted destructions, is
the better poem. *Corsons Inlet* comforts itself (and us) with the perpetually
renewed hope of a fresh walk over the dunes to the sea. *Saliences* rises past
hope to what in the mind is "beyond loss or gain/beyond concern for the
separate reach." Both the hope and the ascension beyond hope return us
to origins, and can be apprehended with keener aptitude after an excursus
taking us deeper into Ammons's tradition. Ammons compels that backward vision of our poetry that only major achievement exacts, and illuminates Emerson and all his progeny as much as he needs them for illumination.
Reading Ammons, I brood on all American poetry in the Romantic
tradition, which means I yield to Emerson, who is to our modern poetry
what Wordsworth has been to all British poetry after him; the starting-
point, the defining element, the vexatious father, the shadow and the
despair, liberating angel and blocking-agent, perpetual irritant and solac-
ing glory.

John Jay Chapman, in what is still the best introductory essay on
Emerson, condensed his estimate of the seer into a great and famous
sentence: "If a soul be taken and crushed by democracy till it utter a cry,
that cry will be Emerson." In the year 1846, when he beheld "the famous
States/Harrying Mexico/With rifle and with knife!", Emerson raised the
cry of himself most intensely and permanently:

> Though loath to grieve
> The evil time's sole patriot,
> I cannot leave
> My honied thought
> For the priest's cant,
> or statesman's rant.
>
> If I refuse
> My study for their politique,
> which at the best is trick,
> The angry Muse
> Puts confusion in my brain.

The astonished Muse found Emerson at her side all through 1846, the year not only of the Channing *Ode*, but of *Bacchus* and *Merlin*, his finest and most representative poems, that between them establish a dialectic central to subsequent American poetry. In *Bacchus*, the poet is not his own master, but yields to daimonic possession. In *Merlin*, the daimonic itself is mastered, as the poet becomes first the Bard, and then Nemesis:

> Who with even matches odd,
> Who athwart space redresses
> The partial wrong,
> Fills the just period,
> And finishes the song.

The poet of *Bacchus* is genuinely possessed, and yet falls (savingly) victim to Ananke—he is still *human*. The poet of *Merlin* is himself absorbed into Ananke and ceases to be human, leaving *Bacchus* much the better poem. To venture a desolate formula about American poetry: our greater poets attain the splendor of Bacchus, and then attempt to become Merlin, and so cease to be wholly human and begin to fail as poets. Emerson and his descendants dwindle, not when they build altars to the Beautiful Necessity, but when they richly confuse themselves with that Necessity. Poetry, Emerson splendidly observed, must be as new as foam and as old as the rock; he might also have observed that it had better not itself try to be foam or rock.

A strain in Ammons, ecological and almost geological, impels him towards identification with the American version of Ananke, and is his largest flaw as a poet. Robert Bly brilliantly parodied this strain by printing a passage from *The Mushroom Hunter's Field Guide* under the title, *A.R. Ammons Discusses The Lacaria Trullisata*:

> The somewhat distant,
> broad, purplish
> to violaceous gills,
> white spore
>
> Deposit, and
> habitat
> on sand distingu-
> ish it. No
> part of the fruit-
>
> Ing body is ever
> glutinous.
> *Edibility*. The question
> is academic: It is

> Impossible to get
> rid of
> all the sand.

And so on. The Ammonsian literalness, allied to a similar destructive impulse in Wordsworth and Thoreau, attempts to summon outward continuities to shield the poet from his mind's own force. *A Poem Is A Walk* is the title of a dark, short prose piece by Ammons that tries "to establish a reasonably secure identity between a poem and a walk and to ask how a walk occurs, what it is, and what it is for," but establishes only that a walk by Ammons is a sublime kind of Pythagorean enterprise or Behmenite picnic. Emerson, who spoke as much wisdom as any American, alas spoke darkly also, and Ammons is infuriatingly Emersonian when he tells us a poem "is a motion to no-motion, to the still point of contemplation and deep realization. Its knowledges are all negative and, therefore, more positive than any knowledge." *Corsons Inlet, Saliences,* and nearly a hundred other poems by Ammons are nothing of the kind, his imagination be thanked, rather than his spooky, pure-product-of-America mysticism. Unlike Emerson, who crossed triumphantly into prose, Ammons belongs to that company of poets that *thinks* most powerfully and naturally in verse, and sometimes descends to obscure quietudes when verse subsides.

Corsons Inlet first verges on, and then veers magnificently away from worshipping the Beautiful Necessity, from celebrating the way things are. "Life will be imaged, but cannot be divided nor doubled," might be the poem's motto; so might: "Ask the fact for the form," both maxims being Emerson's. Ammons's long poem, *Tape for the Turn of the Year,* contains the self-admonishment: "get out of boxes, hard/forms of mind:/go deep:/penetrate/to the true spring," which is the initial impulse of *Corsons Inlet.* The poet, having walked in the morning over the dunes to the sea, recollects later in the day the release granted him by the walk, from thought to sight, from conceptual forms to the flowings and blendings of the Coleridgean Secondary Imagination. Released into the composition of *Corsons Inlet,* he addresses his reader directly (consciously in Whitman's mode) to state both the nature of his whole body of poetry, and his sense of its largest limitation:

> I allow myself eddies of meaning:
> yeild to a direction of significance
> running
> like a stream through the geography of my work:
>   you can find
> in my sayings

> swerves of action
> like the inlet's cutting edge:
>
> there are dunes of motion,
> organizations of grass, white sandy paths of remembrance
> in the overall wandering of mirroring mind:
>
> but Overall is beyond me: is the sum of these events
> I cannot draw, the ledger I cannot keep, the accounting
> beyond the account:

Within this spaced restraint, there is immense anguish, and the anguish is not just metaphysical. Though this anguish be an acquired wisdom, such wisdom proffers no consolation for the loss of quest. The anguish that goes through *Corsons Inlet*, subdued but ever salient, is more akin to a quality of mind in Thoreau than to anything in Emerson or Whitman. What Transcendentalists wanted of natural history is generally a darkness to me, and I resort to the late Perry Miller for some light on "the Transcendental methodology for coping with the multifarious concreteness of nature. That method is to see the particular as a particular, and yet at the same time so to perceive it as to make it, of itself, yield up the general and the universal." But that is too broad, being a Romantic procedure in general, with neither the American impatience nor the American obsession of particularity clearly distinguished from Wordsworthianism. Wordsworth was wonderfully patient with preparations for vision, and was more than content to see the particulars flow together and fade out in the great moments of vision. Emerson scanted preparations, and held on to the particulars even in ecstasy. In Thoreau, whatever his final differences with his master, the Emersonian precipitateness and clarity of the privileged moment are sharpened. When I read in his *Journals*, I drown in particulars and cannot find the moments of release, but *The Natural History of Massachusetts*, his first true work, seems all release, and very close to the terrible nostalgias *Corsons Inlet* reluctantly abandons. William Ellery Channing, memorializing Thoreau clumsily though with love, deluges us with evidences of those walks and talks in which Overall was never beyond Thoreau, but came confidently with each natural observation. But Ammons, who would want to emulate Thoreau, cannot keep the account; his natural observations bring him wholly other evidences:

> in nature there are few sharp lines: there are areas of
> primrose
>   more or less dispersed;
> disorderly orders of bayberry; between the rows
> of dunes,

irregular swamps of reeds,
though not reeds alone, but grass, bayberry, yarow, all . . .
predominantly reeds:

All through the poem beats its hidden refrain: "I was released from
. . . straight lines," "few sharp lines," "I have drawn no lines," "but there
are no lines," "a wider range/than mental lines can keep," "the waterline,
waterline inexact," "but in the large view, no/lines or changeless shapes."
A wild earlier poem, called *Lines*, startlingly exposes Ammons's obsession,
for there nature bombards him, all but destroys him with lines, nothing
but lines:

Lines flying in, out: logarithmic
    curves coiling
toward an infinitely inward center: lines
    weaving in, threads lost in clustral scrawl,
        weaving out into loose ends,
wandering beyond the border of gray background,
    going out of vision,
        not returning;
or, returning, breaking across the boundary
    as new lines, discontinuous,
        come into sight:
fiddleheads of ferns, croziers of violins,
    convoluted spherical masses, breaking through
        ditchbanks where briar
stem-dull will
    leave and bloom:
        haunch line, sickle-like, turning down, bulging, nuzzling
under, closing into
    the hidden, sweet, dark meeting of lips:
        the spiraling out
or in
    of galaxies:
        the free-running wavy line, swirling
configuration, halting into a knot
    of curve and density: the broken,
        irreparable filament: tree-winding vines, branching
falling off or back, free,
    the adventitious preparation for possibility, from
        branch to branch, ash to gum:
the breaker
    hurling into reach for shape, crashing
        out of order, the inner hollow sizzling flat:
the longnecked, uteral gourd, bass line
    continuous in curve,

melodic line filling and thinning:
concentrations,
   whirling masses,
      thin leaders, disordered ends and risks:
explosions of clusters, expansions from the
   full radial sphere, return's longest chance:
      lines exploring, intersecting, paralleling, twisting,
noding: deranging, clustering.

This is Ammons's Mad Song, his equivalent of Stevens's A *Rabbit As King of the Ghosts*, another poem of the mind's mercilessness, its refusal to defend itself against itself. "Deranging, clustering" is the fear and the horror, from which *Corsons Inlet* battles for release, mostly through embracing "a congregation/rich with entropy," a constancy of change. The poet who insists he has drawn no lines draws instead his poem out of the "dunes of motion," loving them desperately as his only (but inadequate) salvation, all that is left when his true heaven of Overall is clearly beyond him. Yet this remains merely a being "willing to go along" in the recognition not of the Beautiful but the Terrible Necessity:

the moon was full last night: today, low tide was low:
black shoals of mussels exposed to the risk
of air
and, earlier, of sun,
waved in and out with the waterline, waterline inexact,
caught always in the event of change:
   a young mottled gull stood free on the shoals
   and ate
to vomiting: another gull, squawking possession, cracked a crab,
picked out the entrails, swallowed the soft-shelled legs, a ruddy
turnstone running in to snatch leftover bits:

risk is full: every living thing in
siege: the demand is life, to keep life: the small
white blacklegged egret, how beautiful, quietly stalks and spears
   the shallows, darts to shore
      to stab—what? I couldn't
   see against the black mudflats—a frightened
fiddler crab?

This great and very American passage, kin to a darker tradition than Ammons's own, and to certain poems of Melville and Hart Crane, is *Corsons Inlet's* center, the consequence of the spent seer's consignment of order to the vehicle of change. I remember, each time I read it, that Ammons is a Southerner, heir to a darker Protestantism than was the immediate heritage of the New England visionaries or of Whitman. But our best Southern poets from Poe and Timrod through Ransom, Tate, Warren, have not affected his art, and a comparison to a Southern contemporary like James Dickey indicates sharply how much Ammons is the conscious heir of nineteenth-century Northern poetry, including a surprising affinity to Dickinson in his later phase *Uplands* and *Briefings*. But, to a North Carolinian one hundred years after, Transcendentalism comes hard and emerges bitterly, with the Oversoul reduced from Overall to "the overall wandering of mirroring mind," confronting the dunes and swamps as a last resource, the final form of Nature or the Not-me.

From the nadir of "every living thing in/siege," *Corsons Inlet* slowly rises to a sense of the ongoing, "not chaos: preparations for/flight." In a difficult transitional passage, the poet associates the phrasal fields of his metric with the "field" of action on every side of him, open to his perception "with moving incalculable center." Looking close, he can see "order tight with shape"; standing back, he confronts a formlessness that suddenly, in an extraordinary epiphany, is revealed as his consolation:

> orders as summaries, as outcomes of actions override
> or in some way result, not predictably (seeing me gain
> the top of a dune,
> the swallows
> could take flight—some other fields of bayberry
>   could enter fall
>   berryless) and there is serenity:
>
>   no arranged terror: no forcing of image, plan,
> or thought:
> no propaganda, no humbling of reality to precept:
>
> terror pervades but is not arranged, all possibilities
> of escape open: no route shut, except in
>   the sudden loss of all routes:

"No arranged terror" is the crucial insight, and if we wish to inquire who would arrange terror except a masochist, the wish will not sustain itself. The poem's final passage, this poet's defense, abandons the really necessary "pulsations of order," the reliable particulars, for what cannot suffice, the continued bafflement of perceiving nothing completely. For Ammons, the seer of *Ommateum* and the still-confident quester of the *Hymn*, this bafflement is defeat, and enjoying the freedom that results from scope eluding his grasp is hardly an enjoying in any ordinary sense. The poem ends bravely, but not wholly persuasively:

> I see narrow orders, limited tightness, but will
> not run to the easy victory:
>> still around the looser, wider forces work:
>> I will try
> to fasten into order enlarging grasps of disorder, widening
> scope, but enjoying the freedom that
> Scope eludes my grasp, that there is no finality of vision,
> that I have perceived nothing completely,
>> that tomorrow a new walk is a new walk.

Origin is still his original sin; what his deepest nature longs for, to come to unity and yet remain material, is no part of *Corsons Inlet*, which grants him freedom to choose, but no access to that unity that alone satisfies choice. The major poem written immediately after *Corsons Inlet* emerges from stoic acceptance of bafflement into an imaginative reassurance that prompts Ammons's major phase, the lyrics of *Uplands*, *Briefings*, and the work-in-progress:

> Consistencies rise
> and ride
> the mind down
> hard routes
>> walled
> with no outlet and so
> to open a variable geography,
>> proliferate
> possibility, here
> is this dune fest
>> releasing,
> mind feeding out,
> gathering clusters,
> fields of order in disorder,
> where choice
> can make beginnings,
>> turns,
>> reversals,
> where straight line
> and air-hard thought
> can meet
> unarranged disorder,
>> dissolve
> before the one event that
> creates present time
> in the multi-variable
>> scope:

Saliences thus returns to *Corsons Inlet*'s field of action, driven by that poet's need not to abide in a necessity, however beautiful. Saliences etymologically are out-leapings, "mind feeding out," not taking in perceptions but turning its violent energies out into the field of action. If *Corsons Inlet* is Ammons's version of *The Idea of Order at Key West* (not that he had Stevens's poem in mind, but that the attentive reader learns to compare the two), then *Saliences* is his *The Man With the Blue Guitar*, a discovery of how to begin again after a large and noble acknowledgement of dark limitations. *Saliences* is a difficult, abstract poem, but it punches itself along with an overwhelming vigor, showing its exuberance by ramming through every blocking particular, until it can insist that "where not a single single thing endures,/the overall reassures." Overall remains beyond Ammons, but is replaced by "a round/quiet turning,/beyond loss or gain,/beyond concern for the separate reach." *Saliences* emphasizes the transformation of Ammons's obsessive theme, from the longing for unity to the assertion of the mind's power over the particulars of being, the universe of death. The Emersonianism of Ammons is constant; as did Whitman, so his final judgment of his relation to that great precursor will be: "loyal at last." But *Saliences* marks the *clinamen;* the swerve away from Emerson is now clarified, and Ammons will write no poem more crucial to his own unfolding. Before *Saliences*, the common reader must struggle with the temptation of naming Ammons a nature poet; after this, the struggle would be otiose. The quest that was surrendered in *Guide*, and whose loss was accepted in *Corsons Inlet*, is internalized in *Saliences* and afterward.

    Saliences approximates (indeliberately) the subtle procedure of a subtradition within Romantic poetry that goes from Shelley's *Mont Blanc* to Stevens's *The Auroras of Autumn*. The poet begins in an austere, even a terrifying scene of natural confrontation, but he does not describe the scene or name the terror until he has presented fully the mind's initial defense against scene and terror, its implicit assertion of its own force. So *Saliences* begins with a vision of the mind in action "in the multi-variable/scope." A second movement starts with the wind's entrance ("a variable of wind/among the dunes,/making variables/of position and direction and sound") and climaxes at the poem's halfway point, which returns to the image of the opening ("come out of the hard/routes and rust,/pour over the walls/of previous assessments: turn to/the open,/the unexpected, to new saliences of feature." After this come seventy magical lines of Ammons upon his heights (starting with: "The reassurance is/that through change/continuities sinuously work"), lines that constitute one of a convincing handful of contemporary assurances that the imagination is capable always of a renovative fresh start.

The dune fest, which in the poem's opening movement is termed a provocation for the mind's release from "consistencies" (in the sense of Blake's Devourer), is seen in the second movement as *Corsons Inlet's* baffled field of action:

> wind, a variable, soft wind, hard
> steady wind, wind
> shaped and kept in the
> bent of trees,
> the prevailing dipping seaward
> of reeds,
> the kept and erased sandcrab trails:
> wind, the variable to the gull's flight,
> how and where he drops the clam
> and the way he heads in, running to loft:
> wind, from the sea, high surf
> and cool weather;
> from the land, a lessened breakage
> and the land's heat:
> wind alone as a variable,
> as a factor in millions of events,
> leaves no two moments
> on the dunes the same:
> > keep
> free to these events,
> bend to these
> changing weathers:

The wind has gone beyond the wind of *Guide*, for it has given up everything to eternal being, even direction, even velocity, and contents itself to be shaped and kept by each particular it encounters. Knowing he cannot be one with or even like this wind, knowing too he must be more than a transparency, an Eye among the blind particulars, the poet moves to a kind of upper level of Purgatory, where the wind ceases to be his guide, and he sees as he has not seen before:

> when I went back to the dunes today,
> > saliences,
> congruent to memory,
> spread firmingly across my sight:
> the narrow white path
> rose and dropped over
> grassy rises toward the sea:
> sheets of reeds,
> tasseling now near fall,
> filled the hollows
> with shapes of ponds or lakes:

bayberry, darker, made wandering
chains of clumps, sometimes pouring
into heads, like stopped water:
　　much seemed
constant, to be looked
forward to, expected:

It is the saliences, the outleapings, that "spread *firmingly* across my sight," and give him assurances, "summations of permanence." The whole passage, down through the poem's close, has a firm beauty unlike anything previous in Ammons. Holding himself as he must, firmly apart from still-longed-for unity, he finds himself now in an astonishing equilibrium with the particulars, containing them in his own mind by reimagining them there:

　　　　　　　　. . . in
　　the hollow,
　where a runlet
　　makes in
　at full tide and fills a bowl,
　extravagance of pink periwinkle
　along the grassy edge,
　and a blue, bunchy weed, deep blue,
　deep into the mind the dark blue
　　constant:

The change here, as subtle as it is precarious, only just bears description, though the poet of *Uplands* and *Briefings* relies upon it as though it were palpable, something he could touch every way. The weed and the mind's imaginative constancy are in the relation given by the little poem, *Reflective*, written just afterward:

　　I found a
　　weed
　　that had a

　　mirror in it
　　and that
　　mirror

　　looked in at
　　a mirror
　　in
　　me that
　　had a
　　weed in it

In itself this is slight; in the context provided by *Saliences* it is exact and finely wrought. The whole meaning of it is in "I *found*," for *Saliences* records a finding, and a being found. Because of this mutual finding, the magnificent close of the poem is possible, is even necessary:

> where not a single single thing endures,
> the overall reassures,
> deaths and flights,
> shifts and sudden assaults claiming
> limited orders,
> the separate particles:
> earth brings to grief
> much in an hour that sang, leaped, swirled,
> yet keeps a round
>   quiet turning,
> beyond loss or gain,
> beyond concern for the separate reach.

I think, when I read this passage, of the final lines of Wordsworth's great Ode, of the end of Browning's *Love Among the Ruins*, of the deep peace Whitman gives as he concludes *Crossing Brooklyn Ferry*, and of Stevens closing *As You Leave the Room*:

> An appreciation of a reality
>
> And thus an elevation, as if I left
> With something I could touch, touch every way.
>
> And yet nothing has been changed except what is
> Unreal, as if nothing had been changed at all.

This is not to play at touchstones, in the manner of Arnold or of Blackmur, but only to record my experience as a reader, which is that *Saliences* suggests and is worthy of such company. Firm and radiant as the poem is, its importance for Ammons (if I surmise rightly) transcends its intrinsic worth, for it made possible his finest poems. I pass to them with some regret for the splendors in *Selected Poems* I have not discussed: *Silver, Terrain, Bridge, Jungle Knot, Nelly Myers, Expressions of Sea Level*, and for the long poem, *Tape for the Turn of the Year*, a heroic failure that is Ammons's most original and surprising invention.

Uplands, published in the autumn of 1970, begins with a difficult, almost ineluctable lyric, *Snow Log*, which searches for intentions where they evidently cannot be found, in the particulars of fallen tree, snow, shrubs, the special light of winter landscape; "I take it on myself," the poet ends by saying, and repeats the opening triad:

> especially the fallen tree
> the snow picks
> out in the woods to show.

Stevens, in the final finding of the ear, returned to the snow he had forgotten, to behold again "nothing that is not there and the nothing that is." *Snow Log* seems to find something that is not there, but the reader is left uncertain whether there is a consciousness in the scene that belongs neither to him nor to the poet. With the next poem, *Upland*, which gives the volume both its tonality and title, the uncertainty vanishes:

> Certain presuppositions are altered
> by height: the inversion to
> sky-well a peak
> in a desert makes: the welling
>
> from clouds down the boulder fountains:
> it is always a
> surprise out west there—
> the blue ranges loose and aglide
>
> with heat and then come close
> on slopes leaning up into green:
> a number of other phenomena might
> be summoned—
>
> take the Alleghenies for example,
> some quality in the air
> of summit stones lying free and loose
> out among the shrub trees: every
>
> exigency seems prepared for that might
> roll, bound, or give flight
> to stone: that is, the stones are
> prepared: they are round and ready.

A poem like this is henceforth Ammons's characteristic work: shorter and more totally self-enclosed than earlier ventures, and less reliant on larger contexts. He has become an absolute master of his art, and a maker of individual tones as only the greater poets can accomplish:

> . . . the stones are
> prepared: they are round and ready.

Upland does not attempt to define "some quality in the air" that alters presuppositions and makes its stones prepared for anything at any time. The poem disturbs because it compels us to accept the conflicting notions (for us) of surprise and preparation as being no conflict for the intentionality held by those summit stones. It satisfies as much as disturbs because something in us is not wholly apart from the summit stone's state-of-being; a natural apocalypticism is in the air, and pervades our rare ascensions to the mind's heights. Ammons, who is increasingly wary of finalities, praises hesitation in the next lyric, *Periphery*:

> One day I complained about the periphery
> that it was thickets hard to get around in
> or get around for
> an older man: it's like keeping charts
>
> of symptoms, every reality a symptom
> where the ailment's not nailed down:
> much knowledge, precise enough,
> but so multiple it says this man is alive
>
> or isn't: it's like all of a body answering
> all of pharmacopoeia, a too
> adequate relationship:
> so I complained and said maybe I'd brush
>
> deeper and see what was pushing all this
> periphery, so difficult to make any sense
> out of, out:
> with me, decision brings its own
>
> hesitation: a symptom, no doubt, but open
> and meaningless enough without paradigm:
> but hesitation
> can be all right, too: I came on a spruce
>
> thicket full of elk, gushy snow-weed,
> nine species of lichen, four pure white
> rocks and
> several swatches of verbena near bloom.

All the poems in *Uplands* have this new ease, but the conscious mastery of instrument may obscure for us the prevalence of the old concerns, lightened by the poet's revelation that a serach for saliences is a more possible quest than the more primordial romancing after unity. The concerns locate themselves still in Emerson's mental universe; Ammons's *Periphery*, like Dickinson's *Circumference*, goes back to the astonishing *Circles* of 1840 with its insistence that "the only sin is limitation" and its repeated image of concentricity. The appropriate gloss for Ammons's *Periphery* (and for much else in *Uplands*) is: "The natural world may be conceived of as a system of concentric circles, and we now and then detect in nature slight dislocations which apprise us that this surface on which we now stand is not fixed, but sliding." Ammons calls so being apprised "hesitation," and his slight dislocation is the radiant burst of elk, snow-weed, lichen, white rocks, and verbena that ends *Periphery* so beautifully.

In *Uplands* and the extraordinary conceptions of the recent volume, *Briefings*, the motions of water have replaced the earlier guiding movements of wind. *If Anything Will Level With You Water Will*, the title of one fine poem, is the credo of many. "I/mean the telling is unmediated," Ammons says of a rocky stream, and his ambition here, enormous as always, is an unmediated telling, a purely visionary poetry. It is not a poetry that discourses of itself or of the outward particulars, or of the processes of the poet's mind so much as it deals in a purer representation than even Wordsworth could have wanted. The bodily eye is not a despotic sense for Ammons (as it became for Thoreau) who has not passed through a crisis in perception, but rather has trained himself to sense those out-leapings later available to the seer (like Emerson) who had wisdom enough to turn back from Unity. For pure representation in the later Ammons, I give *Laser* (from *Uplands*) as a supreme example:

> An image comes
> and the mind's light, confused
> as that on surf
> or ocean shelves,
> gathers up,
> parallelizes, focuses
> and in a rigid beam illuminates the image:
>
> the head seeks in itself
> fragments of left-over light
> to cast a new
> direction,
> any direction,
> to strike and fix
> a random, contradicting image:
>
> but any found image falls
> back to darkness or
> the lesser beams splinter and
> go out:
> the mind tries to
> dream of diversity, of mountain
> rapids shattered with sound and light,
>
> of wind fracturing brush or
> bursting out of order against a mountain
> range: but the focused beam

> folds all energy in:
> the image glares filling all space:
> the head falls and
> hangs and cannot wake itself.

I risk sounding mystical by insisting that "an image" here is neither the poetic trope nor a natural particular, but what Ammons inveterately calls a "salience"; "the image glares filling all space." Not that in this perception there is no perceiver; rather the perceiving is detached, disinterested, attentive without anxiety or nostalgia. Perhaps this is only Ammons's equivalent of the difficult "half create" of *Tintern Abbey* or Emerson's "I am nothing; I see all," but it seems to ensue from the darker strain in him, that goes back to the twenty-sixth poem in *Ommateum*, "In the wind my rescue is," which stated a hopeless poetic quest: "I set it my task/to gather the stones of earth/into one place." In *Uplands*, a profound poem, *Apologia pro Vita Sua*, makes a definitive revision of the earlier ambition:

> I started picking up the stones
> throwing them into one place
> and by sunrise I was going far away
> for the large ones
> always turning to see never lost
> the cairn's height
> lengthening my radial reach:
>
> the sun watched with deep concentration
> and the heap through the hours grew
> and became by nightfall
> distinguishable from all the miles around
> of slate and sand:
>
> during the night the wind falling
> turned earthward its lofty freedom and speed
> and the sharp blistering sound muffled
> toward dawn and the blanket was
> drawn up over a breathless face:
>
> even so you can see in full dawn
> the ground there lifts
> a foreign thing desertless in origin.

"Distinguishable" is the desperate and revelatory word. To ask, after death, the one thing, to have left behind "a foreign thing desertless in origin," the cairn of a lifetime's poems, is to have reduced rescue into a primordial pathos. Yet the poem, by its virtue, renders more than pathos, as the lyric following, on the same theme, renders more also:

> Losing information he
> rose gaining
> view
> till at total
> loss gain was
> extreme:
> extreme & invisible:
> the eye
> seeing nothing
> lost its
> separation:
> self-song
> (that is a mere motion)
> fanned out
> into failing swirls
> slowed &
> became continuum.

Offset is the appropriate title; this is power purchased by the loss of knowledge, and unity at the expense of being material. *Uplands*, as a volume, culminates in its last lyric, *Cascadilla Falls*, placed just before the playful and brilliant long poem, *Summer Session 1968*, in which Ammons finds at last some rest from these intensities. Despite its extraordinary formal control and its continuous sense of a vision attained, *Uplands* is a majestically sad book, for Ammons does not let himself forget that his vision, while uncompromised, is a compromise necessarily, a constant knowing why and how "unity cannot do anything in particular." The poet, going down by Cascadilla Falls in the evening, picks up a stone and "thought all its motions into it," and then drops the stone from galactic wanderings to dead rest:

> the stream from other motions
> broke
> rushing over it:
> shelterless,
> I turned
>
> to the sky and stood still:
>
> I do
> not know where I am going
> that I can live my life
> by this single creek.

From this self-imposed pathos Ammons wins as yet no release. Release comes in the ninety delightful lyrics gathered together in *Briefings* (first entitled, gracefully but misleadingly, *Poems Small and Easy*), this poet's finest book. Though the themes of *Briefings* are familiarly Ammonsian, the mode is not. Laconic though transfigured speech has been transformed into "wasteful song." The first poem, *Center*, places us in a freer world than Ammons would give us before:

> A bird fills up the
> streamside bush
> with wasteful song,
> capsizes waterfall,
> mill run, and
> superhighway
> to
> song's improvident
> center
> lost in the green
> bush green
> answering bush:
> wind varies:
> the noon sun casts
> mesh refractions
> on the stream's amber
> bottom
> and nothing at all gets,
> nothing gets
> caught at all.

The given is mesh that cannot catch because the particulars have been capsized, and so are unavailable for capture. The center is improvident because it stands at the midmost point of mind, not of nature. *Briefings* marks an end to the oldest conflict in Ammons; the imagination has learned to avoid apocalyptic pitch, but it has learned also its own painful autonomy in regard to the universe it cannot join in unity. With the confidence of this autonomy attained, the mind yet remains wary of what lurks without, as in *Attention:*

> Down by the bay I
> kept in mind
> at once
> the tips of all the rushleaves
> and so
> came to know
> balance's cost and true:
> somewhere though in the whole field
> is the one

> tip
> I will someday lose out of mind
> and fall through.

The one particular of dying remains; every unmastered particular is a little death, giving tension to the most triumphant even among these short poems. *Hymn IV*, returning to the great *Hymn* and two related poems of the same title, seals up the quest forever:

> You have enriched us with
> fear and contrariety
> providing the searcher
> confusion for his search
>
> teaching by your snickering
> wisdom an autonomy
> for man
> Bear it all
> and keep me from my enemies'
> wafered concision and zeal
> I give you back to yourself
> whole and undivided

I do not hear bitterness in this, or even defiance, but any late Emersonian worship of the Beautiful Necessity is gone. With the going there comes a deep uncertainty in regard to poetic subject, as *Looking Over the Acreage* and several other poems show so poignantly. The ironically moving penultimate poem of *Briefings* still locates the poet's field of contemplation "where the ideas of permanence/and transience fuse in a single body, ice for example,/or a leaf," but does not suggest that the fusion yields any information. The whole of *Briefings* manifests a surrender of the will-to-knowledge, not only relational knowledge between poetic consciousness and natural objects, but all knowledge that is too easy, that is not also loss. Amid astonishing abundance in this richest of his volumes, I must pick out one lyric as representative of all the others, for in it Ammons gives full measure of a unique gift:

> He held radical light
> as music in his skull: music
> turned, as
> over ridges immanences of evening light
> rise, turned
> back over the furrows of his brain
> into the dark, shuddered,
> shot out again
> in long swaying swirls of sound:

reality had little weight in his transcendence
so he
had trouble keeping
his feet on the ground, was
terrified by that
and liked himself, and others, mostly
under roofs:
nevertheless, when the
light churned and changed

his head to music, nothing could keep him
off the mountains, his
head back, mouth working,
wrestling to say, to cut loose
from the high, unimaginable hook:
released, hidden from stars, he ate,
burped, said he was like any one
of us: demanded he
was like any one of us.

It is the seer's horror of radical light, his obduracy to transcendence, that moves the seer himself, moves him so that he cannot know what he should know, which is that he cannot be like ourselves. The poem's power is that we are moved also, not by the horror, which cannot be our own, but by the transcendence, the sublime sense we long to share. Transcendent experience, but with Emerson's kind of Higher Utilitarianism ascetically cut off by a mind made too scrupulous for a new hope, remains the *materia poetica* of Ammons's enterprise. A majestic recent poem like *The City Limits* suggests how much celebration is still possible even when the transcendent moment is cruelly isolated, too harshly purified, totally compelled to be its own value. Somewhere upon the higher ridges of his Purgatory, Ammons remains stalled, unable for now to break through to the Condition of Fire promised by *Ommateum*, where instead of invoking Emerson's Uriel or Poe's Israfel he found near identity with "a crippled angel bent in a scythe of grief" yet witnessed a fiery ascent of the angel, fought against it, and only later gained the knowledge that "The eternal will not lie/down on any temporal hill."

RICHARD HOWARD

"The Spent Seer Consigns Order to the Vehicle of Change"

All of a sudden, with an unheralded and largely unacknowledged cumulus of books, a poet who accounts for himself with laconic diversity as the holder of the B.S. degree from Wake Forest College in North Carolina, as the principal of an elementary school in that State at the age of 26, as an executive, thereafter and inconsequently, in the biological glass industry:

> (how you buy a factory:
> determine the lines of force
> leading in and out, origins, destinations of lines
> determine how
>   from the nexus of crossed and bundled lines
>   the profit is
> obtained, the
> forces realized, the cheap made dear,
> and whether the incoming or outgoing forces are stronger)

and currently as an English teacher:

> (I'm waiting to hear if
> Cornell will give me
> a job: I need
> to work &
> maybe I write
> too much)

From *Alone with America*. Copyright © 1969, 1980 by Richard Howard. Atheneum Press.

—suddenly, then, A. R. Ammons has exploded into the company of American poets which includes Whitman and Emerson and articulates the major impulse of the national expression: the paradox of poetry as process and yet impediment to process. More honestly than Whitman, acknowledging his doubts as the very source of his method ("teach me, father: behold one whose fears are the harnessed mares of his going!"), though without Whitman's dramatic surface, Ammons has traced out the abstractive tendency, the immaterialism that runs through all our *native strain,* in both acceptations of the phrase: to suffer or search out immersion in the stream of reality without surrendering all that is and makes one particularly oneself. The dialectic is rigorous in Ammons' version—the very senses which rehearse the nature of being for the self, the private instances of the sensuous world, must be surrendered to the experience of unity:

> we can approach
> unity only by the loss
> of things
> a loss we're unwilling
> to take—
> since the gain of unity
>   would be a vision
> of something in the
> continuum of nothingness:
> we already have things:
>   why fool around?

And how avoid the "humbling of reality to precept?" "Stake off no beginnings or ends, establish no walls," the poet urges, addressing that Unity: "I know if I find you I will have to leave the earth and go on out . . . farther than the loss of sight into the unseasonal, undifferentiated stark"—a region, a Death, to speak literally, where there is no poetry, no speech to one's kind, no correspondence perceived and maintained, but only the great soft whoosh of Being that has obsessed our literature from its classical figures, as Lawrence saw so clearly, down to Roethke, Wright Morris, Thornton Wilder.

In 1955, A. R. Ammons, a native and occasional resident of North Carolina, issued a wispy first book of poems and then held his peace, or rather his pugnacity, for ten years. When he next broke the silence, with a triad of voluble and original books at the age of forty, the development from that initial and inconclusive—certainly unconcluded— effort, the achievement in the terms of means and meaning reached so far that it is difficult, now, to see *Ommateum* for what it is, rather than an omen, a symptom.

The title means *compound eye*, as in an insect, and to the magnifying vision of such "irridescence of complex eyes" Ammons returns in the posterior books:

> I see how the bark cracks and winds like no other bark
> chasmal to my ant-soul running up and down . . .

I suppose the thirty-some litanies in *Ommateum* are to be taken as so many various lenses, ways of looking at landscape, history and deity which together make up one of those strange bug-eyed views wherein the world is refracted into various but adjacent fragments. The book is dedicated to Josephine Miles, the distinguished poet and teacher Ammons had met during his studies (three semesters) at the University of California, and is prefaced by an arrogant, unsigned foreword which asserts that the poems "rather grow in the reader's mind than exhaust themselves in completed, external form." It is just such exhaustion, "the coercive charm of form" as Henry James called it, which the collection lacks, for all its nicely witnessed natural movements:

> and the snake shed himself in ripples
> across a lake of sand

or again, more wittily:

> The next morning I was dead
>   excepting a few peripheral cells
> and the buzzards
> waiting for a savoring age to come
> sat over me in mournful conversations
> that sounded excellent to my eternal ear . . .

and despite its many fine passages, aspirations to share yet shed a nature regarded, throughout, as a goal and equally as a prison, the pitch is insistently wordy and too shrill:

> But the wind has sown loose dreams
> in my eyes
>   and telling unknown tongues
> drawn me out beyond the land's end
>   and rising in long
>   parabolas of bliss
> borne me safely
> from all those ungathered stones

After many such vociferations, one wonders whose voice it is that utters these hymns to—and against—Earth. The sapless lines, terminated only by the criterion of conversational or rhetorical sense, cannot beat against a stiffening rhythmic constant, and we are reminded of Miss Moore's prescription, taking her words in whatever pejorative sense they may bear: "ecstasy affords the occasion, and *expediency determines the form.*" Whose, then, is the voice that chants these prayers to the unstringing of all harps? The only aid the young poet affords is the assumption in several poems of the identity of the prophet Ezra. In a later book too, "I Ezra" returns, "the dying portage of these deathless thoughts," and we recall that this prophet is generally regarded as responsible for the revision and editing of the earlier books of Scripture and the determination of the canon. The persona appears in Ammons' poems, I think, when he is desperate for an authoritative voice; the nature of his enterprise is so extreme, and the risks he is willing to take with hysterical form and unguarded statement (unguarded by image, as Coleridge said that "a whole Essay might be written on the Danger of *thinking* without Images") so parlous, that the need for such *authority* must be pretty constant:

> I am Ezra
> as a word too much repeated
> falls out of being . . .

Yet even in this first book, especially as we tend to read it with the later work in mind, as a propaedeutic function of that work, it is evident that Ammons has discovered his tremendous theme: putting off the flesh and taking on the universe. Despite a wavering form, an uncertain voice, Ammons means to take on the universe the way Hemingway used to speak of taking on Guy de Maupassant—the odds, it is implied, more than a little in favor of the challenger. Here in *Ommateum*, then, is the first enunciation of the theme, in the crude form of a romantic pantheism:

> Leaving myself on the shore
> I went away
> and when a heavy wind caught me I said
>   my body lies south
> given over to vultures and flies
> and wrung my hands
> so the wind went on . . .
> The flies were gone
> The vultures no longer searched
> the ends of my hingeless bones . . .
> Breathing the clean air
> I picked up a rib
>   to draw figures in the sand . . .

And more decisively, in one of the finest early pieces, with its many echoes of Pound's diction and of course the metric of Dr. Williams, properly assimilated to the poet's own requirements which are speed, ease, and the carol of the separate phrase:

> Peeling off my being I plunged into
> the well
> The fingers of the water splashed
> to grasp me up
> but finding only
> a few shafts
> of light
> too quick to grasp
> became hysterical
> jumped up and down
> and wept copiously
> So I said I'm sorry dear well but
> went on deeper
> finding patched innertubes beer cans
> and black roothairs along the way
> but went on deeper
> till darkness snuffed the shafts of light
> against the well's side
> night kissing
> the last bubbles from my lips.

By the time, ten years later, of his second book, *Expressions of Sea Level*, Ammons had extended and enriched this theme to stunning effect—not only in versions of nature and the body, but in terms of poetics as well, enforcing the substitution of the negative All for the single possibility of being:

> go back:
> how can I
> tell you what I have not said: you must look for it
> yourself: that
> side has weight, too, though words cannot bear it
> out: listen for the things I have left out:
> I am
> aware
> of them, as you must be, or you will miss
> the non-song
> in my singing.

Here Ammons has found, or fetched out, besides a functioning arrangement of words on the page, the further device of the colon, which he

henceforth wields in its widest application as almost his only mark of
punctuation—a sign to indicate not only equivalence, but the node or
point of passage on each side of which an existence hangs in the balance:

> a tree, committed as a tree,
> cannot in a flood
>   turn fish,
> sprout gills (leaves are
> a tree's gills) and fins:
>   the molluscs
> dug out of mountain peaks
> are all dead . . .

This observation, from a long poem called "Risks and Possibilities"—one
of the penalties of his method, of course, is that Ammons requires length
in order to indulge his effects, lacking that compression of substance
which amounts to a "received form"—exhibits, too, a curious and rueful
connivence with the universal doxology that to represent any one form of
life is a limitation, a limitation that cannot be transcended beyond the
mere consciousness of it. For only limited forms of life *matter*, and I intend
the pun—are of *material consequence*. In one of his saddest poems, an
astonishing meditation called "Guide," Ammons admits that it is not,
really, worth "giving up everything to eternal being but direction," as the
wind has done. With the humility of a man whose enormous ambitions
have been chastened by a constatation of his restricted place in the
world—and the chastening has been a religious experience, in the literal
sense of religion: a linking, a binding, even a fettering—the poet returns
to his body, his particular geography and even his rather bleak sociology.
Stretching his long legs on late-afternoon walks down the Jersey coast, he
has learned that "when I got past relevance the singing shores told me to
turn back":

> What light there
> no tongue turns to tell
> to willow and calling shore
> though willows weep and shores sing always

In *Expressions of Sea Level* we are given a lot more to go on, and
consequently go a lot farther, than the persona of Ezra and some rhapsodic
landscapes of apocalypse. We are given, with great attention to vegetable
detail and meteorological conditioning, the scenes of the poet's childhood
in a North Carolina backwoods, the doctrine and rationale of his metaphysical aspirations:

```
        the precise and
    necessary worked out of random, reproducible,
    the handiwork redeemed from chance . . .
        I will show you
    the underlying that takes no image to itself,
        cannot be shown or said,
    but weaves in and out of moons and bladderweeds,
        is all and
    beyond destruction
    because created fully in no
    particular form . . .
```

and the resignation, the accommodation of himself to the tidal marshes of
New Jersey as the site of the poet's individual drama. Here is a man
obsessed by Pure Being who must put up with a human incarnation when
he would prefer to embody only the wind, the *anima* of existence itself:

```
        So it came time
            for me to cede myself
        and I chose
        the wind
            to be delivered to

        The wind was glad
            and said it needed all
        the body
        it could get
            to show its motions with . . .
```

With the acknowledgment of these limitations has come an interest in
other, equally limited, possibilities. One of Ammons' most interesting
sidelines, a lagoon of his main drift, is a concern with archaic cultures whose
aspect often reminds us, in its amalgam of the suggestive detail and the
long loose line, in its own prose music, of Perse:

```
    Returning silence unto silence
    the Sumerian between the rivers lies.
    His skull crushed and molded into rock
        does not leak or peel.
    The gold earring lies in the powder
    of his silken perished lobe.
    The incantations, sheep trades, and night-gatherings
        with central leaping fires,
    roar and glare still in the crow's foot
    walking of his stylus on clay.
```

But not until a more recent book, *Corsons Inlet*, would this mode be
brought into accord with the main burden of Ammons' song—the made

thing of his impulse. Song may seem an odd word for a verse in which I have descried the music of prose, a verse which is as near as words can get us to our behavior, no more than a fairly cautious means of putting down phrases so that they will keep. Yet though the iambic cadence, and all it implies and demands by way of traditional lilt, has been jettisoned as utterly as Dr. Williams ever decreed, there *is* a song in Ammons' windy lines, a care for the motion of meaning in language which is the whole justice of prosody; consider this invocation to the wind, one more of many, and perhaps the loveliest:

> When the tree of my bones
>   rises from the skin
> come and whirlwinding
> stroll my dust
>   around the plain
> so I can see
>   how the ocotillo does
> and how the saguaro-wren is
> and when you fall
>   with evening
>
> fall with me here
>   where we can watch
> the closing up of day
> and think how morning breaks

There is another strand of discourse in *Expressions of Sea Level*, whose very title gives an idea of Ammons' use of a new vocabulary, one that Kenneth Burke would call "scientistic," I guess, to mean the dramatic use of an exact nomenclature, in Ammons' case a use quite properly managed:

> An individual spider web
>   identifies a species:
> an order of instinct prevails
>   through all accidents of circumstance
>   though possibility is
> high along the peripheries of
> spider
>   webs:
>   you can go all
>   around the fringing attachments
>   and find
> disorder ripe,
> entropy rich, high levels of random,
>   numerous occasions of accident . . .

this poem concludes:

> if the web were perfectly pre-set
> the spider could
> never find
> a perfect place to set it in: and
> if the web were
> perfectly adaptable,
> if freedom and possibility were without limit,
> the web would
> lose its special identity . . .

The dangers of this kind of thing, the dangers of which Coleridge spoke, were evident, of course, to the author of "River," whose mastery of natural imagery and vocalic music is exact and generous, as in this example of what Hopkins called "vowelling off":

> I shall
> go down
> to the deep river, to the moonwaters
> where the silver
> willows are and the bay blossoms,
>
> to the songs
> of dark birds
> to the great wooded silence
> of flowing
> forever down the dark river
>
> silvered at the moon-singing of hidden birds.

The repetition of the short *i* and the variants on the sound of "river" in "forever" and "silvered" in the last two lines—not to sound too much like the late Dr. Sitwell—indicate and insure a consciousness of effects that become the living twist of things we call idiom.

Insurance is what we shall mostly need in dealing with Ammons' next book. Mooning around the house and waiting for *Expressions of Sea Level* to come off the press in December of 1964, the poet produced, in a two month period, and with a determination to reach an end that became more than obsessive, became self-destructive, "a long thin poem" written on a huge roll of adding-machine tape run through the typewriter to its conclusion ("I am attracted to paper, visualize kitchen napkins scribbled with little masterpieces: so it was natural for me . . ."). The "serious novelty" of the enterprise is unquestionable, and there are many beautiful tropes in this long *Tape for the Turn of the Year*, chiefly in the form of pious assurances that the undertaking is or will be worthwhile:

let this song
    make
complex things salient,
saliences clear, so
        there can be some
    understanding

Enough to suggest that the text is not so much a poem as the ground of a
poem, the dark backing of a mirror out of which all brightness may, as a
condition, come. There are two moments of confrontation, when Ammons
links his 200-page transcribed tape with the generality of his gift as a poet:

ecology is my word: tag
me with that: come
in there:
    you will find yourself
in a firmless country:
    centers and peripheries
    in motion,
    organic
        interrelations!
    that's the door: here's
the key: come in,
    celebrant,
    to the one meaning
that totals my meanings . . .

The other moment of address follows closely:

my other word is
    provisional . . .
        you may guess
the meanings from *ecology:*
don't establish the
    boundaries
    first . . .
    and then
    pour
    life into them, trimming
off left-over edges,
ending potential . . .
    the center-arising
    form
    adapts, tests the
        peripheries, draws in,
    finds a new factor,
    utilizes a new method,

gains a new foothold,
responds to inner and outer
change . . .

This is the poet arguing himself onward. His book arrives, the Muse ("a woman in us who gives no rest") reassures him (if not us), and in acknowledgment he turns, a moment, to address us before returning to his vocation in the most luscious of his books so far, *Corsons Inlet*:

> I've given you the
> interstices: the
> space between . . .
> I've given you
> the dull days
> when turning and turning
> revealed nothing . . .
> I've given
> you long
> uninteresting walks
> so you could experience vacancy: . . .
> our journey is done:
> thank you
> for coming:
> the sun's bright,
> the wind rocks the
> naked trees . . .

Published almost simultaneously with the indiscreet, revelatory *Tape*, *Corsons Inlet*, from the title poem with its sure grasp of site ("the 'field' of action with moving, incalculable center") to the farewell to the reader, to poetry and to the spirit of place given at the end ("surrendered self among unwelcoming forms: stranger, hoist your burdens, get on down the road"), stands as the farthest and still the most representative reach into, upon, and against Being which the poet has yet made. It opens with a poem that nicely illustrates the perfected diction Ammons has now achieved, a rhythmical certainty which does not depend on syllable-counting or even accentual measure, but on the speed and retard of words as they move together in the mind, on the shape of the stanzas as they follow the intention of the discourse, and on the *rests* which not so much imitate as create the soft action of speech itself. There is a formality in these gentle lines which is new to American poetry, as we say that there is a draughtmanship in the "drip-drawings" of Pollock which is new to American painting: each must be approached with a modulated set of expectations if we are to realize what the poet, the painter is about.

Consider the close of this first poem, "Visit," in Ammons' fourth book, and compare its resonance—reserved but not evasive, convinced but not assertive—with the heartier music of a similar passage, too famous to quote, in Frost:

> . . . or you can come by shore:
>
>> choose the right: there the rocks
>> cascade less frequently, the grade more gradual:
>> treat yourself gently: the ascent thins both
>>> mind and blood and you must
>>>> keep still a dense reserve
>
>> of silence we can poise against
>> conversation: there is little news:
>> I found last month a root with shape and
>>> have heard a new sound among
>>>> the insects: come.

The device of the colon helps keep a dense reserve of silence to poise against the "conversation" here, and the reason for the visit—finding a root with shape and hearing a new sound—is a kind of compressed *ars poetica* of Ammons' enterprise, that understanding of natural process which will include the negative moment: "what destruction am I blessed by" the poet asks in "the moment's height," but his prosody asks the question in a firmer, more axiological *set*, the resources of imagism that are generally employed to accommodate a natural movement here made over to a powerful abstraction:

> exhilaration
> sucking him up,
>
> shuddering and
> lifting
>
> him
> jaw and bone
>
> and he said
> what
>
> destruction am I
> blessed by?

Then comes the book's title poem, like so many of Ammons' largest statements the account of "a walk over the dunes" which is also a natural history of the poem itself:

the walk liberating, I was released from forms,
from the perpendiculars,
    straight lines, blocks, boxes, binds
of thought
into the hues, shadings, rises, flowing bends and blends
    of sight:

the interrelations of *making* and of a beneficent destruction are here
followed out ("I was released from forms"), the actions of sea and land
serving as the just emblem of the mind's resources, so that the poet can
discuss his undertaking precisely in the terms of his locus, and indeed
acknowledges his inability to wield any terms *except* those afforded him by
what Kenneth Burke calls the scene-agent ratio:

                    I allow myself eddies of meaning:
    yield to a direction of significance
    running
    like a stream through the geography of my work:
        you can find
    in my sayings
                        swerves of action
                        like the inlet's cutting edge:
            there are dunes of motion,
    organizations of grass, white sandy paths of remembrance
    in the overall wandering of mirroring mind:

    but Overall is beyond me: is the sum of these events
    I cannot draw, the ledger I cannot keep, the accounting
    beyond the account . . .

It is characteristic that so many of these poems—and in the previous book
as in the one to come—take up their burden from the shore, the place
where it is most clearly seen that "every living thing is in siege: the
demand is life, to keep life"; whether he investigates the small white
blacklegged egret, the fiddler crab, the black shoals of mussels, the reeds,
grass, bayberry, yarrow, or "pulsations of order in the bellies of minnows,"
Ammons is concerned to enunciate a dialectic, "the working in and out,
together and against, of millions of events," and *event* is precisely his
word—

                no finality of vision,
    I have perceived nothing completely,
        tomorrow a new walk is a new walk

he insists: Ammons rehearses a marginal, a transitional experience, he is a
littoralist of the imagination because the shore, the beach, or the coastal

creek is not a *place* but an *event*, a transaction where land and water create and destroy each other, where life and death are exchanged, where shape and chaos are won and lost. It is here, examining "order tight with shape: blue tiny flowers on a leafless weed: carapace of crab: snail shell" that Ammons finds his rhythms, "fastening into order enlarging grasps of disorder," and as he makes his way down the dunes, rhythms are "reaching through seasons, motions weaving in and out!"

The rebellion against Being and into eternity is put down by the body itself on these expeditions the poet makes, safaris into mortality which convince him that "the eternal will not lie down on any temporal hill," and that he must "face piecemeal the sordid reacceptance of my world." It is not acceptance, but *re*acceptance which must be faced, the world which must be learned *again* as the poet, borrowing Shelley's beautiful image, "kindles his thoughts, blowing the coals of his day's bright conscious" in order "to make green religion in winter bones." In *Corsons Inlet* doctrine has been assimilated into "one song, an overreach from which all possibilities, like filaments, depend: killing, nesting, dying, sun or cloud, figure up and become song—simple, hard: removed." That is Ammons' definition of his aspiration—a long way from the breezy expostulations in *Ommateum*—and, I believe, of his achievement as well: his awareness and his imagination have coincided. Not that the poet has lost his initial impulse—for example, the close of the finest poem in that first volume, quoted earlier—"night kissing/ the last bubbles from my lips" —finds itself enlarged and suited to the poet's wider utterance here, so that the poem called "Libation" in *Corsons Inlet* ends: "Now keep me virile and long at love: let submission kiss off/the asking words from my lips." There is a loyalty to finite being, "losing the self to the victory of stones and trees, of bending sandpit lakes, crescent round groves of dwarf pine," Ammons says in the last poem of the book, "Gravelly Run," a central impulse that "extends the form, leads us on," and if there is also a freedom to explore an eccentric impulse, as in the brilliant poem "The Strait," it is a freedom granted because the divergent "filaments" have been braided back into the main strand, a rope of sand indeed. The poem concerns a worshipper at the phythoness' cave, questioning the ways of receiving the oracle, and ends with the kind of "simple, hard: removed" words which so often suggest, in this poet, the pre-Socratic impulse:

> go
> to your fate:
> if you succeed, praise the
> god:
> if you fail,
> discover your flaw.

Yet such terrors of self-knowledge are generally, by this climax of submissive response in the poet's work, abated by his more habitual reference to the design, the order, the form of the natural world: "for it is not so much to know the self," Ammons admits,

> as to know it as it is known
> by galaxy and cedar cone,
> as if birth had never found it
> and death could never end it.

In 1966 Ammons published his fifth book, in which again "events of sense alter old dunes of mind, release new channels of flow, free materials to new forms": *Northfield Poems* enacts Ammons' now familiar insurgence against finitude, and his resignation, once the impossibilities of both macrocosm and molecule are confessed, to the demands of form as *the vehicle of change*:

> unlike wind
> that dies and
> never dies I said
> I must go on
> consigned to
> form that will not
> let me loose
> except to death
> till some syllable's rain
> anoints my tongue
> and makes it sing
> to strangers:

"some syllable's rain" intimates this poet's trust in language, when any confidence in the body's identity, as in that of bog and bay, is lost; in all these "riding movements" the transformation finally relied on is the transformation of process into words; as Valéry said in the canonical utterance about such littoral metamorphoses, the poet comes to learn *le changement des rives en rumeur*, the change of shores to sound. For Ammons, there is a liberation as well as an acknowledgment of inadequacy about his failure to reduce himself to singleness or to swell to a "savage" chaos:

> when I tried to think by what
> millions of grains of events
>   the tidal creek had altered course,
>   when I considered alone
> a record
> of the waves on the running blue creek,
>   I was released into a power beyond my easy failures:

the power is the strength, the wit, the *balance* of mind which enables him to fall back on his verbal nature, acknowledging that "the dissolved reorganizes to resilience" in his language, that reflexive tool of his specific incarnation:

> only the book of laws founded
>   against itself
> founded on freedom of each event to occur as itself
> lasts into the inevitable balance events will take.

Ammons' poems are that book of laws founded against itself, perpetually questioning not only the finality, but the very finitude of the world, deploring in an almost Catharist way the "fact" that "coming into matter, spirit fallen trades eternity for temporal form," asserting that it is their part to consummate—by the "gist of 'concrete observations,' pliant to the drift"—the world's body which, as in "February Beach," is in constant modification:

>   creation may not be complete,
> the land may not have been
> given
> permanently,
>   something remains
> to be agreed on,
> a lofty burn of sound, a clamoring and
>   coming on . . .

In this metaphysical breviary, the self is forever giving itself instructions about its own disembodied aspirations—"if you must leave the shores of mind," Ammons adjures his "Discoverer," reverting to his familiar accommodation of the Sea of Being in the salt marshes of Northfield,

>   if to gather darkness
> into light, evil into good,
> you must leave the shores of mind,
> remember us, return and rediscover us.

The dissident Ezra, who reappears in one or another of these poems, is said to listen from terraces of mind "wind cannot reach or weedroots"—and at once we know this is not the Way: for Ammons, only what comes back into being by an eternal yet secular reversion—remembered, returned to, rediscovered—is viable:

>   The world is bright after rain
> for rain washes death out of the land and hides it far
> beneath the soil and it returns again cleansed with life
>   and so all is a circle
> and nothing is separable . . .

Indeed, the prophetic lurch to the edges of being—into that "scientific" area of "cytoplasm's grains and vacuoles" on the one hand, and the pulsing, shooting abstractions of "matter and energy" on the other—is repudiated in the final statement of *Northfield Poems*, though there are no final statements in this world of Ammons', of course, only articles of belief, only a mastered credulity:

> energy's invisible
> swirls confused, surpassed
> me: from that edge
> I turned back,
>
> strict with limitation,
> to my world's
> bitter acorns
> and sweet branch water.

Uplands: New Poems (The Nation, 1971)

What was it like, to bear witness to the articulation of a great career in American poetry, to account for volume as it succeeded volume, revision as it focused vision, until the trajectory was complete, the canon fulfilled? What did a critic *feel* in the presence of the new work (including "Acquainted with the Night") when in 1928 Frost's sixth book *West-Running Brook*, followed his *Selected Poems* at a five-year interval? We can look it up: a shift was remarked, was lamented, a shift to a more "philosophic" mode among the short poems which chiefly composed the book, the title poem now the sole "characteristic" regional dialogue once so distinctive in Frost's work. "Slight" is used in three of the reviews to dismiss Frost's escape from his own previous selection. In other words the sliced-apple effect was evident: as soon as new work was exposed, it turned brown in the open air, and it was the *preceding* poems, mysteriously digested meanwhile, which were declared to exhibit the poet's true mastery, his authentic character, while the immediate achievement represented a wrong turning, a misapprehension, a falling off. If it is true, as Wordsworth said, that a poet must create the taste by which he is enjoyed, it is also true that he must continually dislodge himself if he is to create more than taste.

We can look up what the critics said of Frost's sixth book, or Stevens', or Auden's—indeed, it is a humbling exercise—but the retrospective, with regard to feeling, is always a category of bad faith, and we had better examine our own feelings *now*, for we are faced with just such an occasion, just such an opportunity. Here is Ammons' sixth book, two years after his

Selected Poems, four years after his last new work. The situation, then, is parallel to Frost's in 1928: the poet reaches that stalled place in his career where it is necessary to inventory his resources, to take stock—what else is a Selected Poems?—of his possibilities, those behind him and those ahead. And then he must move, must find—invent—what there is in himself which will make further work identifiable yet not identical. It is the crisis of middle life which he must emblematically resolve: to acknowledge not only his future but his past, betraying neither:

> the problem is
> how
> to keep shape and flow

No wonder so many of these new poems are concerned with initiations, submissions to motion, giving way, getting started. But before Ammons wrests himself free, by so many "scoops scopes scrimps and scroungings," by the geological energies of "fill, siftings, winnowings, dregs,/cruds, chips," let me rehearse in a paragraph the mountainous achievements at his back, from which he is setting forth.

In 1955, Ammons' first book, *Ommateum*, discovered his tremendous theme: putting off the flesh and taking on the universe. For this poet, there is no windy abstraction in the notion, but a wonderful and rustling submission to the real, the incidental and the odd. Indeed, the poignance of momentary life in its combat with eternal design so haunted the poet that a decade later, in his magnificent second and third books, *Expressions of Sea Level* and *Corsons Inlet*, he had not yet come down on the side of transcendence, nor even taken off. Determined rather to suffer or search out immersion in the stream of reality without surrendering all that is and makes one particularly oneself, Ammons devised a notation of events as faithful to the wavering rhythm of metabolism as it might be to the larger fixities of celestial order:

> for it is not so much to know the self
> as to know it as it is known
> by galaxy and cedar cone,
> as if birth had never found it
> and death could never end it:

that terminal colon is a characteristic of Ammons' verse—a sign to indicate not only equivalence but the node or point of passage on each side of which an existence hangs in the balance; and the balance is the movement of the verse itself, a constant experiment with the weight of language the line can bear, can meaningfully break beneath, so that the enjambment will *show* something more than completion or incompletion. Between these two books, Ammons published a kind of satyr play of selfhood, *Tape for the Turn of the Year*, "a long thin poem" written on a huge roll of adding-machine tape run through the typewriter to its conclusion, a poem about the specifications of identity by the very refusal to prune or clip. And these mediations led, or prodded, the poet to a further collection, *Northfield Poems*, in which the provisional is treasured as an earnest (though hardly a solemnizing) of survival: "no finality of vision,/I have perceived nothing completely,/tomorrow a new walk is a new walk." And then in 1968 Ammons chose from all these books (except for the indiscreet, revelatory *Tape*) a splendid series of *provisions*, stays against chaos as against finality, articles of belief, a mastered credulity, his *Selected Poems*. Insufficiently attended to, this book is a masterpiece of our period, the widest scope and the intensest focus American poetry has registered since Frost, since Stevens, since Roethke.

And now we have a new book, three dozen lyrical pieces, mostly no more than a page long, and two extended texts, the erotic experiment "Guitar Recitativos" and the superb dedication poem called "Summer Session" which closes "with trivia / I'll dispense dignity, a sense of office, /formality they [the poet's students] can define themselves against." A collection necessarily *slight* if measured against the massive accumulation of Ammons' past, yet if we recall the original sense of the word—*plain, simple*—then we can say, with Pope, "slight is the subject, but not so the praise," for in these sudden, attractive fits and starts the poet urges himself into a new economy, a bright particularity of diction entirely *gainful* to his panoply, a way of handling verse without giving up conversation:

> arriving at ways
> waters survives its motions.

The way is enjambment, a wizardry in working with the right-hand margin, so that the line never relinquishes its energy until it can start up its successor. "Certain presuppositions are altered," Ammons announces talking about the look of "summit stones lying free and loose/out among the shrub trees" in the Alleghenies. We are no longer on the beach in these poems, but in the mountains, among masses, solids, fixities, and the problem is how to get moving again. It is the poet's situation, the poet's dilemma, to make the mountain come to Mohammed, and he has started the pebbles rolling:

> every
> exigency seems prepared for that might
> roll, bound, or give flight

> to stone: that is, the stones
> are prepared: they are round and ready.

Thus the book itself is an account—scrupulous in its details, its hesitations, its celebrations of minor incidents, lesser claims—of how a landscape or a man comes to realize motion, comes to be *on the way* rather than in it.

Briefings: Poems Small and Easy (Partisan Review, 1972)

Hard upon *Uplands* appears *Briefings: Poems Small and Easy*. Small and easy! Ever since his deprecating "Foreword" to his first book and his embarrassed asides braided right into his adding-machine epyllion, it has been evident that Ammons is a great craftsman in his poems, but an erratic stage director or prompter from the wings. What he calls "small and easy" may not be anything of the kind, and need not be called anything at all. He is ever uneasy, this poet of what David Kalstone once identified as subversive bravado, as he walks his way into "song's improvident/center/ lost in the green bush"; and like Ammons we shall be at a loss to say much that is to the point about his genre, about his poetics, though the affinities are there, the spectral precursors and the *a posteriori* spooks— Emerson, Dickinson, Whitman, then Pound, Williams, Stevens. It is not to the *point* that we are to speak, anyway, as Ammons keeps telling us—rather it is out of muddle and even mud that we get what matters; it is out of chaos that cosmos comes:

> between life and me obtrude
> no symbolic forms:
> grant me no mission . . .
> leave me this black rich country
> uncertainty, labor, fear: do not
> steal the rewards of my mortality.

We are, then, to be at a loss with Ammons, and happy to be there, for it is only when losses are permitted, invited even, that there are possibilities invoked. In the poem called, crucially, "Poetics", Ammons admits how he goes about making, precisely, by leaving off as much as by inventing, by finding:

> I look for the forms
> things want to come as
> from what black wells of possibility,
> how a thing will unfold: . . .
> not so much looking for the shape
> as being available

to any shape that may be
summoning itself
through me
from the self not mine but ours.

The search is for a poetic incarnation, but it is also an abandonment of
the search, a hope of poetic disincarnation, a way of overcoming by
literally *undergoing* the separate self. In this, Ammons' energies are dedicated concurrently with those of his fellow American poets. But it is only
in Ammons that I find all three moments—the changing from, the changing, and the changing to—exalted equally. Only Ammons, I think, of all
American poets today, has—when he is not diverted into his hip asides—
the capacity to endow the moment of loss, the moment of metamorphosis
and the moment of release with an equal light, "the blue obliteration of
radiance".

Indeed the three moments are what Ammons calls, in his account-
ing for events, for outcomes, for irreversible exits and recurrences alike,
ambiance, salience, radiance. These are his three favorite words for the
phenomenon signified (there is a place), then for the phenomenon abandoned (the place can be left), then for the phenomenon sanctified (only
loss reveals what the reward was to be). It is no accident, except insofar as
everything in Ammons is literally an accident, a falling-to, a befalling, it
is no accident that the greatest poem in this latest book is the last, and
neither small nor easy, the cross-titled poem "The City Limits", which
begins its 18-line single sentence "When you consider the radiance" and
ends with the acknowledgment that each thing is merely what it is, and
all that can be transcended is our desire for each thing to be more than
what it is, so that for such a consideration of the losses of being, the very
being of loss, "fear lit by the breadth of such calmly turns to praise." It is
all there in Ammons—the fear and the light, the calm and the breadth,
the turning and the praise, and that is why he is a great poet.

Collected Poems 1951–1971 (Boundary 2, 1973)

I have published an account of each of Ammons' books as they appeared,
following a first long essay on his work; I have taught, or been taught by,
the poetry in seminars at two universities, where it became clear to my
students as it became incontrovertible to me that for all our probable
ignorance of the ruddy turnstone and its habits, here was a great poet,
surely one of the largest to speak among us, today, of what we are and are
not, speaking wherever we troubled to listen in a voice so reticent in all
its authority, so gorgeous in all its immediacy, that we could scarcely miss

the accents of its persuasion, overheard, underlying, central. My intention here, therefore, is not one of summing up what is in every sense a going concern; it is not yet appropriate to tabulate results, for the poet is still very much ahead of us, making his way by the light of what he calls *the noons of recurrence*. Rather I should like to record my sense, merely, of a stunned gratitude for the work as it masses thus provisionally, my response to a recent rereading of the territory covered so far, always with the understanding that as Ammons ruefully admits, "less than total is a bucketful of radiant toys."

It is difficult to speak of any quantity of Ammons' poems without employing spatial metaphors—he is the poet of walking, and his is the topography of what one pair of legs can stride over, studies in *enjambment* indeed—and I have not resisted the difficulty: in all its guises, Ammons' poetry is never disguised—it takes a spiral trajectory, so that wherever we take it, his art is complete *that far*. In fact, it is the nature of this book's unrelenting course ("I like the order that allows," is how Ammons puts it) to describe that arc between the impossible and the necessary which will be this poet's particular balance, his special poise: between metaphor (saying that something is something else) and identity (saying that something is what it is). This is an old argument in our poetry—the argument between Thoreau and Emerson, between nature and vision, between the natural and the visionary, and no one has more shrewdly *drawn the line* than Ammons by this showing of twenty years work. It is no accident that the word *coil* and the word *collection* writhe upward to the surface from the same root.

"The war of shape and loss" is Ammons' Homeric conflict, the beach his Troy, though in the later poems a backyard will do: any *place* is an event for this bordering imagination, and what comes as something of a surprise in the discovery of his solitude, his singleness (there are no friends in this poetry, no other people, in fact; most dialogue is with the wind, with mountains, and when Ammons turns away from "cytoplasm's grains" or from "energy's invisible swirls," what he turns *back* to is not any human bond:

> I turned back
> strict with limitation,
> to my world's
> bitter acorns
> and sweet branch water.)

—what comes as an astonishment, I was saying, with the poet's solitary contemplations is his sociability of *form*. Ammons is a great inventor of forms, and his poetry murmurs and glitters with the sensuality of his "boundaried vacancies." I think our expectation would be that a man of such lonely confrontations would have devised a sort of paradigm of utterance, an exemplary discourse by which to speak his piece, and would *by now* have settled down to "a perfect carriage/ for resolved, continuous striving." Nothing of the kind. "Firm ground is not available ground," he observes, and risks his prosody in all the quicksands of variation. The characteristic somatic gesture in Ammons is that of testing his weight, seeing how much traffic any particular utterance can bear, from the favored mark of punctuation, the colon, to the endless open hexameters of "Hibernaculum":

> a poem variable as a dying man, willing to try anything,
> or a living man, with the consistency of either direction:
> just what the mind offers to itself, bread or stone:
>
> in the swim and genesis of the underlying reality things
> assume metes and bounds, survive through the wear
> of free-being against flux, then break down to swim and
>
> genesis again: that's the main motion but several
> interturns have been concocted to confuse it: for example . . .

and Ammons is off again. *Pages of examples,* his book might be called, and indeed it is exemplary, at a time of recipes and formulas, to find this supreme artificer inventing an unheard-of prosody each time he writes a poem. "Versification or diversification," he propounds, thereby suggesting that what has already been achieved is merely a chain—what Ammons cares about is the forging of new links, the finding of the next connection.

It is why so much of his poetry is given over—given away, as he likes to say—to erasure, destruction, loss, "the chant of vacancies, din of silences." Only when you have unmade something is there room for new making: "listen for the things I have left out." "Arrange me into disorder," Ammons implores his "Muse", and it is because his poetry hovers and shivers, in all its intonations (Ammons can be vatic, pop, sheepish, dogged, even kittenish, but the exactitude of his vocabulary makes his best poems geological, they are the *words of earth*), on the line, the arc, the curve between arrangement and chaos, that he is not merely a collected poet but a *collecting* one, that he keeps gathering within his circumference new reaches of the same substance, the same energy.

In the eight years since I began to read, and study, and love this man's poetry, I have had the opportunity to know the poet as well, and I presume it is appropriate to friendship that I "extend the form" of his collection, his coil, by adding to it a poem Ammons has not collected, but which he wrote after a visit I had made to his classes at Cornell, a poem which is a major provision—because provisional—for understanding the nature of his enterprise, the quality of his undertaking:

UNTELLING

Poetry is the word that has no other words,
the telling indistinguishable from the told:

it is all body (spirit) until it moves
and moving only is its declaring, divisible

neither into mind nor feeling, mind-felt,
form only if motion stays an instant into form,

otherwise form-motion, the body and the void
interpenetrating, an assuming, a perfect allowance:

how it moves away, returns, settles or
flashes by, how it works its worked space

into memory's body may tell tellings,
narratives, progressions beyond,

surrounding an instant's telling, though
only body-in-motion can place them there:

being is its afterlife whose life was becoming:
mind and other words confront, untell its dream.

It is sufficient excuse, this offering of an uncollected poem by A.R. Ammons, for my exultation over his collection: the poet who asks "what/ destruction am I/blessed by?" is thereby a master maker of his period, and by the working together of his movement and his stillness, leaves us the monument we need; "and fear lit by the breadth of such calmly turns to praise."

JOHN ASHBERY

In the American Grain

The pure products of America don't always go crazy: Dr. Williams himself is a demonstration of this. But the effort of remaining both pure and American can make them look odd and harassed—a lopsided appearance characteristic of much major American poetry, whose fructifying mainstream sometimes seems to be peopled mostly by cranks (Emerson, Whitman, Pound, Stevens), while certified major poets (Frost, Eliot) somehow end up on the sidelines. This is suggested again by the unexpected appearance of two voluminous *Collected Poems* by two poets who now seem destined to pass abruptly from the status of minor to major cranks.

Both John Wheelwright and A. R. Ammons are full of tics and quirks; both frequently write as though poetry could not be a vehicle of major utterance, as though it were itself a refutation of any such mythic nonsense; in both the poem is not so much a chronicle of its own making as of its unmaking. Often, as in Ammons's "Working Still" or Wheelwright's "North Atlantic Passage," the final product looks like a mess of disjointed notes for a poem. Yet each poet finishes by stretching our recognition of what a poem can be and in so doing carries the notion of poetry a little higher and further. Each seems destined to end up, albeit kicking and struggling, as classic American. . . .

A. R. Ammons's *Collected Poems* comes almost as unheralded as Wheelwright's sudden belated materialization. Ammons's first book, *Ommateum*, published in 1955, seems not to have attracted much attention; his second appeared nine years later. Recently he has been more

From *The New York Review of Books* (February 22, 1973). Copyright © 1973 by *The New York Review of Books*.

prolific, and critics, particularly Harold Bloom and Richard Howard, have considered his work seriously and at length, but few had probably anticipated a *Collected Poems* of such dimensions (almost 400 pages, to which must be added the recent Norton reissue in a separate volume of his 200-page poem *Tape for the Turn of the Year*). If his importance was suspected before, it is now, as so often happens, confirmed merely by the joining of several volumes in one—not only because the solidity and brilliance are at last fully apparent but because, as also often happens, the occasionally weaker early poems somehow illuminate and give access to the big, difficult later ones.

Without wishing to fall into the trap of comparing Wheelwright and Ammons merely because of the hazards of publication, one cannot help being struck by certain resemblances. Both are American originals (in the French sense of *un original* as someone who is also quite eccentric), and they are products as much of the American landscape as of its poetic tradition, in devious ways. Wheelwright's relation to New England is as tenuous but as real as Ives's cacophonous *The Housatonic at Stockbridge* is to the bucolic scene which prompted it. The relation lies deeper than resemblance. Ammons's landscape is American sidereal; a descendant of Emerson, as Bloom has pointed out, he is always on the brink of being "whirled/Beyond the circuit of the shuddering Bear" from the safe confines of backyard or living room. But the fascination of his poetry is not the transcendental but his struggle with it, which tends to turn each poem into a battleground strewn with scattered testimony to the history of its making in the teeth of its creator's reluctance and distrust of "all this fiddle."

Reading the poems in sequence one soon absorbs this rhythm of making-unmaking, of speech facing up to the improbability of speech, so that ultimately Ammons's landscape—yard, riverbed, ocean, mountain, desert, and soon "the unseasonal undifferentiated empty stark"—releases the reader to the clash of word against word, to what Harold Bloom calls his "oddly negative exuberance." The movement is the same, from the visible if only half-real flotsam of daily living to the uncertainties beyond, but one forgets this from one poem to the next; each is as different as a wave is from the one that follows and obliterates it. One is left, like the author at the end of his best-known poem, "Corsons Inlet," "enjoying the freedom that/Scope eludes my grasp, that there is no finality of vision,/ that I have perceived nothing completely,/that tomorrow a new walk is a new walk."

The poet's work is like that of Penelope ripping up her web into a varicolored heap that tells the story more accurately than the picture did. And meanwhile the "regional" has become universal, at an enormous but unavoidable cost, the destructiveness of the creative act in Ammons ("what/destruction am I/blessed by?")permits him to escape, each time, the temptations of the *paysage moralisé*. Much has been written about the relation of the so-called "New York School" of poets to the painting of men like Pollock, but in a curious way Ammons's poetry seems a much closer and more successful approximation of "Action Painting" or art as process. ("The problem is/how to keep shape and flow.")

Marianne Moore pointed out that "inns are not residences," and a similar basic corrective impulse runs throughout Ammons, giving rise to a vocabulary of pivotal words. "Saliences" (the title of one of his best poems), "suasion," "loft," "scary," "motion," and "extreme" are a few which assume their new meaning only after a number of encounters, a meaning whose sharpness corrects a previous one whose vagueness was more dangerous than we knew. A "loft" (also frequently used as a verb) is not a summit, but a way station and possibly the last one; saliences are pertinent and outstanding but not necessarily to be confused with meanings; suasion is neither persuasion nor dissuasion. The corrective impulse proceeds as much from prudence as from modesty; in any case it can coexist with occasional outbursts of pure egotism: "I want a squirrel-foil for my martin pole/I want to perturb some laws of balance/I want to create unnatural conditions" (but the poem of which this is the beginning is entitled "The Imagined Land"), just as Ammons's frugality and his relentless understatement are countered by the swarming profusion of the poems.

This austerity could lose its point in the course of such a long volume: the restricted palette; the limited cast of characters (bluejays, squirrels, and other backyard denizens figure prominently, along with the poet's wife, child, and car, not to forget the wind with whom he has dialogues frequently in a continuing love-hate relationship); the sparse iconography of plant, pebble, sand, leaf, twig, bone, end by turning the reader back from the creature comforts he might have expected from "nature" poetry to the dazzlingly self-sufficient logic which illuminates Ammons's poetry and in turn restores these samples from nature to something of their Wordsworthian splendor—but Wordsworth recollected in the tranquillity of midcentury mindless America, and after the ironic refractions of Emerson, Stevens, and Williams. For despite Ammons's misgivings, his permanent awareness of "a void that is all being, a being that is void," his "negative exuberance" is of a kind that could exist only after the trials of so much negation.

> I can't think of a thing to uphold:
> the carborundum plant snows
> sift-scum on the slicks outgoing river
> and along the avenues car wheels
> float in a small powder: my made-up
> mind idles like a pyramid. . . .
>
> ("Working Still")

But if he is unable to find a saving word for the polluted (in so many ways) American scene, his speech elevates it even as it refuses to transform it. "No American poet," writes Harold Bloom in an essay on Ammons, "When You Consider the Radiance," in his book *The Ringers in the Tower*, "not Whitman or Stevens, shows us so fully something otherwise unknown in the structures of the national consciousness as Ammons does." And for Americans who feel that America is the last truly foreign country, this something comes startlingly alive in poem after poem, as in the magnificent "One: Many":

> . . . and on and on through the villages.
> along dirt roads, ditchbanks, by gravel pits and on
>   to the homes, to the citizens and their histories,
> inventions, longings:
> I think how enriching, though unassimilable as a whole
> into art, are the differences: the small-business
> man in
>   Kansas City declares an extra-dividend
> and his daughter
>   who teaches school in Duquesne
> buys a Volkswagen, a second car for the family:
> out of many, one:
> from variety an over-riding unity, the expression of
> variety: . . .

How perfect and how funny in its Whitmanesque nod to the automotive industry is that "buys a Volkswagen, a second car for the family": it seems as much by its music as by its sense to sum up everything that is beautiful and wrong in our vast, monotonous, but very much alive landscape. And Ammons knows this well; he ends the poem with an unemotional summation that, in its reluctant acceptance of the "opaque" world that is still "world enough to take my time, stretch my reason, hinder / and free me," can also stand for the work:

> no book of laws, short of unattainable reality itself,
> can anticipate every event,

control every event: only the book
of laws founded against itself,
founded on freedom of each event
    to occur as itself,
lasts into the inevitable balances
    events will take.

HYATT H. WAGGONER

Notes and Reflections

My title is not modest, simply descriptive. Mr. Boyers asked me about a year ago to contribute an essay on a contemporary poet to this issue of *Salmagundi* and I agreed to do so if possible, but circumstances of several sorts now make it impossible to write the full-length, fully worked out, appreciative and interpretive article Ammons' poetry deserves and I should like to do. What follows is simply some of the thoughts, and a few reflections on those thoughts, that have come to me as I have read through seven volumes of the poetry, the product of something more than a decade of writing. I do not own, am not near a library that contains, and so have not seen Ammons' first volume, *Ommateum* (1955), an omission which must qualify anything I may say about Ammons' development.

I write these notes seated in a mountain meadow, facing north toward a spruce woods fringed with poplar and balsam fir, the short-lived forward units of the woods as it edges across an unused pasture beyond the meadow. I have been watching the woods take over the pasture for more than thirty years now but have seen no movement. All I know is that the woods are a hundred or so feet closer to engulfing the spot where I sit and the house behind me than they used to be, and from that I can deduce that they are coming toward us all the time, moving in stillness.

So much for the permanencies of nature. I find this helping me to understand and respond to a good deal of Ammons' poetry, in which nature is the subject, the exemplum, or the setting of a good many of the best passages and poems.

Ammons is a visionary poet in the Neoplatonic tradition intro-

---

duced and best represented in our (American) poetry by Emerson. I would guess that he has read a good deal of Emerson and pondered much on what he has read. Maybe not. Maybe he has read only a little and gotten all his Emersonianism from that little, working out for himself, as Emerson did, the consequences of a few major ideas about the relations of the Many and the One. Or maybe it has come to him at second and third hand, through Pound and Williams, Whitman and Frost, all of whom make their appearance in his poetry. It is clear at least though that he has read "Brahma"—which could have been sufficient for the right kind of mind—for he alludes to it and paraphrases it in "What This Mode of Motion Said" in *Expressions of Sea Level*. Emerson: "When me they fly, I am the wings"; Ammons: "I am the wings when you me fly"; Emerson: "I am the doubter and the doubt"; Ammons:

> I am the way by
> which you prove me
> wrong,
> the reason you
> reason against me.

Some other "Emersonianisms" in the poetry. (This could be a full-length article itself. It would have to treat important poems in each of the seven volumes I have read.) "Raft," the opening poem in *Expressions of Sea Level*, a somewhat self-consciously Romantic poem in which the sought-for unity with nature—or with the undefinable Reason behind nature—is distanced by a tone of playful makebelieve, is central Emerson: let go, yield, be blown by the winds of spirit. *Spiritus:* breath, wind. The Muse, the deeper self, the Holy Spirit. The boy on the circular raft is swept out to sea by the tides to where the winds control his motion toward the east, the rising sun. Neoplatonists: sun, source of light, life, and goodness; emanation. Christian Neoplatonists: sun = Son. . . . The Romantic sea-voyage; the "innocent eye" of the child. Several poems in the same volume make explicit what "Raft" implies by the story it tells. For instance, "Guide": "the wind that is my guide said this"; and "Mansion":

> So it came time
> for me to cede myself
> and I chose
> the wind
> to be delivered to.

The word *soul* can be used only in actual or implied quotation marks by contemporary poets. Since Ammons takes what the word refers to very seriously, he seldom uses it: there is nothing "so-called" about spirit in his work. Like Emerson, he is ambiguous about what he refuses to name. Emerson usually preferred to define the "Over-Soul," "World-Soul," "The Spirit," "The Real" in negative terms, as he does in the opening of the essay on the subject, following the long tradition of "negative theology." He was surer about Immanence than about Transcendence: "A light from within or from behind," with the ambiguity kept. Only in "Circles," in the early essays, does he drop the subjective-objective ambiguity and attribute unqualified Transcendence to the One: "the eternal generator of circles," that is, the Creator of the circles of physical and spiritual reality. Ammons' poetry keeps both Emerson's theoretic ambiguity and the intensity of Emerson's search for vision.

Ammons has a *mind*, too good a mind to be content with the kinds of superficial Romanticism that are becoming fashionable in contemporary poetry. I would like to call him a philosophical poet—except that description might turn away some of those who should read him, and except also that the phrase is in part intrinsically misleading in its suggestion that he deals principally in abstractions. He deals with the perfectly concrete felt motions and emotions of the particular self he is and, like Emerson again, looks for and often sees "Correspondences" between these motions and those of animate and inanimate nature, both nature-as-observed (winds, tides, seeds, birds) and nature-as-known-about (the chemistry of digestion, entropy).

The title poem of *Corsons Inlet* is such a philosophical poem, treating the relations and claims of logic and vision, order created and order discovered, being and becoming, art and nature. Rejecting any "finality of vision," it still prefers the risk of vision to any "easy victory" in "narrow orders, limited tightness." The poet's task is to try to "fasten into order enlarging grasps of disorder," the task Emerson set before the poet in "Merlin" and "Bacchus." I find significance in the fact that the poem was first entitled "A Nature Walk." If there is no order discoverable in nature, the order of art is a contrivance without noetic value. Ammons, like his Romantic and Transcendental poetic forebears, is not content to make pretty, or even interesting because intricately fashioned, poems. "Corsons Inlet" seems to me at once one of the finest and one of the most significant poems written by any of our poets in recent years. It is a credo, a manifesto, a cluster of felt perceptions, and a demonstration that, up to a point at least, vision *can* be both achieved and conveyed.

Though I am persuaded that my frequent mentions of Emerson up to this point do not distort but rather illuminate Ammons' work, still they might prove misleading if I failed to mention the ways in which the poet's vision is *un*like Emerson's. (Emerson, I should explain, is very fresh in my mind these days, for I have just spent a year rereading and writing about him. But I am still not importing my own preoccupation into Ammons' poetry: Emerson is there, and I happen to be well prepared to notice his presence—in many more ways, and more poems, than I have mentioned or will mention.) Let me try to generalize the difference first. Ammons comes as close to rediscovering the Romantic Transcendental vision of Emerson as any thoughtful and well-informed man of the late twentieth century is likely to be able to, but as a man of our time he simply cannot be a "disciple," he can only learn from, be stimulated by, walk the paths of, and be honest about his differences with, the poet who more than any other foreshadows him, as I see it.

A few of the differences. Ammons allows to come into consciousness, and so into his poetry, much more freely than Emerson did, the existential *angst* that Emerson must have felt but usually repressed. (See "1 Jan." in *Tape for the Turn of the Year* for Ammons' statement on this. The point he makes there—"I know the/violence, grief, guilt,/despair, absurdity"—is clear in all the volumes without being stated.) Death, disorder, entropy (one of his few technical philosophical terms) are never far from the surface of any of Ammons' poems, and frequently they are central in them. Poetry, he says in *Tape*, has "one subject, impermanence." Never unaware of "a universe of horror," Ammons knows that "we must bear/the dark edges of/our awareness," but the goal of his search remains "a universe of light" (*Tape*, "1 Jan.")

A different man in a different age, Emerson erected his defenses against fear and grief stronger and taller than Ammons', though I should say that in his best poetry—in prose as well as in verse—he was sufficiently open to all his feelings, even these, to allow his wonderful intelligence to work freely. Still, it is true, however one may take the fact, that Ammons does not transcend so easily or so far.

Related to this as a symptom is to a cause is the much greater concreteness of the way Ammons' imagination works, and so of his poetic language. As Emerson was more concrete, specific, even local (think of the first line of "Hamatreya") than the Pre-Romantics whose style his often resembles, so Ammons is more concrete, specific, local, and *personal* than Emerson. On this matter, as on style in general, Ammons' affinity seems to be with Pound and Williams, but of course Pound and Williams were more Emersonian than they knew.

A difference that is more strikingly obvious but I think finally less important is that of verse-forms. Emerson's theory, at least the part of it we are most likely to remember, called for organic or open form, but only a few of his best poems put the theory successfully into practice, and then only partially. Ammons, like most of his best contemporaries, has moved all the way toward practicing the theory announced in "The Poet" and elaborated in "Poetry and Imagination." Still, there is not an immeasurable gap, formally speaking, between "Merlin" and "Poetics" in *Briefings*.

Tape for the Turn of the Year, Ammons' "long thin poem" typed on a roll of adding-machine paper, a poetic journal which keeps turning into a poetic meditation, is the most continuously interesting, the strongest, the finest long poem I have read in I don't know how many years. It is as concrete as the *Cantos*, but the facts in it are not exotic lore out of the library and they are not illustrations of theories. It is at once personal and historical, like *Paterson*, but I don't feel, as I do in that poem at times, any attempt to impose the larger meanings. The meanings rise from the facts of personal history, the life the poet led from December 6 to January 10, the meals, the weather, the news, the interruptions, the discrete perceptions, and are presented for just what they are, felt thoughts. *Tape* proves—for me, anyway—the point Ammons makes in it somewhere, that poetry is "a way of/thinking about/truth" even while, as an art form, its distinctiveness is its way of "playing" with language to create untranslatable meanings.

Stylistically, *Tape* is "good Emerson," not so much in resembling Emerson's poems (though it does resemble them in certain ways, at times) as in following-out Emerson's theory. Transcendental poetic theory puts enormous emphasis on the single word, the single image, the discrete perception that may become an intuition. The short lines of the poem would seem merely stylish if they could not be justified in terms of this aspect of Transcendental Poetics. "Stylish" they may be, but the reason for the style emerges from the lines surprisingly, astonishingly. Prosaic, lyric, meditative, philosophic by turns, *Tape* is a wonderful poem. Read it.

Ammons' latest poems strike me as showing two developments. Stylistically, they are somewhat less "open," more thought-out, "reasonable," logically disciplined. They have pulled back a little from the letting-go and letting-out of the earlier work. There is less abandon, more control. Stylistically firmer perhaps, they seem to me less daring. Their style might be described as more "mature," but maturity brings losses as well as gains. The transparent eyeball narrows slightly to shield itself against the too-dazzling light. Ammons said toward the end of *Tape* that after the long, in a sense "dictated," poem he wanted to write short, artful lyrics, and he's doing it. And of course art is artificial. But I hope he will continue to leave openings, cracks maybe, in his conceptual boxes.

In any poet as fine as Ammons, a stylistic change signals a change in sensibility and vision. "Transaction" in *Uplands* ("I attended the burial of all my rosy feelings") describes the new "resignation" (Is this the right word? I'm not sure.) explicitly, but a good many of the poems in the two latest volumes exhibit it.

In *Tape* he reminded us—warned us?—that "I care about the statement/of fact" and suggested that "coming home" meant "a way of/going along with this/world as it is:/nothing ideal," but he still invited us to the dance. Wisdom involves a kind of resignation, I suppose, as one of its elements, but I think of it as contrasting with rashness and inexperience rather than as first cousin to prudence. I should hate to see Ammons become too prudent. I don't think he will.

The most recent poems may be less ambitious philosophically and less openly Romantic-Transcendental in their imaginative questing, but the quest itself has not been abandoned and the conception of how the journey should be undertaken—how thinking, feeling, imagining, responding can find expression and thus be realized, recognized, identified, and shared in a particular verbal object we call "this poem"—has not essentially changed. In the inseparable union of physics and metaphysics in Ammons' imagination, the emphasis may have shifted a little from the *meta* to the *physics*, but the union has not been dissolved, as of course it must not be if poetry is to continue to have noetic value. (Heidegger's "What Are Poets For?" in his recent *Poetry, Language, Thought* is relevant here. What are poets for in a dark time?) "Poetics" in *Briefings* should send any readers of it who don't remember the essay back to Emerson's "Poetry and Imagination." "Ask the fact for the form." Imagination and circles, imagination and possibility, the expanding spheres of possibility—of apprehension, of recognition, of meaning—finding their forms in poems. Here's the poem:

> I look for the way
> things will turn
> out spiralling from a center,
> the shape
> things will take to come forth in
>
> so that the birch tree white
> touched black at branches
> will stand out
> wind-glittering
> totally its apparent self:
>
> I look for the forms
> things want to come as

from what black wells of possibility,
how a thing will
unfold:

not the shape on paper—though
that, too—but the
uninterfering means on paper:

not so much looking for the shape
as being available
to any shape that may be
summoning itself
through me
from the self not mine but ours.

Harold Bloom is quoted on the back cover of *Briefings* as saying that the lyrics in the book "maintain an utterly consistent purity of detached yet radiant vision." Right on target. But I'd like to shrink the ambiguities of this a bit if I can without putting us and Ammons into a mentalistic box. "Consistent": consistent with all the other lyrics in the volume, yes, but not entirely consistent, in tone or statement, with the best of the earlier lyrics or even with the prayer ("14 Dec.") and the several credos (*credo*: I believe) in *Tape*. A little more defensive, more guarded, more "intellectually prudent." There's a concern with defining differences: ". . . keep me from my enemies'/wafered concision and zeal" ("Hymn IV," *Briefings*). A fear almost that vision may harden into doctrine.

"Purity": Yes, of style, of tone, of vision too. The wonderful thing is that the purity is at once a purity of style and a purity of vision, in both cases (or perspectives: two sides of the same coin) a unique balance maintained between conflicting perceptions of the One and the Many, the Real and the Actual, etc.—to borrow some Emersonian terms for what is not easily talked about in any terms.

"Detached": "Wafered concision" suggests that the detachment is from High Church zealots who localize "the eternal generator of circles" (Emerson's term in "Circles") in the manageable little round wafer of Communion. But the detachment is equally, I think, from the rationalistic formulations of the ineffable that betray an idolatrous attitude not toward a common substance, bread, but toward the results of a process, directed abstract thought. I say this not from the evidence of this poem, which, by its emphasis, might not seem to prompt it, but from the evidence of the whole corpus of the poetry as I have read it.

"Radiant": No need for clarification (if that's the word for what

I'm trying to do) here. "Radiant" in the sense that applies to Blake, Emerson, Whitman, Cummings, Roethke.

"Vision": Right again, of course. But "vision" and "visionary" can be a way of throwing positivistic enemies off the scent. Vision of what? Assuming that God is not a "being" among other beings, and so, being unlimited spatially and temporally ("God is the circle whose center is everywhere and circumference nowhere"—the practitioners of the "negative theology," and Emerson, said), is undefinable, still I'd say a sense of God's reality, whether as immanent or as *deus absconditus*, is everywhere present in the poems and should be recognized, for it does more than anything else (of the many factors at work, some unknown, some unknowable,) to give the poems their special *kind* of "vision." Heidegger, "What Are Poets For?" again.

I'd like to make the word *religious* respectable once again among literary critics, rescue it from Frued ("the future of an illusion") and give it to Jung, who used the word not to clobber the naively pious but to point to something real and permanent in human experience. ("Permanent" until *now*, maybe.) Ammons is a poet of religious vision who is as wary of intellectualist abstractions as he is of pious dogmas. *That's* the peculiar feature of the "purity" of his "vision," it seems to me. Peculiar in our time, not peculiar if we think of the poetic visionaries who are his ancestors, whether he knows it or not—and he probably does, for he seems to know everything.

The "veracity" of Ammons' poetry (his word, and Emerson's before him, in "Poetry and Imagination"), the sense it creates in us that the radiance, when it comes, is real, discovered, not invented or faked, is causally related, I suspect, to the steadiness with which the poet has looked into the Abyss. The gains for the imagination from such looking are incalculable, but it must be hard on the nerves. One wants to survive as well as write "short rich hard lyrics," as Ammons is doing now. I want Ammons to do both—that is, survive and write. Perhaps the slight narrowing of the eyelids over the transparent eyeballs I seem to detect in the later work is necessary for the survival. But the transparency remains essential to his kind of vision. Dilemma. Poets age, like the rest of us.

I don't try very conscientiously to "keep up" with all the new poetry in the magazines and the slender volumes, but I can say that of the "new" poets I've read since Roethke's death, Ammons seems to me at or near the top. His poetry is, among other things, more important, a "sign" granted for the strengthening of the faith, the faith that in a dark time light may still be seen, not invented (no "Supreme Fiction," no fiction at all), by the unguarded eye.

At his best (I don't much like "Summer Session 1968"), Ammons is a highly distinguished poet of religious vision who grants the Transcendence but finds his occupation chiefly in searching out the traces of the Immanence. May he survive, save himself for this, and be visited often by the Muse, indulging as little as may be in the writing of merely fashionable poems.

HELEN VENDLER

Ammons

PART I

In *Briefings* (1971) Ammons brought
his difficult form of short poetry to perfection. The poetry he is best able
to write is deprived of almost everything other poets have used, notably
people and adjectives. (Where would Whitman have been, shorn of his
soldiers, sleepers, and shipwrecked women, not to speak of his incandes-
cent palette of adjectives?) Ammons has written some poems about "people," including his mule Silver, and even permits himself an adjective
now and then, but rarely one more subjective than an adjective of color or
measurement. "Half-dark," "massive," "high," "giant," "distant," "long,"
"broad," "noticeable," "late," "dry," "diminished," "passable" (implying
height of hills), and "quiet" are the crop gleaned from two pages chosen at
random in the *Collected Poems*, and these "objective" adjectives, Ammons'
own, are balanced by only one "subjective" adjective on the same pages
("taxing"—an opinion imputed to a hill ·trying to be a mountain and
finding it hard). Such word-counts are perhaps not very gripping, but I
found myself reduced to them in trying to understand what new language
Ammons is inventing. (If he never succeeded, it wouldn't matter what he
was up to, but since he does bring it off, we need to know how he is
working out for us "a new knowledge of reality.") What he does is remarkable both in its sparseness and in its variety. One can't say "richness"

I. From *The Yale Review* 62 (Spring 1973). Copyright © 1973 by Yale University Press.
II. From *The Yale Review* (Autumn 1977). Copyright © 1977 by Yale University Press.

because there is no sensual "give" in this poetry—but it does attempt an imitative re-creation, no less, of the whole variety of the natural world, if not regrettably, of what Stevens called its "affluence." But if, as Ammons seems to think, affluence is brought rather by the perceiving and receptive mind, as a quality, rather than inhering in nature itself (nature, who perceives herself singly, we may say, as an acorn here, a brook there, rather than corporately congratulating herself on all her brooks), then a poetry attempting this ascetic unattributiveness must refrain from celebrating the multiplicity of the world in human terms. Why it should be so wrong to let in human gestalt-making is another question; Ammons permits himself entry when the poem is about himself, but he won't have any of those interfering adjectival subjectivities when he's occupied with morning glories or caterpillars or redwoods. This discipline of perfect notation is almost monklike, and, monklike, it takes what comes each day as the day's revelation of, so to speak, the will of God. Ammons wakes asking what the world will today offer him as a lesson and he is scarcely permitted choice: if it is snowing, he has to deduce the mantra in the snow; if it is a night with a masked aurora, it is to the aurora that he must compose that night's address. He is like a guitarist presented every day with a different señorita in the balcony, and commanded, like some latter-day Sheherezade, to think up each day different but appropriate serenades reflecting the lady's different looks.

In one way, given the fertile changingness of the external world, and its numberless inhabitants animal, vegetable, and mineral, this is a very rich discipline. On the other hand, it risks being merely fussy. If one should stop caring just what the weather is doing day after day in Ithaca, all is lost:

it's snowing now with

the sun shining: squalls with clearings: today is Tues-
day: yesterday there were 9 hrs and 2 minutes of
daylight, sunup to sundown: that means light is

broadening: right here at the edge of winter-beginning's
winter-ending: today will probably be 9 hrs and 3 minutes:
tomorrow will be different, maybe 9 hrs and 4 minutes.

There is a fair amount of this sort of thing, especially in the rather willed long poem *Tape for the Turn of the Year* (you buy a roll of adding-machine tape and type on it for a couple of weeks until the tape is all typed and then you have finished your poem). There is also a trust that everything you do, like everything the weather does, has its part in the configuration

of the whole. Ammons' gas station tells him his car is ready and he goes to
get it:

> the total parts came to $7.79, 1 push rod ($1.25), 1
>
> rocker arm ($1.35), rocker retainer ($0.50), 1 set 2
> gaskets @ $2.10 ($4.20), and 1 roll electrical tape ($0.49):
> the total labor was $10.50: r & r (remove and repair?)
>
> 1. (left?) valve cover, r & r both valve covers, replace
> rocker arm, push rod, & retainer on #4 cyl intake valve:
> all in all I thought I got off easy: one thing interesting
>
> is that Ned's Corners Station is at 909 Hanshaw Road
> and I'm 606 Hanshaw Road: that's configuration.

Only if you think it is, is it configuration, and for all Ammons'
jauntiness, he carries this Wordsworthian notion of everything-adding-up
to an extreme. In Wordsworth, it sounds rather saner:

> How strange, that all
> The terrors, pains, and early miseries,
> Regrets, vexations, lassitudes interfused
> Within my mind, should e'er have born a part,
> And that a needful part, in making up
> The calm existence that is mine when I
> Am worthy of myself!

Ammons' version of this omnivorousness is offered us in "Hibernaculum,"
one of the several long poems he has recently and self-consciously written:

> In the swim and genesis of the underlying reality things
> assume metes and bounds, survive through the wear
> of free-being against flux, then break down to swim and
>
> genesis again.

And so he writes his "poem variable as a dying man, willing to try
anything," even catalogues of spare parts. Very often, in his later poetry,
Ammons tries to reassure himself on the value of his poetics by comparing
it to the geological and organic motions of the universe, so molecularly
deep and so cosmically all-embracing: we hear about the genetic code and
double helices, cryogenic events and supernovas, colloidal floats and
platelets, estuary populations, nucleations, defoliations, the underground
mantle, and so on, through all the vocabulary, one might say, of *Scientific
American.* "*Ecology* is my word," declares Ammons adding "my other
word is / *provisional,*" and he says elsewhere, half in play and half in
earnest:

> I get lost for fun,
> because there's no chance of getting lost: I am seeking the
> mechanisms physical, physiological, epistemological, electrical,
>
> chemical, esthetic, social, religious, by which many, kept
> discrete as many, expresses itself into the
> manageable rafters of salience, lofts to comprehension.

This "Essay on Poetics" is presented with an unusual amount of candor, summing up what we had had glimpses of in "Motion" and "Poetics" and "Zone," and any critic would be glad if one day he understood Ammons as well as Ammons, rather exceptionally among poets, understands himself. "I was thinking last June," he confesses, "so multiple and diverse is the reality of a tree, that I/ought to do a booklength piece on the elm in the backyard here:/wish I had done it now because it could stand for truth, too." In fact, he even begins the tree poem, and in a burst of fancy imagines how he would have to determine the tree's place in space by longitude, lattitude, distance from the earth's core, and other methods. Never has there been a poetry so sublimely above the possible appetite of its potential readers. Genial as Ammons' programs are, and impressive as his lava-flows of language become in the long poems, these longer efforts are less likely to win an audience (except those of us captive enough to listen like a three-years' child to anything new and personal being done with words) than the shorter poems.

It is with his short poems, where he does obstinate battle with both multiplicity and abstraction at once, being fair to the weeds and the vines and the grasses and the worms, and at the same time rising to grand speculations on man's nature and the design of life, that Ammons will win a permanent audience. Ammons' conversations with mountains are the friendliest and most colloquial conversations with the inanimate recorded in poetry since Herbert talked to his shooting-star ("Virtu," "Classic," "Reversal," "Schooling," and "Eyesight" belong to this group); another group includes poems rejoicing in the world, like the beautiful "This Bright Day"; others retell, over and over, with a satisfying variety in imagery, the climb up to perspective and the slide back down to particularity, that process out of which lyric is built (and these include the splendid "Two Possibilities," "One More Time," and "High and Low," with its Emersonian determination and its rueful country debacle):

> A mountain risen
> in me
> I said
> this implacability

must be met:
so I climbed
the peak:
height shook and
wind leaned
I said what
kind of country is
this anyhow and
rubbled
down the slopes to
small rock
and scattered weed.

Then there is another group, not making points at all, just seeing how things are: these are the ones I like best, and would first anthologize, the ones like "Treaties," where Ammons' instinctive identification with earthly events affords a symbolism which remains natural and, though clear, inconspicuous:

My great wars close:
ahead, papers,
signatures, the glimmering
in shade of
leaf and raised wine:
orchards, orchards,
vineyards, fields:
spiralling slow time while
the medlar
smarts and glows and
empty nests
come out in the open:
fall rain then stirs
the black creek and
the small leaf slips in.

Such poems, though perhaps not Ammons' superficially most ambitious, are the ones that last in the mind, drawing as they do on his feeling that "if a squash blossom dies, I feel withered as a stained/zucchini and blame my nature." Ammons has taken into the realm of nature Donne's "any man's death diminishes me," and so can write about the lives and deaths in nature as though they were (and they are) his own. It is a severe poetry, attempting the particularity of Hopkins with none of what Hopkins' schoolmates called his "gush," trying for the abstraction of Stevens without Stevens' inhuman remove from the world of fact, aiming at Williams' affectionateness toward the quotidian without Williams' romantic drift. Since Ammons is still in mid-career, we can watch the experiment, we hope, for a good while yet: if he can succeed (even granting the absurdity of some of the niches and odd corners of his enterprise), he will have written the first twentieth-century poetry wholly purged of the romantic.

PART II

Perhaps only someone who has lived through the full interminableness of winters in upstate New York can feel, as I did, the weight of A. R. Ammons' *Snow Poems*. Unsentimentally, from the snow-threat at the end of September to the final sleet of May, they chronicle an Ithaca snow-season, often with a fine dry comedy ("today continues the tropical/ extravaganza—up to 45″"). Ammons is a diarist here, like Thoreau, not wishing to make well-made poems (though he can do those expertly whenever he wants), but rather to write down life as it is at fifty, during a long winter, in a solitary epoch. He runs through all his repertory of styles, from mock-Negro (in one brilliant flash) to Emersonian reflection to Thoreauvian accuracy. Open the book anywhere and there is a ripple of thought, a weather report, a lament, a curious observation of the out-of-doors, and a hard inquiry. The individual poems are named only for their first line: no titular summings-up allowed. The book needs to be lived in for days, reread after the first reading has sorted out its preoccupations and methods, and used as a *livre de chevêt* if its leisurely paths are to be followed in their waywardness. Ammons has developed an annoying tic of turning clichés mechanically around ("being there is the next best/thing to long distance") and a somewhat distracting habit of doodling on the typewriter ("overwhelm whelm helm elm"). All poets do those things in the margins, but they usually leave them behind when the poem reaches the printed page; in accord with some present principle of aesthetic nudity, Ammons has let them remain. His fluency is unstoppable, as always, but here it appears in short lines rather than his recent long ones in *Sphere*. An extremely attractive mind—full of sights, science, quirks, questions, and a million words—appears to unroll itself to us as one would unroll an endless scroll—another "tape for the turn of the year."

Ammons' current of language flows (to mix a metaphor) from his perpetual attempt to draw nectar in a sieve; like Warren, he sees drops trickling through his fingers, but writes of that loss as the only motive for life:

                    how
grateful we must be that as we reach to take the
much desired in hand it loses shape and color and
drifts apart and must be looked for all over again
        so are we shoveled
        forward half unwillingly
        into the future (where futurity is lost)

The voice reasonable in loss is one Ammons; the eviscerated Ammons,
doggedly writing down the weather day after day, is something else,
Beckett-like, hard on himself as ice:

            who who had
            anything else
            to be interested
            in would be
            interested in
            the weather

"Sick with a pure/ interest in beauty," Ammons lives off the land, but
admits that for anyone hungering for love, "this beauty, though very /
beautiful, is an inconsiderable / feast." Nonetheless, all Ithacans and
ex-Ithacans will recognize that Ammons has delineated that landscape
and that climate for good and all, with an Emersonian wintriness of voice
diluting the ebullience he inherited from Williams. Since the sound of
Ammons is deservedly well-known, I will quote, instead of a more characteristic passage, the opening of his inspired blackface excursus on being
born different from the American herd. It might be spoken by the bad
fairy at the christening of a doomed genius:

            the average person is average
            the common people is common
            the straight people is straight
            you gone be the crooked weird
            rare intelligent bird creep type
            that what you gone be, honey
                    you gone look funny
                    when they put you in your
                    coffin
                    like you something
                    unright
                    like you ain't
            worth dying
            like every day when they passes out the
            honey
            you gone get a little vial of fear and
            you gone drink it yes you is

This is allusive poetry for the middle-aged, expecting from its audience a nod of recognition:

> you have to feel pretty
> good to have a good time:
> the aspirant spiral: you remember
> the aspirant spiral

Uh huh, we remember the aspirant spiral; we felt pretty good; we had a good time. And so we talk back to Ammons' mumble over the one-way telephone of verse. He has changed the "we" of poetry from the high philosophical mode ("We live in an old chaos of the sun") to the mode of refugees caught together in a bad time. He probably cannot escape what he fears—"the outbreak of destructive clarification" from critics—but more than most poets, he is, though offhand and compressed, a man speaking. "Do you not see," Keats wrote, "how necessary a world of pains and troubles is to school an intelligence and make it a soul?" Ammons has his version:

> to be made of steel!
> so bullets and aches and
> pains and sorrows
> the sorrows of knowing and
> not knowing and witnessing
> bing off you
> that would be so fine
> provided you did not
> remain stiff and
> uneducated.

As poets accompany their discipline of pains and troubles with the discipline of expressive form, an enormous superfluity, it would seem of ingenuity is required in order to convey the lessons of the Keatsian world-hornbook. How odd it remains that the solitaries who are bedeviled by the possibilities of words remain the chief chroniclers of the emotional history of mankind.

PATRICIA A. PARKER

Configurations of Shape
and Flow

There are no fixtures in nature. The universe is fluid and volatile.
Permanence is but a word of degrees.

—EMERSON, *Circles* (1840)

These poems are, for the most part, dramatic presentations of thought
and emotion, as in themes of the fear of the loss of identity, the
appreciation of transient natural beauty, the conflict between the individ-
ual and the group, the chaotic particle in the classical field, the creation
of false gods to serve real human needs. While maintaining a perspective
from the hub, the poet ventures out in each poem to explore one of the
numberless radii of experience. The poems suggest a many-sided view of
reality; an adoption of tentative, provisional attitudes, replacing the
partial, unified, prejudicial, and rigid; a belief that forms of thought, like
physical forms, are, in so far as they resist it, susceptible to change,
increasingly costly and violent.

—A. R. AMMONS, *Ommateum* (1955)

T he poet who speaks in the Foreword
to his own first volume of "the chaotic particle in the classical field," goes
on to dazzle us with a profusion of such titles as "Nucleus," "Bourn,"
"Center," "Periphery," "Circles," and "Round," and begins the longest
and most difficult of his recent poems, "Hibernaculum," with an evocation of the "timeless relations" of "center to periphery," "core-thought to

---

From *Diacritics* 3 (Winter 1973). Copyright © 1973 by Diacritics, Inc.

consideration" is of all the present generation of poets not only the most strikingly Emersonian in his own way, but the one most conscious of the dynamics and metamorphoses of his tradition's most persistent emblem, from Emerson's essay *Circles* and Whitman as "encompasser of worlds" to Dickinson's "Circumference" and "Circumstance" and the ninth of Stevens' "Thirteen Ways of Looking at a Blackbird": "When the blackbird flew out of sight,/It marked the edge/Of one of many circles."

Even the early *Ommateum* poems betray a fascination with what Dickinson called the "Wizardry" of "Geometry." The diagrammatic easiness of these poems is provided by the two axes inevitable no matter where the poet stands—the earth's horizontal surface and that upright animal man, in "the boost of perpendicularity,/directional and rigid" ("Doxology"). Because of this upright position, a stance as challenging to entropy as the mountainous coiffures in Wallace Stevens' "Le Monocle de Mon Oncle," the "I" of these desert dramas inhabits a plainisphere and, judging all things from his own vertical precipice, naturally sees the earth as flat and the sun as sinking into an abyss. These axes are still the implicit setting of the later poem "Recovery," with its shadow "hardened into noon," and in the twenty-seventh of the *Ommateum* poems Ammons seems to delight in geometric wizardry almost for its own sake:

> waterfalls
> humbling in silent slide
> the precipice of my effrontery
>   poured libations of arms
> like waterwheels
> toward the ground but
> knowing the fate of sunset things
> I grew desperate and entertained it
>   with sudden sprints
>   somersaults
> and cartwheels figuring eight
>
> It would not stay
>   Ring of cloud I said
> high pale ringcloud
> ellipsis of evening moment's miracle
> where will I go looking for your return
> and rushing to the rim
> I looked down into the deep dissolution

This is not the best of the early Ammons and is, quite rightly, not included in the *Collected Poems*, but it takes us, both in image and concern, all the way forward to the "anguish perfect/that the sun still/took its gold away" in "Wagons" and the persistent westwardness of everything that gives a very recent poem the title "Left." The poet who knows the fate of sunset things and from the western rim looks down into the deep dissolution is, of course, simply reminding us of the obvious visual extensions of the first sentence of Emerson's remarkable essay *Circles*—"The eye is the first circle; the horizon which it forms is the second"—and of the fact that, as far as poets are concerned, the Copernican revolution has not occurred, that all of us, visually at least, belong to one or another flat earth society by whose conventions the sun rises and sets. Inhabiting a flat earth gives Stevens the "trash can" for the "rejected things" which have "Slid over the western cataract" in "The Well Dressed Man with a Beard." And when Ammons in the *Ommateum* poem uses "entertained" in the root sense of holding within the present circumference of sight, we may remember the entertainers fetched out of air in "The Auroras of Autumn" and their failure.

Diagram is not always a virtue in poetry and within this tradition revealed its limitations early in Whitman's very bad poem "Chanting the Square Deific." But when Ammons provides us with a profusion of such titles, he is clearly inviting us to explore the wizardry of this geometry and to discover in some of his best lyrics that diagram itself can be delight— and revelation. One of the revelations which emerges in the persistence and explicitness of Ammons' "wizardry" is that of his own relationship to his tradition. The poet who tells us that "The unassimilable fact leads us on" ("The Misfit") knows the exhilarations of the never-ending expansion of circumference that led Emerson to speak in *Circles* of "the inevitable pit which the creation of new thought opens for all that is old" and of the challenge of "the Unattainable, the flying Perfect." But he also knows the terror in this "pit" that Stevens took to its logical and absurd conclusion in "The Man on the Dump" and the sorrows of the "bird that never settles," which in Stevens' "Somnambulisma" ensure that any paradise sought in nature will be a lost one:

> it all adds up to zero only
> because each filled day is shut away, vanished: and what
> memory keeps it keeps in a lost paradise
>
> ("Hibernaculum")

The poet who raises in the late poem "Summer Session" the problem of how to keep both "shape & flow" inherits his tradition's deepest concern and its most persistent emblem. At the same time he invites us to see it in a different way, a gift that, as Harold Bloom has written, "compels that backward vision of our poetry that only major achievement exacts" and yet enables us to return to find in the poet a freshness that we find nowhere else, as Ammons' own recent poem "Precursors" so disarmingly suggests.

That the perpendicular axis should be the rigid one reminds us of the perils of the upright stance in a world which does not like sharp lines and takes us all the way forward to "Corsons Inlet" and its discoveries. The opposition between "shape & flow" will later become the series of devastating if delightful encounters with the mountain's "massive symmetry and rest" ("Mountain Talk") and with the wind which "has given up everything to eternal being but/direction" ("Guide") and the identity crisis these encounters represent for the poet who is one of the "intermediates of stone and air" ("Delaware Water Gap"). The problem of "Identity" in the poem of that name will be the topic of a meditation on the spider web and the "disorder ripe" along its "peripheries." But when the center of "identity" will not hold in Ammons' very earliest poems, the "I" becomes a self given up to the victory of stones and trees, the seeker "broken over the earth" in "Rack" and "wasted by hills" in "Look for My White Self." The explorations the poet suggests in the *Ommateum* Foreword become the various strategies of mind in an alien environment— from the furious attempt to entertain the things that will not stay to the determination to fix some immovable center in the midst of constant change.

This attempt to find some shelter for the mind often produces too rigid an order for "unformulable reality's/fall-out insistences" ("Medicine for Tight Spots"), like the oak tree "experiment" in "With Ropes of Hemp" whose Whitmanian ending ("I in the night standing saying oaksongs/ entertaining my soul to me") reveals both the terrible reduction of this encompasser and all there is left to "entertain." The echoes of Whitman in this chant hysterical return in another early poem where the sun's advances recall the "prurient provokers" of section twenty-eight of "Song of Myself" and the contractive movement becomes a mechanism of defense:

> A treeful of cleavage flared branching
> through my flesh and cagey
> I sat down mid-desert
> and heaping hugged up between my knees
> an altarcone from the sand
> and addressed it with water dreams.

The pent-up being of this poem complains that there is no time "to dream real" his "dreams," and at the sound of "time," the sun does its usual disappearing act, leaving this stony idolater to become what he beholds, the "fixed will" of his "bones entombed" with the "dull mound" of his "god/in bliss."

The "altarcone" heaped up against this threat in "A Treeful of Cleavage Flared Branching" becomes, in another early poem, the more active task of gathering "the stones of earth" from "the boundaries of mind" into "one place." This altarcone is to be topped by "a cardinal/ chilled in the attitude of song," and we hardly need the hint of the sparrow's "one / repeated song" in the later poem "Glass" to recognize in this cardinal both of the wrong kinds of order in Wallace Stevens' "Notes Toward a Supreme Fiction"—the "episcopus" and the incessantly calling bird. However, the first stanza, which gives this poem its title, suggests the countering force that finally saves the stonegatherer from himself.

> In the wind my rescue is
> in whorls of it
>   like winged tufts of dreams
> bearing
>   through the forms of nothingness
>   the gyres and hurricane eyes
> the seed safety
>   of multiple origins.

These early poems are still the best introduction to Ammons' ongoing poetic enterprise. The "seed safety/of multiple origins" takes us all the way forward to the poem "Laser" and the fixed image to which the mind finally succumbs in spite of its desperate struggle to "dream of diversity." The dangers of the center already presented in the "altarcone" continue through Ammons' work right up to the decision of a "periphery riffler" to be near enough to the center of things to be "knowingly away," even if it means, geometrically and colloquially, to be a "Square." And when this wariness of the center is extended to what he calls, in the *Ommateum* Foreword, "the drama of rising and falling," he invites us to stretch his circle into a sphere and explore the related dangers of vertex and vortex.

This drama takes as many forms as there are voices in Ammons, from the poet who moves close to the eternal in "The Watch," to the mountain who finds grandeur taxing in "Height," to the Dialogue of Soul and Body in "Touching Down," to the seer who cannot refuse the terrors of his own election in the haunting "He Held Radical Light." When the drama is that of rising to "imagination's limit" ("Two Possibilities"), where "all-is-one" means "nothing is anything" ("Looking Over the Acreage"), the poet's fear is of the immateriality and exclusions of ascent to an

"extreme" gain which is also a "total" loss ("Loft"). One of these potential losses is that once up in "abstraction's gilded loft" ("Levitation"), the
seer will not accept the stiff fact of coming down or perhaps even be able
to. The danger in these moments of dominion for the seer is the same,
whether it is "The Strait" and its fear that the sibyl might lose her
"human hold" or the experience of being sucked up into the "Moment"
which prompts one seer in the poem of that name to ask "what/destruction
am I blessed by?" When, on the other hand, the journey to the center
becomes the drama of "falling," it appears as the dance of death that the
poet steps out of in the early poem "In Strasbourg in 1349," the "universal
law of gravity" in "Choice," and, in "Guitar Recitativos," the kind of
magnetic attraction that reminds us of why Stevens says "Farewell to
Florida":

<blockquote>

why
don't you get yourself together and I'll

get myself together and then we'll sort of shy out
of each other's gravitational field, unstring the
electromagnetism and then sort of just drop this
whole orientation baby.
</blockquote>

When Ammons uses the circle in its plane sense, however, it
becomes in the poems written after the publication of *Ommateum* in 1955
a series of meditations on the relationship of center and periphery, order
and entropy. Emerson begins his essay of 1840 by speaking of the circle as
the "emblem" we are all our lifetime reading, precisely because it connects
so many disparate phenomena. Ammons in "Undersea" uses the more
modern term "paradigm," but his own response to the miracle of micro-
cosm and macrocosm, in poems like "The Constant" and "World," suggests that it is for him a very great "Event" indeed. His fascination with
the rhythm of "diffusion and concentration:/in and out" ("Four Motions
for the Pea Vines") accounts for the diagrammatic and topographical
nature of much of his poetry, a feature some readers have found uncongenial.
But it is resolutely his mode, and "paradigm" becomes literally "topography" in the first part of the recent "Essay on Poetics."

To note that Ammons includes in his meditations on paradigm the
latest in field theory in science or center-margin models in economics, or
again, flirts with Emerson's "circle of compensation" in its modern form of
probability and quantum mechanics, may be simply to point out that he is
the twentieth-century equivalent to what Emerson described in *The Poet*:
"Readers of poetry see the factory-village and the railway, and fancy that
the poetry of the landscape is broken up by these; for these works of art

are not yet consecrated in their reading; but the poet sees them fall within the great Order not less than the beehive or the spider's geometrical web." When the poet of the "Essay on Poetics" tells us that he is "seeking the/mechanisms physical, physiological, epistemological, electrical,/chemical, esthetic, social, religious" by which "many, kept/discrete as many, ex-presses itself into the/manageable rafters of salience," paradigm may seem to have become a kind of mad structuralism. In the best of Ammons' work, it is a mode of revelation. One of the revelations of paradigm is its disclosure of the hidden metaphors of common speech, so that it is not surprising that the double talk of the poem in which Ammons "can't decide whether/the backyard stuff's/central or irrelevant" bears the title "Circles." The delight of poems such as "Right On," "Making Waves," and "If Anything Will Level with You Water Will" is that they speak what Stevens called the "lingua franca et jocundissima" and yet are used with an exactness that takes the dialect of the tribe at its word. The hidden paradigm is the reason why Ammons can speak in one poem of "unwind-ing" as a "Medicine for Tight Spots."

The fact that the circle is both a paradigm of relationship and a submerged figure of speech enables Ammons to move from the problem of the spider web's "Identity" to the peripheral "Expressions of Sea Level" to the dynamics of corporate control in "Nucleus." In the last of these poems, he can use the language of center and periphery precisely because the corporate empire itself has given the ghostly paradigm "A local habitation and a name." The word "nucleus" requires for its appropriation perhaps a little more exposure to the filter of sociological jargon, but "nexus" has long been as much a part of commercial parlance as "profit and loss," and "whether the incoming or outgoing forces are stronger" becomes here the movement of "Lines" as "cash flow":

> how you buy a factory:
> determine the lines of
> force
> leading in and out, origins, destinations of lines;
> determine how
>   from the nexus of crossed and bundled lines
>   the profit is
> obtained

The double time we know from Eliot or Joyce becomes in Ammons' poem a revelation of old and new visions of empire, Cartier travelling up the St. Lawrence to "Hochelaga," his modern counterpart taking " 'The Laurentian' out of New York/first morning after the strike ended." The connection, once again, is the paradigm. Montreal, once a margin on the French empire, is now—except for a little competition from the "Queen" and "parent companies in England and Germany" —a margin on the American one. The "prospect" afforded Cartier by the "panoramic" view from "Mt. Royal" becomes the "prospects" mapped out over breakfast from the twenty-two storey height of " 'The Panorama.' " The easily defendable island Cartier surveys from his mountain of vision becomes the factory location on Linden Street, "four walls, a limited, defined, exact place,/a nucleus,/solidification from possibility." And if the problem of balancing "growth possibility" with sufficient central control is now a more delicate operation than it was for Cartier with his "tin paternosters" and "knives," the present "nucleus" does not appear to be in danger as long as the response from the margins is "Yassuh."

If Ammons reveals in "Nucleus" the dynamic of empires past and present, he also knows with Emerson that the "empire of thought" is an inescapable activity of mind, that every man is an imperialist of the imagination whose sphere of influence, however small, begins in at least some Idea of a Colony. Building in matter a home for mind requires the same balance of shape and flow as the enterprise of "Nucleus," and when "empire" has itself acquired unpleasant associations in the "lingua franca," this too is one of the revelations of paradigm. The relationship of this "periphery riffler" to the "systems analysts,/futurists, technocrats, and savvy managers / who square off a percentage of reality and name their price" ("Reassessing") is a complex one, balanced on as fine a difference as that between the too stony center of "In the Wind My Rescue Is" and the stonegatherer's need, in "Apologia pro Vita Sua," to build some "foreign thing desertless in origin." The poet of "Mission" knows only too well the sorrows of being unable "to make/anything round enough to last" even if he also knows the reply of the wind—"as if anything here belonged to you/as if anything here were your concern." His own mission within the empire of mind seems therefore to be not so much abolishing it as "Conserving the Magnitude of Uselessness" and reminding all shelters of the mind of their contingency:

> I really do not want to convince anyone of anything except
> that conviction is cut loose, adrift and aswim, upon the
> cool (sometimes sweltering) tides of roiling energy:
> that's not to despise conviction, definition, or other
> structure but to put them in their place:
>
> ("Hibernaculum")

The tension between shape and flow in Ammons' poetry continues from the synthesis that "fails (and succeeds) into limitation" in "The

Misfit" to "Hibernaculum" and the "definitions" that produce "about the same/securities and disasters." The most revealing explorations of the grief and glory of living in a world where no circumference is final are, however, the poems written in the decade immediately following *Ommateum*. The tone of "Hymn V" and its demand that all questions be "in/triumphs of finality" categorically "answered and filed" is clearly ironic, but the irony only slightly masks the pain of being without the "old rich usage" of the final lines. It is a pain that we still hear in the later poem "The Eternal City" in its statement of the need to preserve even in ruin "all the old/perfect human visions, all the old perfect loves." In "Joshua Tree," the wasteland quester waiting for "some/syllable's rain," is like similar figures in Stevens the poet's image of himself and his own poetic dilemma, without "eternal city," "liturgy," or "dome."

The poet of the much later lyric "Cut the Grass" knows that for man the encloser, "less than total is a bucketful of radiant toys" and that the only way of taking on the "roundness" is to try, like Whitman in the crucial twenty-fifth section of "Song of Myself," to encompass everything within the circle of "Speech." But he also knows, with the Emerson of *Nominalist and Realist*, that "No sentence will hold the whole truth, and the only way in which we can be just, is by giving ourselves the lie"; and this, in effect, is what he does in the early poem "Unsaid" when he asks his readers to listen for the things "left out." His realization of the futility of trying to define the fluid becomes in a later poem a contempt for "The Confirmers" equal to anything in Dickinson.

When, however, the "disorder ripe" along the "peripheries" of his control becomes what Emerson in *Circles* calls "the Unattainable, the flying Perfect, around which the hands of man can never meet," then the unencompassed is much more menacing. In a poem appropriately entitled "Attention," it becomes the unencompassed as Achilles' heel, the "one/ tip" he will some day "lose out of mind/and fall through." And when the "unassimilable fact" of "The Misfit" becomes "What This Mode of Motion Said," its "leading on" is of a more sinister kind:

> pressed too far
> I wound, returning endless
> inquiry
> for the pride of inquiry:

Emerson in the essay on Plato describes this revenge as that of the "bitten world" on the "biter." Ammons' version of the fatal consequences of this quest both for nature and for her would-be encompasser is the poem "Jungle Knot," where owl— "errors of vision"—and anaconda—"errors of self-defense"—kill each other in a "coiled embrace."

Between "Hymn V" and "Corsons Inlet" fall a great many poems, some of which involve an equally unsatisfactory center, Ammons' version of what Wallace Stevens, in "Notes Toward a Supreme Fiction," calls "the first idea," the "muddy centre before we breathed." Partly because he is as aware as his predecessor that neither the rigidly centered self nor the attempt to encompass everything is a sufficient or even possible way of living constantly in change, Ammons occasionally provides us with his own variation on the Stevensian mode of reduction, as in the early poem "This Black Rich Country," which begins: "Dispossess me of belief: /between life and me obtrude/no symbolic forms." His most serious temptation, however, goes beyond Stevens to Emerson, and it is perhaps for this reason that where he is most tempted he is most ironic. "The Golden Mean" is a brilliant satiric exposure of the argument of Emerson's essay *Experience* and its description of man as "a golden impossibility," just as the later poem "Mean" is a kind of *Compensation* pushed to its extreme. But each of them, like the picture of "Mr. Homburg" in Stevens' "Looking across the Fields and Watching the Birds Fly," says as much about the poet as about his target.

It is, nevertheless, this same irony, or sometimes just whimsical humor, which provides him with the distance from both Emerson and himself that he clearly needs. In one of the later lyrics entitled "Classic," this distance is realized, as it often is in Ammons, by the poem's dramatic context. The "I" here is caught "scribbling again" by the mountain, but protests that by now he has learned the lessons of reduction and can scribble in "a fashion very/like the water here/uncapturable and vanishing." The mountain's reply is to remind him of past sins:

> but that
> said the mountain does not
> excuse the stance
> or diction
>
> and next if you're not careful
> you'll be
> arriving at ways
> water survives its motions.

If the "stream" here is, as I think it is, at least partly like the "flecked river" of Stevens' "This Solitude of Cataracts," one of these past sins is the original one in this tradition: what in the very Emersonian seer of Stevens' poem is the desire to merge with some "permanent realization" at the "azury centre of time."

These glances at the tradition and its central emblem may suggest that if Ammons in some ways suffers the disadvantages of a latecomer—"My hands are old/and crippled keep no lyre," in the most light-hearted treatment of this problem ("Mountain Liar")—he also in one sense shares in the advantages of latecoming: he knows where this tradition's central image led its first circular philosopher and his knowledge makes him wary. The "too/adequate relationship" he protests against in the late poem entitled "Periphery" is at least in one of its senses what Emerson in the essay *Power* describes as "causality" or the "strict connection between every pulse-beat and the principle of being." The decision to go "deeper" and see what is "pushing all this/periphery, so difficult to make any sense/out of, out" takes us all the way back to the poetic motto of Emerson's *Circles* and the "new genesis" such a penetration of earth's "surface" would bring. But the "hesitation" at the end is Ammons' own and brings its own rewards:

> with me, decision brings its own
>
> hesitation: a symptom, no doubt, but open
> and meaningless enough without paradigm:
>   but hesitation
> can be all right, too: I came on a spruce
>
> thicket full of elk, gushy snow-weed,
> nine species of lichen, four pure white
>   rocks and
> several swatches of verbena near bloom.

As a wariness of the center and its fixity, it returns, this time with Emerson named, in a crucial section of "Hibernaculum": "O/Plotinus (Emerson, even) I'm just as scared as comforted/by the continuity, one sun spelling in our sun-made heads."

In some of the early poems, however, Ammons' own greatest temptation is to honor any going thing, to celebrate in a poem like "Mechanism" the "precise and/necessary worked out of random, reproducible, /the handiwork redeemed from chance." When it appears, it is in a language which shows just how much of a fascination for him Emerson's "Balance-loving Nature" and her "bunch of/compensating laws" ("The Wind Coming Down From") could become. In one early poem, the distance he needs takes, once again, the dramatic form of "Ezra," who, tired of being "the dying portage" of "deathless thoughts," interrupts the mountain's lecture to give his own version of a merging with the Beautiful Necessity, "the Way in whose timeless reach/cool thought unpunishable/by bones eternally glides" ("Whose Timeless Reach"). But in "Lines," where "deranging" in the final line captures both the French sense of upsetting an order of some kind and the very graphic English description of the mad as "deranged," there is no interposed "Ezra" or "I" and something much closer to Ammons' own temptation is at stake. The poet who is always asking us to see "the wonderful workings of the world" ("Cut the Grass") constantly apprises us, in his best lyrics, of the kind of perception which is an act of love. But "Lines" is perception itself as madness, a madness not of confusion but of too much lucidity. And it is exactly this "boreal clarity" which leads to the terrible surrender of the "spent seer" at the end of "Prodigal":

> the mind whirls, short of the unifying
> reach, short of the heat
>   to carry that forging:
>   after the visions of these losses, the spent
> seer, delivered to wastage, risen
>   into ribs, consigns knowledge to
>   approximation, order to the vehicle
> of change, and fumbles blind in blunt innocence
>   toward divine, terrible love.

Or that, again, in "Motion for Motion," leads to a "blurred mind overexposed":

> I—lost to an
>
> automatic machinery in things, duplicating, without
> useful difference, some changeless order extending
> backward beyond the origin of earth,
>
> changeless and true, even before the water fell, or
> the sun broke, or the beetle turned, or the still
> human head bent from a bridge-rail above to have a look.

The difficulty of sustaining the burden of these mysteries brings Ammons to the point Stevens reached in the seventh section of "The Auroras of Autumn": the temptation to assume what he calls in "Motion for Motion" some "will not including him" which has "a clear vision of it all" even if he himself does not. It is the flirtation with "the possibility of rule as the sum of rulelessness" that seems to be moving Ammons' best-known poem, "Corsons Inlet," in the same direction and then does not.

"Corsons Inlet" and "Saliences," both written in 1962, appear less than halfway through the *Collected Poems*, but together they are the pivotal point of the collection, marking both the continuity and the difference in the poems written before and since. Both are poems of sea level, the marginal, transitional place that makes Ammons, in Richard

Howard's phrase, a "littoralist of the imagination." "Corsons Inlet," in its refusal of all "arranged terror" and "humbling of reality to precept," takes us all the way back to the *Ommateum* Foreword, and though its promise to be satisfied with the "freedom" that "Overall" and "Scope" elude his grasp is not the final word in Ammons for an order that will suffice, the release it represents here is the necessary outward movement that a later title will call "Countering." "Saliences" read closely holds in potential so much of the poetry written since that we can return to it to illuminate even the longest and most ambitious of Ammons' recent work. The wind that earlier brought "rescue" to the stonegatherer becomes the "variable" that both brings the mind out of its "hard routes/walled/with no outlet" and saves the mechanism of natural change from an eternal sameness. Its "dunes," taken as a releasing perception for "old dunes/of mind," provide an image that will return in the poem entitled "Dunes" and its discovery that "loose" ground is more "available" than "firm" even if "Taking root in windy sand/is not an easy/way/to go about/finding a place to stay." The wind "shaped and kept in the/bent of trees" leads all the way to the later poem "Pluralist" and its maple tree "large/enough to express contrary/ notions," and both provide an indication of how to read the kind of "objectivity" that is always in Ammons only "the objective way of talking about ourselves" ("Extremes and Moderations"). The counsel to mind to "bend to these changing weathers" recalls the dangers of "icebound/mind" in the earlier poem "Thaw." And the preference for "gradual shadings out or in" over the abruptness of "alarm" will be echoed in poems all the way to "Hibernaculum" and its recognition that there must be some law of succession for mental states, some "protection against jolt-change."

"Saliences" is still a decade away from the longer and more difficult of the *Collected Poems*, but both in its refusal to give assertion up and in its realization of the need to "bend," it begins the search for some "Unifying Principle" which will keep the "shape" without damming up the "flow" and for a poetics which will involve a "Countering" of the "crystal of reason" whether or not it actually reaches "the higher/reason" that "contains the war/of shape and loss/at rest" ("Countering"). Whatever else this might mean, it seems to involve in the more recent poetry a new control which is at once a new freedom. In "The Put-Down Come On," it is a search which states that it will be satisfied if probability— "what has always happened"—and possibility—"what/has never happened before"—seem, if only "for an instant," reconciled. In what several readers have sensed as the freer world of these poems, it seems to involve a kind of centering which is not a solipsism, in the same way as the enterprise of the late poem, "Conserving the Magnitude of Uselessness," is not a terrifying or engulfing exercise because its very conservation is an act of mind saving mind from itself.

One beautiful example of this new freedom is a poem written soon after "Saliences," with the significant title "Center":

A bird fills up the
streamside bush
with wasteful song,
capsizes waterfall,
mill run, and
superhighway
to
song's improvident
center
lost in the green
bush green
answering bush:
wind varies:
the noon sun casts
mesh refractions
on the stream's amber
bottom
and nothing at all gets,
nothing gets
caught at all.

This lyric gathers up and removes the burden and threat of so many earlier images that it seems almost to stand as a declaration of this new freedom to the reader who has been following the geography of Ammons' work. Its "mesh" does not entrap realities, nor do its stream's "refractions" bring him a blurred mind overexposed. The symmetry of its "noon sun" does not oppress, and the wasteful capsizing of its "waterfall" need not be furiously entertained. Its "center," finally, is freer because it is neither the destruction of the vertical "moment" nor a bird of glass, hard and removed.

"The Unifying Principle" suggested in the poem of that name recalls the possible "modes of structuring" the spent seer of "Prodigal" failed to "perfect" before consigning all order to the vehicle of change. In the most recent poetry, this principle seems to be emerging as the search for a "balance" which will be not the static tightrope walk of "The Golden Mean" but the constant in and out motion that gives a double meaning to the "ecology" of "Extremes and Moderations." Like the dualities of the earlier poem "Risks and Possibilities," "extreme" here can be either a too-rigid order or a too-sudden change, with the "moderations" providing the countering movement which saves us from each:

circulations are moderations, currents triggered by extremes:
we must at all costs keep the circulations free and clear,
open and unimpeded: otherwise, extremes will become trapped,
local, locked in themselves, incapable of transaction: some

extremes, though, *are* circulations, a pity, in that kinds of
staying must then be the counters.

The fact of this duality helps to clarify what are frequently puzzling contexts for the word "saliences" in Ammons' most recent work and to suggest, finally, what "taking on the roundness," in this poet's continuing fascination with the circle, is coming to mean. Emerson in a Journal entry of 1857 defines "salience" as "the principle of levity [. . .] the antagonist of gravitation [. . .] the balance, or offset, to the mountains and masses." But Ammons, in "Levitation," evokes the perils of ascent in a world where the ground "disastrous to seers/and saints" is always around "eve-ning scores, calling down" and in another lyric entitled "Offset" suggests the losses as well as the gains in one seer's antagonism to gravity. The paradox in "Offset" of an ascent whose "extreme" is both gain and loss is a reminder that perspective is purchased only by the loss of "ground," a danger in the "principle of levity" itself which gives one late poem the title "The Limit":

> the salience,
> in a bodiless arrogance,
> must preserve
> algal tracings or it
> loses further (already scared of loss)
> ground for possible self-imaginings.

The conclusion here that "it's interwork/that pays with mind" subsumes all of the search for "balance" that provides us, finally, with the connection between Ammons' two principle figures—the axes of "High & Low" and the tension between "center" and "periphery"—the four direc-tions "mind can go" in the recent and appropriately entitled "Staking Claim." "Interwork" in the drama of rising and falling seems to mean in the most recent lyrics not a final decision either way, but an ongoing activity of mind, what Ammons calls his "likely schizophrenia" in the poem entitled "One More Time." In "Extremes and Moderations," the seeming contradiction between the statements, "it's impossible anyone should know anything about the concrete/who's never risen above it" and "the lofted's precarious: the ground is nice and sweet and not/at all spectacular," is instead a dialectic necessary in the "economy of the self." When the paradigm is not "High & Low" but concentration and diffusion, this imperative becomes in "Hibernaculum" the "mind" which from "the undifferentiated core-serum" turns "to the definition of its tangles for rescue" and then "back to the core for clarification" and in "The Swan Ritual" an activity which recalls the terrible centering of "Laser" at the same time as it suggests how its menace might be removed:

> Yield to the tantalizing mechanism:
> fall, trusting and centered as a
> drive, following into the poem:
> line by line pile entanglements on,
> arrive willfully in the deepest
>
> fix: then, the thing done, turn
> round in the mazy terror and
> question, outsmart the mechanism:
> find the glide over-reaching or
> dismissing—halter it into
>
> a going concern so the wing
> muscles at the neck's base work
> urgency's compression and
> openness breaks out lofting
> you beyond all binds and terminals.

That the possible dangers of centering here should be those inherent in a poem leads us finally to the one aspect of "shape & flow" that seems to be increasingly the subject of Ammons' ongoing meditations. The late poem "Image" and its "indefinable idol" raises, though obliquely, the problem of how a poet can be at once image-maker and "iconoclast," how, in short, poetry might point to its own contingency at the same time as it necessarily gives shape to the flow. The poet who listens for the "Expressions of Sea Level" or the language of the orange tree in "Communication" frequently senses human speech as intrusion, from the "round/ fury" of "Spindle" and its "violence to make/that can destroy" to the "disturbing, skinny speech" which by "fracturing" nature's "equilibrium" gives another poem the title "Breaks." The search for a poetic that "traps no/realities, takes/no game" ("Motion") leads in Ammons from the early poem "Unsaid" to the curious and delightful ruse of the late "Snow Log," where the decision to take nature's "intention" on himself enables him to get back again everything he seemed to have given up. The delicate balance of this achievement in Ammons' best lyrics is what enables him, as Harold Bloom has remarked, "to have a complete vision of his own heterocosm, at once an alternative world to outward nature and yet also the actuality of nature given back to us again."

As program, this poetic enterprise leads from the suggestion in "Motion" that the "music/in poems" by "the motion/of its motion" may resemble "what, moving, is" all the way to the three long poems which are successful partly because each has, as one of its subjects, the long poem—"Essay on Poetics," "Extremes and Moderations," and "Hibernaculum." The very length of these verse essays suggests that Ammons is far from giving assertion up, and the most recent, "Hibernaculum," is the most moving in its evocation of the continuing need for and need of the poetic word:

> if the night is to be
> habitable, if dawn is to come out of it, if day is ever
> to grow brilliant on delivered populations, the word
>
> must have its way by the brook, lie out cold all night
> along the snow limb, spell by yearning's wilted weed till
> the wilted weed rises, know the patience and smallness
>
> of stones: I address the empty place where the god
> that has been deposed lived: it is the godhead: the
> yearnings that have been addressed to it bear antiquity's
>
> sanction: for the god is ever re-created as
> emptiness, till force and ritual fill up and strangle
> his life, and then he must be born empty again.

This "god" is the "indefinable idol" of "Image," and the poetic "word" situated between "delivered populations" and the "empty place" takes us back to the peripheral being of the early poem "Muse." That the too-centered "majority" in "Image" is described as "unerring" is both ironic and precise; for the wanderings of this poet's "loose speech" are precisely what inform the perambulating mode of the three long poems. The relation of "center" to "periphery" is still very much their dominant configuration, but less as the locked "geometry" of the early poems than as what "The Unifying Principle" calls "loose constellations," "less fierce, subsidiary centers, with the/attenuations of interstices, roughing the salience." These "interstices" are both the mode of a poetry which presents itself as process and the recognition of contingency that leads Ammons to speak in "Hibernaculum" of the void "inside" and "outside" and in the "Essay on Poetics" of the "emptiness" at the center of the "lyric" and of "earth." "Extremes and Moderations" has as its ostensible subject ecology and ends with it as its "chief concern." But the fact that it also disclaims the structure of "beginning,/development" and "end" and suggests in the hesitations of its close the implication in all poetic forms of closure suggests that "ecology" is also the "less fierce center" of the poem's own mode, the "lattice work" stanza "that lets the world/breeze unobstructed through."

These three long poems exemplify the looser order of "The Unifying Principle" at the same time as they reveal on closer reading the figures of their own remarkable coherence, the "circulations" which keep "Extremes and Moderations" moving, the "topography" which the "Essay on Poetics" enables us to "see," and the "timeless relations" which form the gatherings and concentrations of moving mind in "Hibernaculum." Even as recently as the poem "Spiel," the poet is taking lessons from the spider's "open-ended house" and the spider's knowledge that "safety,/closed up to perfection, /traps" finds its counterpart in the open-ended mode of these poems which at once have their own complex "identity" and suggest that the best of Ammons may be still to come. The resolution of "Corsons Inlet" was to stake off no beginnings or ends. For the reader who has been following this poet's configurations of shape and flow, there is no more satisfying or beautiful close to Ammons' most recent volume than the poem, "The Arc Inside and Out," which travels once more the directions of centering and encompassing—"these two ways to dream"—and then opens itself to another beginning:

> and
> every morning the sun comes, the sun.

DAVID KALSTONE

Ammons' Radiant Toys

Less than total is a bucketful of radiant toys.
—A. R. AMMONS, "Cut the Grass"

Pastoral is hard reading today, not simply because we are more removed from "nature" than the city-dwellers who wrote the first pastoral poems, but because it is a genre scored with contradictions. Its language, stripped of social entanglements, can be baffling and abstract, strenuous testings of the mind against a landscape, as if these were the only really telling encounters. Its modern exponents— Frost, Stevens and Ammons among them—seem almost sentenced to write pastoral poems. "Life is an affair of people not of places. But for me," Wallace Stevens wrote, "life is an affair of places and that is the trouble." Companionable eclogues have long since given way to solitary discoveries, thoughtful shepherds to epistemologists.

Modern pastoral exposes the problems of modern poetry in their most extreme forms. Rather than serving as a welcome setting for verse, land-scape presents a test of the poet's ability to see and enter the world, a crisis of observer and object. Poets like Stevens and Ammons satisfy and frustrate us because, drawn to the radiance of things of this world, these writers are also the most ample and abstract witnesses of their own failure to possess them. In Stevens' words, "It is the human that is the alien,/The human that has no cousin in the moon" ("Less and Less Human, O Savage Spirit"). Ammons sees the poet, pastoral or otherwise, as a "surrendered self among unwelcoming forms" ("Gravelly Run"). His large ambitions

From *Diacritics* 3 (Winter 1973). Copyright © 1973 by Diacritics, Inc.

and his frequent fallings away in the face of abundance make Ammons' pastoral poems sound puzzled and urgent, the frustrations of the most willing, the most ardent, the most open observer. I cannot agree with Helen Vendler that Ammons "will have written the first twentieth-century poetry wholly purged of the romantic." His *not* being purged is the problem. He has always had a gift for recalling romantic promises as if there were fresh ways for them to be fulfilled: "for it is not so much to know the self/as to know it as it is known/by galaxy and cedar cone" ("Gravelly Run"). Yet after these exhilarating prospects come the sobering performances, the puzzles of the "surrendered self among unwelcoming forms." What sounded like visionary promptings—lightning weddings of the self to the outside world—become bewilderments before his eyes.

To devise in the face of that sense of nature an ample rhetoric has been Ammons' problem and finally his distinction: to have invented a pastoral poem at once jagged and discontinuous, but still open to radiance; to have found a grammar that almost erases the speaker who uses it. We can see Ammons' claims over landscape at their most minimal in a recent poem like "Further On":

> Up this high and far north
> it's shale and woodsless snow:
> small willows and alder brush
>
> mark out melt streams on the
> opposite slope and the wind talks
> as much as it can before freeze
>
> takes the gleeful, glimmering
> tongues away: whips and sticks
> will scream and screech then
>
> all winter over the deaf heights,
> the wind lifting its saying out
> to the essential yell of the
>
> lost and gone: it's summer now:
> elk graze the high meadows:
> marshgrass heads high as a moose's
>
> ears: lichen, a wintery weed,
> fills out for the brittle sleep:
> waterbirds plunder the shallows.

In this poem summer sensations are almost stunted by reminders everywhere of the approaching inhuman freeze: "the brittle sleep," the cold which "takes the gleeful, glimmering/tongues away." More important, the threat is put in terms of human speech and understanding: "the wind lifting its saying out/to the essential yell of the /lost and gone." Against such odds, against a "yell" that strangles articulation, even the ability to describe, to offer the reader a corner of landscape becomes a form of self-assertion. What serves is an exact sense of the surviving instincts of summer life: "lichen, a wintery weed,/fills out for the brittle sleep:/waterbirds plunder the shallows."

Many of Ammons' short poems—especially those in *Uplands* (1970) and *Briefings* (1971)—end in just such reduced circumstances, whether facing inhuman zero weather, as in "Further On," or doing battle against the "Periphery," the profusion and separateness of the outside world, "thickets hard to get around in/or get around for/an older man." The poem "Periphery," after looking for explanations and for a center that governs the luxuriant border growth, lapses at its close into documentary satisfactions:

> I came on a spruce
>
> thicket full of elk, gushy snow-weed,
> nine species of lichen, four pure-white
>   rocks and
> several swatches of verbena near bloom.

These precise notations are ultimately shrunken relatives of Whitman's famous catalogues—more modest, but announcing some kinship as in another recent poem, "Breaks":

> From silence to silence:
> as a woods stream
> over a
> rock holding on
>
> breaks into clusters of sound
> multiple and declaring as
> leaves, each one,
>
> filling
> the continuum between leaves,
>
> I stand up,
> fracturing the equilibrium,
> hold on,
>
> my disturbing, skinny speech
> declaring
> the cosmos.

This is not one of Ammons' very best poems. With its awkward bow to Whitman, the "I" seems unsettled, uneasily self-assertive, "standing up" when at other moments in the poem the speaker is pointedly guarded: guarded by the parentheses which enclose the poem ("From silence to silence") and by its otherwise self-deprecating tone, the "disturbing, skinny speech" which contrasts so sharply with Whitman's expansive line.

From the title on ("Breaks": noun or verb? ruptures? bits of fortune? glimpses as through a clouded sky?), Ammons courts a certain confusion. The poem fans out, one simile explained by another, the sound of a woods stream over rocks compared to the "declaration" of new leaves. From that simile within a simile, he pops into the poem "fracturing the equilibrium." The grammar is not entirely clear. He "holds on" like the jutting rock but "declares" like the clusters of sound breaking over it. His "disturbing, skinny speech" is a wry deflation of the stream's "multiple" sound and the "declaring" leaves. No need to labor a simple point, one that helps us understand Ammons' more interesting lyrics. After nature's generous sounds, the assertion of self seems both awkward and a little uncontrolled, an odd placing of the ego. Surprised by fluency, he doesn't appropriate the landscape as Whitman would, though the phrase "declaring the cosmos" might well be Whitman's own.

I am talking about the observer's voice and the assurance it offers us over objects and landscapes. Even Robert Frost's country speakers are sociable by comparison with Ammons'. Frost's wit—his secure rhymes, the way he spreads his net over the sonnet's frame, his puns that catch the eye in a conspiracy of meaning—never allows natural terrors to terrorize form. It is good to have his tone in mind for comparison with Ammons'. Something like "One Step Backward Taken" with its near jingles about geological upheavals in a new ice age ("Whole capes caked off in slices") absorbs catastrophe before it occurs (capes into cake):

> I felt my standpoint shaken
> In the universal crisis.
> But with one step backward taken
> I saved myself from going.

Frost's backward step is also a foreseeing one, a witty preparation.

In a more somber version of disaster, "Desert Places," Frost looks at a snow scene which threatens to obliterate everything. From an initial urgency ("Snow falling and night falling fast, oh, fast/In a field I looked into going past"—insistent participles, phrases rather than sentences) the poem gathers to a self-assertion that takes in all the fear:

> They cannot scare me with their empty spaces
> Between stars—on stars where no human race is.
> I have it in me so much nearer home
> To scare myself with my own desert places.

The poem finds a form and assured tone which answer the terror that remains undiminished. Frost can be homely, witty, and desperate in a single line: "The loneliness includes me unawares," asserting by the end a kind of canny control. Balanced sentences and emphatic rhetoric can replace the poem's introductory phrases acting out the mind's growing command as it understands its terrors:

> And lonely as it is that loneliness
> Will be more lonely ere it will be less—
> A blanker whiteness of benighted snow
> With no expression, nothing to express.

Always beleaguered by nature, Frost has his witty standpoint, his one step backward to take. Frost's poems end, have a place to go, come to rest.

This is precisely what we feel Ammons cannot do: "Stop on any word and language gives way:/the blades of reason, unlightened by motion, sink in" ("Essay on Poetics"). He has his doubts about the finished poem and his own place in it. A few years ago he threaded a book-length poem along an adding machine tape—the poem ended when the tape did—producing a December diary, *Tape for the Turn of the Year*. That was his most flamboyant attempt to turn his verse into something beyond neat gatherings. With *Uplands* and *Briefings*, his most recent short volumes, he was obviously resisting summaries and the idea of books marking stages in a poetic career. They were closer to journals of mental states, each poem an entry finding a form and a scene for a very exact encounter or discovery. The point lay not only in single adventures, but in the continuing, sometimes driven effort: "why does he write poems: it's the only way he can mean/what he says [. . .]/he keeps saying in order to hope he will/say something he means [. . .]/poems deepen his attention till what he is thinking/catches the energy of a deep rhythm" ("Hibernaculum"). The oddest part of that statement is how tentative it is; he keeps writing in order at least to "hope" he'll touch "meaning."

Under such pressures Ammons was bound to value a style that kept moving. "Viable" tells part of the story:

> Motion's the dead give away,
> eye catcher, the revealing risk:
> the caterpillar sulls on the hot macadam

but then, risking, ripples to the bush:
the cricket, startled, leaps the
quickest arc: the earthworm, casting,

nudges a grassblade, and the sharp robin
strikes: sound's the other
announcement: the redbird lands in

an elm branch and tests the air with
cheeps for an answering, reassuring
cheep, for a motion already cleared:

survival organizes these means down to
tension, to enwrapped, twisting suasions:
every act or non-act enceinte with risk or

prize: why must the revelations be
sound and motion, the poet, too, moving and
saying through the scary opposites to death.

Looking askance at "revelation," this poem twins it with danger, scales it down to watching for prey, for the smallest movements. Rather than revelation, there is "the revealing risk"; the "dead give away" is the only moment when the currents of life become visible, palpable for us. The puns and playfulness are part of Ammons' game. Observing, catlike, the rippling caterpillar, the startled cricket, the earthworm prey to the robin, his poem mimics their motion with its own chain of clauses and darting participles. It must, above all, sound offhand, the somber truth buried in the casual opening line. Motion is caught as from the corner of the eye.

Ammons had long since, in a poem called "Motion," talked about the impossibility of ever identifying word with thing. Poems are "fingers, methods,/nets,/not what is or/was." Still he had faith in the music of a poem which

by the motion of
its motion
resembles
what, moving, is—
the wind
underleaf white against
the tree.

In "Viable" he is more canny, more reticent, and also more alive to what *compels* him to seek renewals of motion. Poetry—the movement of poetry—comes closer to reflex and to survival; the final line of "Viable" only confirms a shadow we have already felt. Nature's small creatures, the poem admits, are observed not so much for their own sake as to be a pulse for the poet. He attempts, through verse, movements as minute as theirs. Motion reveals; sound, like the robin's call, waits for a reply, tests the air for "an answering, reassuring/cheep, for a motion already cleared." The question that closes the poem is rhetorical; there are no answers to its *why*, only repeated close observation of tiny actions to relieve an innate and natural "tension." The poet is alive to risks, taking his prize, hoping to prove for this moment that he is alive by catching "the energy of a deep rhythm," all the time acknowledging that he too is ultimately prey. In paraphrase this sounds like a desperate enterprise, but in the poem such explicit meanings are subsumed by metaphor until the very end, absorbed in risk and variety—*sulls, ripples, nudges,* and *strikes.*

A poem like "Viable" is very revealing of Ammons' developed style. Natural facts—an enormous repertoire of them, closely observed— tick through his verse and make it seem, at least superficially, a fulfillment of William Carlos Williams' "No ideas but in things." Ammons' measured, skinny lines focus our attention on things and parts of things with the insistence of a slow-motion camera.

Yet he is restless adopting that style, even when setting out its advantages: "I'm doing the best I can,/that is to say, with too many linking verbs: the grandest/clustering of aggregates permits the finest definition" ("Viable"). The superlatives suggest a fussy version of Williams' "objectivity." Certainly Williams' notation pulses through Ammons' short poems, just as the casual, almost random style of the Beats and New York School give him a way to talk about the provisional and constantly changing voices in his long poems. Those voices contribute to his later verse, but also go against a natural bent, a desire that nature signify or "add up." As a reading of "Viable" suggests, objects may seem like counters in a larger game.

Why then adopt voices close to the minimal and casual, styles which seem least suited to ambitious statement? Certainly the constant struggle of realistic notation and visionary pressure charges these later poems with problematic power and beauty, and explains their curious blurring of the ego. But it is only when we look back to Ammons' early work, poems which reach openly for transcendence, that we see how much he needed the concrete resistance of contemporary objective styles.

Harold Bloom has traced the undisguised Emersonianism of Ammons' early poems. From the very start the poems feared threats to speech: "The pieces of my voice have been thrown/away," he complains in "Rack," and he finds the winds and the sea swallowing his voice in "So I Said I am Ezra" which Ammons sets at the opening of his *Collected Poems.*

> I [. . .]
> swayed as if the wind were taking me away
> and said
>   I am Ezra
> As a word too much repeated
> falls out of being
> so I Ezra went out into the night
> like a drift of sand

Two threats, loss of speech and loss of self, are fused in a single haunted image ("As a word"). But what kind of speech is it that is constantly endangered or scattered? In "Rack" the poet sees himself ransacking nature: "I must run down all the pieces/and build the whole silence back." What is yearned for—and here the Emersonianism is most strongly felt—is a spectral voice, so complete as to be equivalent to silence. He envisions a speech beyond words, which will offset the threatened loss of identity, a ghostly voice which replaces the merely human "I."

Such satisfactions, rarified and not a matter of earthly fulfillment, give an entirely different feel to Ammons' early verse. He faces the shattering abundance of the world, its threat to ego, by making a lunge toward vision, as in the last lines of "Prodigal":

>   the spent
>   seer, delivered to wastage, risen
>   into ribs, consigns knowledge to
>   approximation, order to the vehicle
> of change, and fumbles blind in blunt innocence
>   toward divine, terrible love.

Almost ten years later, in "Laser," that same seer trying "to dream of diversity" can admit only one riveting image at a time; and at the close he must suffer an all too human lapse, a fall into a drained and deadened state:

>   the image glares filling all space:
>   the head falls and
>   hangs and cannot wake itself.

The early poems face no such daily re-enacted deaths. One of their frequent gestures is a welcome abandonment of the world: "I closed up all the natural throats of earth/[. . .] and saying farewell/stepped out into the great open" ("Some Months Ago"); "I looked down at the ashes/and rose and walked out of the world" ("In Strasbourg in 1349"); or

>   Turning a moment to say so long
>   to the spoken
>   and seen
>   I stepped into

the implicit pausing sometimes
on the way to listen to unsaid things.
("Turning a Moment to Say So Long")

These poems, awkward and tentative, have not really found the right
language for their transcendent adventures. Full of ceremonies and rituals,
they try to convince us of vision by using the simplest syntax to recount
supernatural events: "I went out to the sun." The effect he is looking for is
something like the casual tone of Herbert's heavenly encounters, which
convince by their comely, secure, childlike reachings for another world.
One of Ammons' characteristic early structures is the declarative "I" with
a verb in the simple past. In another the simple declarative clause is
preceded by a present participial phrase: "Merging into place against a
slope of trees, I extended my arms." Given the high frequency of present
participles in these first poems, there is surprisingly little sense of movement; action is arrested by the completed pasts into tableaux, characters
in a frieze as they reach for or just attain transcendence.

These modes do not completely satisfy Ammons, or so one would
think from some unsettled and unsettling poems sprinkled among the early
rituals. They sound almost masochistic in their desire for change:

> With ropes of hemp
> I lashed my body to the great oak
> saying odes for the fiber of the oakbark
> and the oakwood saying supplications
> to the root mesh
> ("With Ropes of Hemp")

Or:

> A gall-nesting wren took my breath
>
> flicking her wings, and
> far into summer the termites found the heart.
> ("Song")

The second of the two ends in annihilation; the first closes with a
metamorphosis, the melting self "returning" to say odes in the night. But
both poems suggest more than a yearning for escape. They try to force
their way to vision not through ritual exits and tableaux, but by a burial *in*
nature, a smothered union with the world.

The dilemma becomes clear to Ammons in poems like "Ritual for
Eating the World." A rope hangs mysteriously from rocks. At first it is
threatening: a hangman's noose or "god's own private fishing hook."
Then, seized as a lifeline, a rope "old mountain/climbers left/dangling," it
may be a way to the visionary heights. Finally grasped,

> it broke
> and all through the heaving night
> making day I faced
>
> piecemeal the sordid
> reacceptance of my world.

No talk here of reassembling the pieces of his world into a perfect silence. Conflating the hangman's noose—the self-annihilating impulse—and the climber's rope, an active escape, he is able to see the two as related and doomed to failure. The alternative, ever stronger in his poems, is the piecemeal mastery of his *own* world, here awkwardly scorned, but "faced."

Ammons entertains alternatives more fluently in a fine poem of the same period, "Hymn." Genial, free of the pressures which make him want to lash himself to nature "with ropes of hemp," it truly represents, in Bloom's words, "Ammons' second start as a poet." Each choice has its separate moment:

> I know if I find you I will have to leave the earth
> and go on out
>   over the sea marshes and the brant in bays.

And in the second section:

> And I know if I find you I will have to stay with the earth
> inspecting with thin tools and ground eyes . . .
> and going right on down where the eye sees only traces.

"Hymn" does not attempt a resolution. It praises the alternatives and is delicately conditional about ever locating the truth of nature, equally accepting, as Bloom puts it, that "one part of the self will be yielded to an apprehension beyond sight, while the other will stay here with the earth, to be yielded to sight's reductiveness, separated with each leaf."

Poems like "Hymn" seem a relief for Ammons. Irreconcilable tensions have surfaced and win equal and clear-eyed attention. Yearnings once awkward are now absorbed into a style rather than swamping it. They generate a new kind of poem, as he was to announce in "Guide": "You cannot come to unity and remain material:/in that perception is no perceiver:/when you arrive/you have gone too far." The perceiver was realistically to replace the seer as protagonist in his poems, though the ghost of the visionary is always there, hinting at unity, rueful and radiant. In some of his poems the two voices are raised in gentle argument, or can be recognized prompting together or in counterpoint the speaker of the poem. In "Gravelly Run" he is open to both:

I don't know somehow it seems sufficient
to see and hear whatever coming and going is,
losing the self to the victory
        of stones and trees,
of bending sandpit lakes, crescent
round groves of dwarf pine:

for it is not so much to know the self
as to know it as it is known
        by galaxy and cedar cone,
as if birth had never found it
and death could never end it:

the swamp's slow water comes
down Gravelly Run fanning the long
        stone-held algal
hair and narrowing roils between
the shoulders of the highway bridge:

holly grows on the banks in the woods there,
and the cedars' gothic-clustered
        spires could make
green religion in winter bones:

so I look and reflect, but the air's glass
jail seals each thing in its entity:

no use to make any philosophies here:
        I see no
god in the holly, hear no song from
the snowbroken weeds: Hegel is not the winter
yellow in the pines: the sunlight has never
heard of trees: surrendered self among
        unwelcoming forms: stranger,
hoist your burdens, get on down the road.

Central to an understanding of Ammons' verse, "Gravelly Run" is more explicit about its problems (a speaker who reads Hegel and talks about epistemology) than many of Ammons' later lyrics were to be. Being explicit at this stage allows him his casual tone; having aired so much that his earlier poems did not admit, he can accept himself as the stranger who must "get on down the road."

What is remarkable about "Gravelly Run" is the modulation of tone, the range of voices to which it is open. At the beginning seer and observer seem united. The opening rhythms widen to visionary assurance ("as if birth had never found it/and death could never end it"); observation narrows to the utmost particularity (the emphatic consonant-clotted "long/stone-held algal/hair and narrowing roils"). From that exercise, taking a sharper license, he imagines the cedars as spires. A rebuke is prompt and compact. "Reflect," offered as a gesture of understanding, is drained of its meditative meaning before our eyes. Human gesture becomes nothing but a reflection, a mirror; the poem turns everything brutally physical, a world of unconnected particles, his visionary effort merely that of the "surrendered self among unwelcoming forms."

From this time on the placing of self in Ammons' work is one of its oddest features. In "Saliences," one of his best poems, the *I* enters only in its closing third. It has, of course, made earlier veiled appearances, from the moment, in fact, that this poem announces its title, which has to do with the interaction of mind and landscape. Saliences are, as Bloom notes, "outleapings, 'mind feeding out,' not taking in perceptions but turning its violent energies out into the field of action." The ostensible subject of the poem is a dunes walk like that of "Corsons Inlet." But an elaborate syntax keeps the "I" from making assertions in any ordinary way:

> Consistencies rise
> and ride
> the mind down
> hard routes
>   walled
> with no outlet and so
> to open a variable geography,
>   proliferate
> possibility, here
> is this dune fest
>   releasing
> mind feeding out,
> gathering clusters,
> fields of order in disorder,
> where choice
> can make beginnings,
>   turns,
>   reversals.

The very notion of a distanced "mind" is provocative. It both acts (feeding, gathering) and is acted upon (ridden down, released). More important, the distinction between the two is almost erased when the "dune fest" begins. We are to be caught in a whirl of motion, self merging with the outer world. The rhythm, the short lines and relentless alternation of noun and participle practically blot out differences between actions of mind and nature. Nouns are suspended in a chain of participial explosions of equal force ("releasing/mind feeding out,/gathering clusters"). The

maneuver is vital; you almost feel that the verbal motion is more important than the mixture of abstractions and particulars swept along, and that
everything moves, dissolving "before the one event that/creates present
time," an event described in the long second section of the poem, the
palpable "unarranged disorder" of the wind. Tracing the sequence of
tenses here is one way of telling the story: a sweep of present participles
through the landscape ("weathering shells with blast/[. . .] lifting the
spider"); then the wind traced in past participles, a loving dialogue with
objects it touches ("wind/shaped and kept in the/bent of trees,/[. . .] the
kept and erased sandcrab trails"). All this is done with a Whitmanic force,
minimal pauses, the movement constantly aided by repetitions of words
and participial endings—but in a shorter line than Whitman's to acceler-
ate the flow.

Only then, after this virtual effacement of the self, does he begin
in a third movement to lay claim to the experience: with imperatives
("bend to these/changing weathers") and, finally, with his first use of the
simple past tense ("when I went back to the dunes today"). This is the
first real admission of a separate observer and leads to what Bloom
describes as the "firm beauty" of the last seventy lines, a detailed tracing
of "the reassurance [. . .]/that through change/continuities sinuously work."
In a recapitulation of the previous day's sights and sounds, all changed but
with shades of resemblance (the "saliences" of the title "congruent to
memory") he finds "summations of permanence!/where not a single single
thing endures." The confusion of present and past in the memory is full
and fruitful:

> much seemed
> constant, to be looked
> forward to, expected:
> from the top of a dune rise,
> look of ocean salience: in
>   the hollow,
> where a runlet
>   makes in
> at full tide and fills a bowl,
> extravagance of pink periwinkle
> along the grassy edge,
> and a blue, bunchy weed, deep blue,
> deep into the mind the dark blue
>   constant.

Is it full tide? or is the mind thinking ahead to the expected
moment of full tide and ocean salience which it fuses with the present feel

of pink periwinkle and the blue weed that partakes, for the observer, of land and sea? The evasive *where,* some elided verbs covered by obliging commas—these work to blur present and past in a more relaxed confusion of mind and nature than is felt in the first part of the poem. "Saliences" builds to a close as beautiful as that of Stevens' "Sunday Morning."

> desertions of swallows
> that yesterday
> ravaged air, bush, reed, attention
> in gatherings wide as this neck of dunes . . .
>
> earth brings to grief
> much in an hour that sang, leaped, swirled,
> yet keeps a round
> quiet turning,
> beyond loss or gain,
> beyond concern for the separate reach.

The elegiac close allows for the observer's limitations as well as for nature's "deaths and flights." In fact, the spectator's discretion is one of the poem's great secrets. Manipulating rhythms, but particularly verb tenses—energetic displacements at the outset, subtler swellings at the close—is a way of veiling the observer, without whom, on the other hand, he had come to recognize, no poem exists. Ammons is testing another approach to vision: not claiming it as a seer, but invoking or propitiating it; withdrawing, making us forget he is there; appearing to be close to details, yet minimizing the spectator's presence and powers.

It is here that Williams' devotion to "things" would become useful. The stripped-down lists, the focussed notation were indeed to become ingredients of Ammons' *Briefings,* but not, we can see from "Saliences," the only ingredients. Nor, as a poem like "Viable" suggests, was the balance between discrete particular and a suggested visionary pattern always so grandly, so securely achieved as in "Saliences." The pattern elsewhere may be elusive, the details under pressure to yield it up. Ammons' verse is more restless than Williams' lyrics. The most precise details seem only approximate: "there is nothing small enough to conjure clarity with."

"Clarity" is in fact one of Ammons' subjects. But what other poet would illustrate that title with a poem about erosion? Ammons now enjoys giving visionary words like *clarity* a tumble. A rockslide, exposing the stresses beneath what we imagine to be solid, reveals "streaks &/scores of knowledge/now obvious and quiet." The poem deliberately belies its abstract title and the ordinary meanings of *knowledge, obvious,* and *quiet,* scaling down the large questions of philosophy and romantic lyric to answers made sensible by discrete and particular encounters:

> After the event the rockslide
> realized,
> in a still diversity of completion,
> grain and fissure,
> declivity
>   &
> force of upheaval,
> whether rain slippage,
> ice crawl, root
> explosion or
> stream erosive undercut:
>
> well I said it is a pity:
> one swath of sight will never
> be the same: nonetheless,
> this
> shambles has
> relieved a bind, a taut of twist,
> revealing streaks &
> scores of knowledge
> now obvious and quiet.

Though we have an illusion of the utmost particularity, the first-person observer is almost incidental, invoked only by a chatty comment, otherwise absorbed or lost in the poem whose principal effort is a "realization" of motion—the motion latent in every knot of geological structure. Specific words don't seem to matter as much as the total assembly of nouns and the illusion that they trace out all geological contingencies. At first it is even hard to tell whether the opening section is governed by "realized" or by "diversity of," all the nouns parallel to "completion"; both effects are forceful. The exertions and knotting of syntax seem again an effort to blur traditional functions of grammar; the poem strains toward the general by being as toughly particular as possible. Series of details are preferred over a sustained rhetorical structure that might suggest a spectator's control over them.

We can see how precarious these claims are by comparison with Whitman's large gestures, appropriating objects for the self. "I think we are here to give back our possessions before/they are taken away," Ammons says in the searching long poem "Hibernaculum." That attitude makes Whitmanian confidence impossible. No wonder then that the "I" eventually leaves many of Ammons' briefer poems, letting objects take them over, as in "Periphery" and "Further On." The poem exists for him in a continually threatened state, like a sheet of ice

> for language heightens by dismissing reality,

> the sheet of ice a salience controlling, like a symbol,
> level of abstraction, that has a hold on reality and suppresses
> it, though formed from it and supported by it:

> motion and artificiality (the impositional remove from reality)
> sustain language: nevertheless, language must
> not violate the bit, event, percept,

> fact.
> ("Essay on Poetics")

The violation of fact becomes the death of language: "when that happens abandonment/is the only terrible health and a return to bits, retrials/of lofty configurations."

It is true, then, that in recent poems Ammons characteristically narrows attention to find the smallest details which might confirm a relation between self and nature, that his verse's pressured motion seeks the "energy of a deep rhythm."

> I think I'm almost

> down to shadows, yielding to their masses,
> for my self out here, taut against the mere

> suasion of a star, is explaining, dissolving
> itself, saying, be with me wind bent at leaf

> edges, warp me puddle riffle, show me
> the total yielding past shadow and return.
> ("Schooling")

But it is also important and marvellous that in the very best of his recent work his anxiety is either muted or seen in a new light: muted, as in "Peracute Lucidity," where the self builds, but without commenting on it, the very chapel in nature it was prevented from inhabiting in "Gravelly Run."

> clarity's chapel
> bodied by hung-in boughs: and

> widening out over the pond, the blown
> cathedral luminous with evening glass:
> I go out there and sit

> till difference and event yield to
> perfect composure: then the stars
> come out and question every sound, the brook's.

Only at the end is there a slight rebuke to his confidence, a delicate disturbance that ripples but does not overturn his inhabited scene.

Elsewhere he sets anxiety in a new key. The setting of "Peracute Lucidity" had "a perspicuity like a sanctuary." "Triphammer Bridge," one of Ammons' most beautiful new poems, takes the very word "sanctuary" and, turning it over, as if it were a prism, takes an explicit pleasure in the powers of language that Ammons seldom allows himself.

> I wonder what to mean by *sanctuary*, if a real or
> apprehended place, as of a bell rung in a gold
> surround, or as of silver roads along the beaches
>
> of clouds seas don't break or black mountains
> overspill; jail: ice here's shapelier than anything,
> on the eaves massive, jawed along gorge ledges, solid
>
> in the plastic blue boat fall left water in: if I
> think the bitterest thing I can think of that seems like
> reality, slickened back, hard, shocked by rip-high wind:
>
> *sanctuary*, *sanctuary*, I say it over and over and the
> word's sound is the one place to dwell: that's it, just
> the sound, and the imagination of the sound—a place.

Sanctuary: the word itself is the subject, as if Ammons were for once enjoying the separation of self and nature. Imagination creates its sanctuaries: the bell echoing in gold; the cloud beaches free of eroding seas and piercing mountain peaks; but also—and given co-ordinate place— "jail." Still, confinements are shapely—"massive," "jawed"—transformed despite reminders of an adverse life: the rains of autumn, the bitter shaping force of wind, inseparable from the palpable pleasure he takes in shapes it has made. The poem itself is like the ice of which he speaks: its past participles, like ice crystals, take the sting out of bitter action. The difference between real and apprehended, bitter and sweet, includes all reminders of frailty and a joy, finally, in repeating the word that has evoked them all, "sanctuary [. . .] the one place to dwell." The exaltation of the final line, its real abandonment to the force and pleasure of imagination, recalls the late, great poems of Wallace Stevens.

Recently, then, Ammons has found ways to step back from the whirl of the provisional and particular to which, of necessity, his work has been committed. Perhaps his long poems have satisfied his need for "movement," and he has new notions of what the short poem can do. "The City Limits," which Bloom praises so highly, suggests all the hidden threats and difficulties of vision prominent in *Briefings*, but suspends them in a wonderfully sustained rhetorical structure almost like that of the most controlled and contemplative of Shakespeare's sonnets. Five clauses, repeating, "When you consider the radiance [. . .] when you consider [. . .] When you consider the abundance,"—the *whens* tensing rhetorical springs for an expected *then*, each clause taking in another corner of abundance and vicissitude—finally license the high pleasure and relief of the closing lines: "then [. . .] the dark/work of the deepest cells is of a tune with May bushes/and fear lit by the breadth of such calmly turns to praise." "The Arc Inside and Out," which closes *Collected Poems*, is another example, with its controlled rhetoric, of a firmer meditative order.

But Ammons is unpredictable, full of the subversive bravado of natural and even random facts. There is no way of knowing whether (or when) you will find him desperate to get back to them ("wrestling to say, to cut loose/from the high, unimaginable hook") or on the contrary full of the yearning which Stevens expressed for things beyond "the separate reach":

> Unreal, give back to us what once you gave:
> The imagination that we spurned and crave.
>   (Wallace Stevens,
>   "To the One of Fictive Music")

JEROME MAZZARO

Reconstruction in Art

At the end of *Tape for the Turn of the Year*, A. R. Ammons tells his readers that he has given them "long/uninteresting walks" so that they "could experience/vacancy." The statement follows earlier comparisons of the long poem to an "interstice: the space between/electrons" and to "the dull days/when turning & turning revealed nothing." The poet returns to these images two years after the poem's appearance, in an address before the International Poetry Forum in Pittsburgh. There he recalls more relevantly the ways in which the poem resembles a walk. Both tend to involve "the whole person" and are not really reproducible. They have shapes which occur or unfold in the ongoing way and characteristic action of a moving observer. What tends to be ignored one day becomes observable the next, and the very familiarity of the terrain makes it possible to observe the novel and ephemeral. This quality of dulling recurrence has led to critical statements like Marius Bewley's that the poems "are not afraid of repeating themselves, which they often do with conviction and without monotony" and to the placing of Ammons among that company of writers who are "obsessed with one or two central themes [. . .] to which they return on every creative occasion." The talk also repeats the notion of the poem as a "betweenness," citing Coleridge's statement in the *Biographia Literaria* (1817) that the imagination "reveals itself in the balance or reconciliation of opposite and discordant qualities." This "betweenness" is here described [by Ammons] in Platonic terms; it is a vehicle for overcoming "concrete and universal, one and many, similar and diverse," and it is "capable of bridging the duality and of bringing us the experience of a 'real' world that is also a reconciled, a unified, real world."

From *Diacritics* 3 (Winter 1973). Copyright © 1973 by Diacritics, Inc.

Thus, Ammons sees his own work in terms of a process which is both accretive and dialectic and in which the mind repeats the function of the Metaphysical poet's in being the medium through which opposites may be contained. In contrast, however, to those of the Metaphysical poets, the experiences Ammons undergoes do not lead to an "active" identity—a self which like the individualism of the Renaissance tries to impose its uniqueness on the world. Rather, as his Pittsburgh talk makes clear, the poet considers walks and consequently poems "meaningless": "The answer is that a walk doesn't mean anything, which is a way of saying that to some extent it means anything you can make it mean—and always more than you can make it mean." In fact, as Ammons is fond of saying, he finds himself "ingesting," the end of which process—unlike that of the Renaissance persona—is a new longing that only remotely relates to nature. Harold Bloom's *The Ringers in the Tower* suggests that the process may relate more intimately to previous literature, that as Ammons' poetry is a record of mental activity, it validates prior records of the same process. Certainly the emphasis which the poetry places on mental activity as it leads to consciousness allies it more to previous processes than to a validation of externals, but this does not necessarily limit the relationship to one with previous literature or preclude the possibility of the poetry's leading to a kind of action. Ammons is far more than a poet of sensibility—even a poet of wide-ranging sensibility; he is, as many critics have already maintained, a philosophical poet, one whose very methods of accretion and dialecticism exceed literary considerations and like the considerations of a Robert Creeley become important to an understanding of what possibilities may exist for unity, knowledge, and being in the world.

Critics have contented themselves so far with stressing Ammons' antecedents in the "central" American literary tradition. His indebtednesses to Ralph Waldo Emerson, Walt Whitman, Ezra Pound, William Carlos Williams, and Wallace Stevens have provided entrances into the major problems of dialecticism and Ammons' relation to idealism. Here, as in the case of Bewley's "Modes of Poetry," a quotation from Emerson's "Nature" (1836) will serve as a gloss on "Mountain Liar" or, as in the case of Hyatt Waggoner's "The Poetry of A. R. Ammons: Some Notes and Reflections" (1973), Emerson will be cited as the source for lines in "What This Mode of Motion Said." Even the rhythms of a poem like "Hymn" will be connected with Whitman's *Leaves of Grass* (1855), although in every instance the scholars will rightly insist on Ammons' having transmuted his influence "into an original strength and idiom" (Bewley). Less has been said about what Bloom terms "the anxiety of influence," particularly as it relates to the efforts of Pound, Eliot, Williams, and Theodore Roethke to create a long poem for the present or to lingering Rilkean elements that tie Ammons crucially to both the modernist and post-modernist movements of American poetry. Even less has been said of Ammons' relation to philosophers like Charles Peirce and John Dewey as well as to modern science. Like other poets of his generation, Ammons seems intent upon incorporating the latest discoveries of science and technology into poetry. As he said in a science and technology issue of the *Chelsea Review*, "Much of what is impersonally, flatly new to us arises from scientific insight and technological innovation. It is part of the result of a poem to personalize and familiarize, to ingest and acquaint—to bring feelings and things into manageable relationships."

The comparisons that critics have made of Ammons to his often idealistic precursors have been neglectful as well of his final refusal of an idealistic synthesis like that proposed by Emerson. As Ammons states early in "The Golden Mean," "not too much/mind over body or/body over mind;/they are united in this life and should/blend to dual good or ill." More recently "Hibernaculum" repeats the sentiment: "my little faith, such as it is, is that mind and/nature grew out of a common node and so must obey common/motions [. . .] I depend utterly/on my body to produce me, keep me produced, don't you:/the autonomy of the mind! who could desire it." How different these reconciliations are from Emerson's view of the poet as one who "conforms things to his thoughts" and esteems nature "as fluid, and impresses his being thereon," despite occasional recurrences to this view by Ammons in poems like "So I Said I Am Ezra," "In the Wind My Rescue Is," and "Raft." In a universe drifting into the mutual destruction of body and soul through entropy, it seems foolish to make too much of Emerson's separation of sensuous man and poet other than as *Tape for the Turn of the Year* does: "I feel ideas—as forms of/beauty: I describe/the form as/you describe a pear's/shape." But even here, the poet carefully separates "idea" and "ideal": "not idea as ideal [that is, boundless] —/ideas are human products,/temporal & full of/process;/but/ideas as per-ceptions of form." Being human products, poems, too, must exist somewhere between the uncontained ideal that the poet may have adumbrated and the body which creates him. Like Dante's paradise, poems regather "from height and depth" to come out "onto the soft, green, level earth" ["Bridge"].

Assuredly, Ammons has taken from Emerson in principle and Whitman in practice the view that the poem must be comprehensive and that this comprehensiveness might be achieved by a kind of cosmic ingestion or embracing, as the case may be. *Tape for the Turn of the Year*, for example, describes the process of composition as the making of a "dense, tangled trellis so/lovely & complicated that/every kind of variety will/find a place in it or on/it." "Hibernaculum" restates the notion in culinary terms. The consistency of poetry becomes that of soup—clear consommé, shadowy broth, bits of carrot, pea and rice, and finally chunks of beef and long bean—a mélange equally various and complicated. Just as certainly, Ammons derives from Emerson the mystical paradox of a Oneness that lies both at the still center and the circumference of experience as well as a tendency to identify this Oneness with seeing, but not as the "transparent eyeball" of Emerson's "Nature" so much as the multiple vision of the insect eye—the ommateum of Ammons' first collection of poems (1955). Realizing the difficulty of simply rejecting subjectivity, he is willing to accept a view like Williams' that truth lies at "the intersection of loci," and often the "repetitions" in a poem are devices by which Ammons determines these intersections. In defining the particular problems of language that will allow for the long poem, Ammons rejects in addition Emerson's attachment of words "to visible things" for more contemporary linguistic attitudes.

When, in the course of *Tape*, Ammons is willing to make pronouncements like "only the lively use of/language lives:/can live/on dead words/& falsehood: the /truths poetry creates/die with their language," one thinks of Pound's views in *How to Read* (1929) on the danger to individual and social thought when language "becomes slushy or inexact, or excessive or bloated." Pound prescribes as one function of the writer the preservation of meaningful language. For him, the corruption of language precedes that of man and thus assumes the reverse order of Emerson's view that "the corruption of man is followed by the corruption of language." Ammons, too, sees man shaped by language as well as the shaper of words, and in "Essay on Poetics," he speaks of a poem so contained that "the mind can travel around in it and/know its sound and motion." Still, in "Alternatives" he is willing to admit that the capacity of words to move the world, at least in his experience, is limited, and *Tape*, his first effort at a book-length poem, openly rejects the particular methods that Pound uses for his *Cantos:* "no muffled talk, fragments/of phrases, linked/without logical links,/strung/together in obscurities/supposed to reflect/density." His language will be quiet and "immersed in the play of events"; his method of accretion, different from that heightened tangle of culture and prophecy that Pound proposes. He will be keeping more to a doctrine of change than one of will, to Peirce's belief that meaning in language relies more on how objects that words signify are used than on traditional res-verba connections. Thought and language are as much a part of biochemical processes as they are parts of abstract systems, and unlike nineteenth and early twentieth century writers who believed that great men determined history, Ammons is willing to give preference to democracy and concede a degree of the determining power behind history to body chemistry and accident.

Similarly, when Ammons says in *Tape* that "I've been/looking for a level/of language/that could take in all/kinds of matter/& move easily with/light or heavy burden," one thinks of Eliot's equation of "classic" and "common style" in "What Is a Classic?" (1945). There Eliot describes "classic" as having "within its formal limitations" the ability to express "the maximum possible of the whole range of feeling which represents the character of the people who speak that language" and characterizes English as "being the most various of great languages in its constituents" and therefore tending "to variety rather than perfection." Eliot concludes by sensing that English may need "a longer time to realize its potency" however much it may still have left in the way of "unexplored possibilities." He describes the efforts of current writers as inclining toward both monotony and eccentricity: "monotony because the resources of the language have not yet been explored, and eccentricity because there is yet no generally accepted standard." But again, the structure of a poem like *Tape*—though not necessarily of Ammons' later poems—owes less to Eliot than to someone like Williams, and even the more recent "poetic essays" would prove too "various" and "eccentric" for Eliot's designation of Pope's style as the nearest to classic in English. Yet, Ammons' inclinations toward philosophical poetry suggest an affinity with the later Eliot more than they do with any other contemporary poet, just as statements like "The mind seeks the new object that can adequately reflect and interpret the new feelings" in "A Note on Incongruence" seem to restate Eliot's principle of the "objective correlative."

Williams, who is mentioned in the course of *Tape*, is the subject as well of a poem in *Briefings*. Ammons shares with him a desire to include in poetry current scientific theory and language in addition to a belief that long poems may be built from ordinary experiences. These ordinary experiences, as Williams' "Shadows" maintains, are of "two worlds/one of which we share with the/rose in bloom/and one,/by far the greater,/ with the past" (*Pictures from Brueghel*). For both poets the violent experience of these worlds which is the subject of Ammons' "WCW" results in the need to experiment with traditional theories of meter. Williams went for a time to a variable foot and triadic line in order to trace the movements of sense and mind in a relative universe where verification constitutes truth, and Ammons, as "A Note on Prosody" indicates, shows a comparable consistency by choosing a pendulous rhythm in which both ends of a poetic line "are being played against a middle." For Ammons an imaginary point or vacancy that exists "between the two points of beginning and end" becomes the "center of gravity." This vacuum creates "a downward pull [. . .] that gives a certain downward rush to the movement, something like a waterfall glancing in turn off opposite sides of the canyon, something like the right and left turns of a river," or, to return to his image of the poem as walk, the beginning and ends of his lines become non-linear "glancing off points" for his strolling narrator whose movement is like the poem's "not across the page but actually, centrally down the page."

Still, as Bloom indicates, the result of Ammons' experiment with prosody is not Williams' view of a poem as "a machine made out of words." There is nowhere evident anything like a structure borrowed as were *Paterson*'s from coding practices and contemporary art and imposed *ab exteriore* on experience despite Ammons' making clear in "A Note on Incongruence" that he shares Williams' belief that "a poem is a construct of language," one composed not "out of 'reality' but out of an invented system of signs," and that like Williams, he considers language "an invented instrument" which is not "identical with what it points to," although it remains "one of the best ways of pointing we have." Discrepancy between word and thing never resolves in a depersonalized methodology—not even that of science—in order that the gap between the events which prompt the poem and the stasis it achieves resolve into a kind of formalism. Rather, one awareness leads in turn to a second, larger awareness in a continuous process of enlargement whose formal controls are never divorced from the intelligence which produces the work, and this lack of separation explains why it is easier to understand Ammons' poetry in bulk than in single poems.

The dynamics of such a process of accretion as it achieves long poems may derive practically from works like *Leaves of Grass,* but it receives its theoretical scientific support from views of subjectivity like William James' "stream of consciousness." John Dewey converted the notion early into a principle of esthetic "contexts of experience," in which such "contexts" mirror a view of life wherein continuous, gradated qualitative fusions are here and there broken by analysis and discrimination. Integrity in art becomes as an outgrowth a similar system of fusions, including those with "fringe" elements, that exists so long as a problematic situation does not arise to interrupt the flow with a discontinuous counter quality of analysis and discrimination. In *Art as Experience* (1934), Dewey depicts the rhythms which reinforce these contexts as relational rather than substantial: "Relationships rather than elements recur, and they recur in differing contexts and with different consequences so that each recurrence is novel as well as a reminder. In satisfying an aroused expectancy, it also institutes a new longing, incites a fresh curiosity, establishes a changed suspense." Thus, in the winter of 1963 when Ammons went out and purchased a roll of adding machine tape to record the contexts and consequences that occurred between December 6th and January 10th, he may have begun with what some critics might feel is an arbitrary, external device for containment, but the very rhythms of recurrence, vacillating between immanence and memory, build into a unity of consciousness that is unquestionably a major accomplishment. The daily, "metaphysical" compositions of time and place—diary entry and description of weather—become so habitual and undisruptive that they prove no more intrusive than chapter breaks in a novel. As Dewey had foreseen, unless emphasized, temporal disjunctions blur before the "contexts" of continuous consciousness.

It is perhaps to Roethke and ultimately to the Rilkean elements in Roethke's work that Ammons may be most indebted for his emphasis on temporary closures that awaken into probes of farther ranging consciousness. Of the immediately preceding generation and at the peak of his popularity when Ammons began publishing, Roethke is the least urban of the post-modernist poets who emerged in the forties and the most given to using nature as a guide to psychic states. He saw Rilke's notion of death as "the other, the unilluminated side of life" in terms of what he called "the underside" of life and shared with the German poet the belief in an essential unity of subjective and objective resulting from "an essential connaturality of the depth of things and the depth of self." Rilke's conception of death as "an extension of human life into the infinite" (*Duino Elegies*) is ultimately Platonic and connaturality is common to a number of Romantic writers including Emerson, but their articulation by Roethke immediately prior to Ammons in terms not only of contemporary psychology but also of animism and apostrophe could not avoid influencing someone as sympathetic as Ammons by offering him an ongoing quest for psychic wholeness that would serve as a model for his own reconstruction in art of "the whole person."

One might also add to these basic American influences, the influence of Dylan Thomas, who seems to prompt the rhetoric of poems like "Prodigal" and the opening of "Hardweed Path Going." Here the unusual abundance of descriptive detail combined with an onrush of phrases, intensifying and kept off-balance, and ending in "Prodigal" in an affirmative main clause, recalls Thomas' "A Refusal to Mourn" as well as the poetry of Gerard Manley Hopkins. Nevertheless, much of this tracing of what Bloom would term "poetic misprisions" is not so much to indicate derivation as to support the contention that Ammons is central to his generation because no other poet has been able to incorporate into his poetry so much diverse material from the nineteenth and twentieth centuries. Certainly, no other poet of his generation has "made a heterocosm, a second nature in his poetry" (Bloom). The creation of this "heterocosm" has involved, as Richard Howard indicates, the invention of more forms than any other poet. Still, this "heterocosm" is not, as Bloom would have one believe, primarily directed to a poem-begetting-poem tradition; it is vitally concerned with a preservation of nature that, like Emerson's, is biological as much as cultural. Ammons inveighs against natural waste in "Extremes and Moderations," claiming that man has tripped nature's balance "and gone into exaggerated/possession," and in a review of Ed Saunders' *Peace Eye*, he complains of the loss of culture that poets like Saunders advocate: "If Energy costs so much, if it diminishes man to a rod, woman to an orifice, if it obliterates all surface and personality, then the good is brutally, devastatingly compromised." Man's products, as "Apologia pro Vita Sua" indicates, are expected to introduce positive "foreign things" into nature.

One has only to trace Ammons' sensibility from his earliest poems to observe how much variety attaches to his major themes and how many of them are devoted to an upholding of both segments of nature. The opening poem of *Ommateum*, for example, proposes the crucial dialectic between Being and identity that Ammons enlarges on in his Pittsburgh address and which at heart is Emersonian. This dialectic first appears as a personal tension between a now dead hunchback, childhood playmate and the poet, but the talk enlarges its meaning to include Poseidon or total view and Proteus or knowledge. Ammons tells his audience, "You remember that Proteus is a minor sea god, a god of *knowledge*, an attendant on Poseidon. Poseidon is the ocean, the total view, every structure in the ocean as well as the unstructured ocean itself. Proteus, the god of knowledge, though, is a minor god. Definite knowledge, knowledge specific and clear enough to be recognizable as knowledge, is, as we have seen, already limited to a minor view." Ezra, a hunchback who by dying in the war has joined the eternal, invisible half of life that Rilke writes of, opposes the speaker of "So I Said I Am Ezra" whose element is wind. Ezra's "total view" loses its identity "among the windy oats/that clutch the dunes/of unremembered seas" rather than let its traits "become too much repeated" by aligning its nature with the gaming winds. For the speaker, something inherent in life acts as a check on such totality and, in subsequent poems like "Coming to Sumer," "Whose Timeless Reach," and "The Wind

Coming Down From," Ammons returns to probe just what it is that death seems to achieve.

By losing his identity in the wind and becoming "too much repeated" and hence "vacant," the poet, however, forms the major emphasis of Ammons' subsequent work. His pursuit of knowledge as expansions into periphery epitomizes the underlying rhythm which "Rack" depicts as a running "down all the pieces and build[ing] the whole silence back." "Gravelly Run" shows the ranges of this rhythm in the self caught among "unwelcoming forms" and the wiser, silent galaxy and cedar cone, and "Mansion" repeats the poet's need to move by joining himself to the wind which requires "all/the body/it [can] get/to show its motion with." From this wandering, as "Guide" establishes, the poet comes to unity, for "you cannot come to unity and remain material." In each, the poet's Protean transformations give way to the knowledge that one can make the leap to Poseidon or total view only by abandoning the spoken and seen; by peeling off one's being and plunging into a well where, as "Turning to Say So Long" asserts, the few shafts of light give way finally to darkness and death in a Wordsworthian "oneing" of human and universe. "Hibernaculum" even posits a hoped-for link between the places of origin and those of ending. Ammons complains there of being buried where, "once underground," his feet would not be free to "travel through the earth to [his] sweet home country" and concludes by realizing that "death's/ indifference will absorb living nostalgias," for the "earth's a single mother and all who lie in her are brothers/and sisters."

Just as the outline of these themes constitutes what is informational in Ammons' early poems, the elaboration of these themes in terms of an evolving methodology from simple, almost Imagistic objectifications to depictions of process comprises much of Ammons' efforts between 1961 and 1965. Yet it is only recently that he has been able to treat such process in terms of the short poem. The early poems betray a pattern which is largely mechanical: they open on places—a plateau, a desert, a dark woods, a reed patch, Sumer, Strasbourg, Antioch—and, after a brief description, move into some action—laughter, notation, discovery—before concluding in a summary statement or a second, dissolving action. In later pieces like "Sitting Down, Looking Up" and "Communication" this pattern changes; the speaker of the poem has become the place, defined in Imagistic terms by the actions and objects that surround him. The poems of connaturality, such as "Mountain Liar," undergo similar and corresponding alterations. Rather than the mutual intersubjectivity that the early poem suggests is man's reality, "Mountain Talk" proposes a disinterested central intelligence that is reaffirmed in "Kind" and replaced by resistance in "Height."

Tape for the Turn of the Year seems to have provided the break-through for these changes as well as for the preoccupation with process that Ammons' subsequent work has shown. The very self-consciousness of *Tape*—its being about the efforts of a poet to write a poem under certain conditions as well as its being the poem written—allows it to assume a sense of process despite the compositions of time and place that diary entries and weather reports contribute. Ammons can write movingly, as conditions dictate, about "the business of/getting started," of having "to take a leak," of being "bushed," about selecting Christmas trees, about his boyhood or his feelings for his wife as well as about language and individu-alism and poetry. He can be lyrical, anecdotal, witty, playful, and typo-graphically and verbally funny. What emerges is a comprehensive record of a poet, living in a rural area outside of Philadelphia with his wife and son and caught up in domestic and professional concerns while awaiting the publication of his second book of poems. Both in its tendency to include necessary but trivial actions, menus, prices, and daily annoyances, and in its allowing the personality of the poet to come through by means of what the Renaissance would call "predicaments," *Tape* allows for a persona that makes the figure of the later, more specialized essay poems, seem anemic. The poet is here quiet, warm, intense, and considerate although by no means unbelievably so, and one gathers that much of what goes on in the course of the work is intended to run through the reader's life and exist there "like a protein/molecule"; it is to provide some inkling for moral growth.

A critic like Randall Jarrell might say of *Tape* as he did of both Pound's *Cantos* and Williams' *Paterson* that it embodies "the Organization of Irrelevance (or, perhaps, the Irrelevance of Organization)" (*Poetry and the Age*), that the placing of the thoughts gives no sense of necessity or narrative, and that, as a consequence, there is something vitally wrong with the value system that emerges. He might also add that Dewey's notion of closures that awaken in an ongoing evolution is merely an esthetic equivalent for industry's "built-in obsolescence," that poets should not "rest (or at least [. . .] thrash happily about) in contradictions, doubts, and general guesswork, without ever climbing aboard any of the monumental certainties that go perpetually by, perpetually on time." But such objections would be ignoring—as Jarrell was wont to do—recent philosophical, scientific, and linguistic positions. Roman Jakobson, for instance, is willing to posit man's tendency toward speech in his genetic make-up and to propose that like the web-spinning spider's, the patterns of man's thought may have an instinctual regularity. This certainly is Ammons' position and the reason for the various patternings on the page of what are intended to be "ventilated lattice works." One must reject the terms of Jarrell as being outmoded as Jarrell himself rejected abstract and action painting on the grounds that they tended to play down the superego and ego in their executions. If, as Ammons proposes in "Extremes and Moderations," superego and ego, as they are presently composed, are precisely those elements that prevent an alignment of "psychic forces with the natural," then there can be no common ground between the positions.

In any case, the machinery of *Tape for the Turn of the Year* allows for a number of excellent small poems—"Ground Tide," "Translating," "Sorting," "Delaware Water Gap"—as well as for three long poems which Bloom is willing to pronounce among the best things Ammons has written. Certainly Bloom is right in seeing that these poems will eventually end in a unity or monism of process and that this end has already allowed Ammons in "Extremes and Moderations" a prophetic strain. Nevertheless, the poems do raise questions about the essay form. Usually one expects either originality of thought or fineness of expression as a characteristic of the genre. Pope's "What oft was thought, but ne'er so well expressed" is a commonplace of the tradition; but aphorisms such as one finds in Pope or in Sir Francis Bacon are calculated to arrest, to be commonplaces or independent kernels of wisdom. Fine expression tends to act in direct opposition to "temporary resolutions" and the "provisional" nature of Ammons' work; moreover, the essay form has inclined to be either logical or anecdotal, and neither technique is overwhelmingly present in Ammons' poems. Rather, he chooses to remain associational. Therefore, when he entitles a work "Essay on Poetics," he is writing a very strange "essay"—more a journal or notebook really than anything else, and a journal calculated to stress process above personality, activity over meditation. One can accept the long poem when, as in the case of *Tape*, it ends as do many Romantic essays in personality, but when it ends in process without vision, then one—as Bloom is—should be careful. In the absence of originality and fine expression, the essay poem works best when, as in "Extremes and Moderations," Ammons has an action to propose—in this case, the reconstruction of life in the same process in which art is created.

Of the poets about Ammons' age, only Robert Creeley may be said to share Ammons' involvement with the "central" American literary tradition and the struggle for unity, knowledge, and being in a world dominated by scientific and philosophical ideas. The origin of Creeley's positions may also be traced to Emerson, Dewey, Williams, Pound, and thermodynamics but unlike Ammons, Creeley has preferred the interior austerity of an Emily Dickinson to the expansive nature of Whitman. Of late Creeley, too, has moved into journal poems like *Tape*, but he still manages to interpret his line in terms of breath rather than of chance, writing out of the same silence as Ammons, but with the hesitancy of one who has had a speech impediment and finds the flow of words less rapid than does Ammons. Much as this parsimony with language produces in Creeley a tendency to border on monotony, in Ammons, the generosity of language brinks ever on the chaos of variety. One may say of Ammons' line what he once wrote of Allen Ginsberg's, that it doesn't "shape, predict, and limit whole-poem forms," and what the painter Franz Klein indicates is the condition of art at the present time: "Well, look, if I paint what *you* know, then that will simply bore you, the repetition from me to you. If I paint what I know, it will be boring to myself. Therefore I paint what I don't know." Ammons' openness in his line and stanza to "total acceptance" ["Extremes and Moderations"] and his not knowing beforehand what he will write (*Tape*) create conditions of ongoingness that he shares with no other poet of his generation. He seems less tied to what he has done and more likely than any of his contemporaries to strike out on each of his poetic walks for greater understanding than that already vast wisdom he has already achieved. This condition of itself more than justifies his particular approach to writing.

LINDA ORR

The Cosmic Backyard
of A. R. Ammons

Solitary at midnight in my back yard, my
thoughts gone from me a long while.

—WHITMAN, "Song of Myself"

Never before has the abundance of a backyard entered into such a mutually productive relationship with poetry. If Jarrell was astounded at Stevens' ability to write about whatever he chose, Jarrell had not seen anything yet: "Stevens has learned to write at will, for pleasure; his methods of writing, his ways of imagining, have made it possible for him as it is impossible for many living poets—Eliot, for instance. Anything can be looked at, felt about, meditated upon, so Stevens *can* write about anything." Why is Ammons so prolific? "In my yard's more wordage than I/can read" ("Summer Session"). His backyard is perhaps only slightly more active and encumbered than the ordinary American phenomenon: with its bluespruce, elm, peartree, picnic table, marble bench, quincebush, holly, hedgebrush, sandbox, petunias, tomato plants, hose left out and lots of weeds; I might even recognize it unless, of course, there are the usual inventions. From the Sumerian desert, to Carolina fields, to Jersey shore, Ammons has backed or been backed up into his backyard for a reason. He justifies his move by saying he's really quite pleased, "some universe" drops by every day, and "it's world enough to take my time, stretch my reason, hinder/and free me" ("Hibernacu-

From *Diacritics* 3 (Winter 1973). Copyright © 1973 by Diacritics, Inc.

lum"). Often he's concealing other motives and this time he lets us in on
a little more of himself:

> by the time I got the world cut down small enough that
> I could be the center of it, it wasn't worth having:
> but when I gave up center, I found I was peripherally
>
> no bigger than a bit: now, I have decided the former
> was the better: I must re-mount the center and force
> the world to subside about me:
>
> ("Hibernaculum")

That's tough language, sounds as if someone has his eye on power and will
make a last stand to get it. A small world can be controlled from its
imaginary center but large forces and a score of events pouring into a
limited space, while increasing energy and pressure, heighten an already
volatile situation, for the central problem—the self and its well-being in
the world—is barely disguised in this mixing of motives. Ammons' poems
are a jockeying of an elaborate self-consciousness to come to expression
without being seen, a consciousness of an essential discontinuity and
doubleness which is pried out of the "nooks and crannies" of his poetry by
the very act of hiding: "how much revelation concealment necessitates"
("Cut the Grass"). Ammons is rather foxy and his smoke screen of ink
gives the illusion of complete "disarmament." Indeed sooner or later the
changing shapes do inform. Ammons' first poems already parry with this
consciousness, but *Tape for the Turn of the Year* (1965) and the recent long
"essay" poems especially emerge as a kind of dark face to his Whitmanian
hope that all the universe is one glorious intersubjective relationship. The
"fall" into consciousness occurs when one recognizes a Not-Self and a
non-human world around him; this may be called Nature or, if the idea of
two "selves" is to carry over: an empirical self. One can talk about the
Not-Self and Self together only in terms of differentiation, never of
hierarchy and control, for a total transference from one self to the other is
a miracle. Man is strictly a "thing" in nature's terms; nature can never be
humanized nor man naturalized. That selfhood of man apart from nature is
defined by language; through language is the process of continual differentiation accomplished. An entity in itself, language is profoundly ambiguous; the "luminous ideal image-tree" Ammons speaks of in "Essay on
Poetics" resembles the elm in his backyard but *is* not that elm (Shakespeare "never got it straight that in talking about the/actual king and the
symbolical king he was merely/engaging a problem in rhetoric," ["Hibernaculum"]). Language is both referential and autonomous and must keep
this duality intact:

motion and artificiality (the impositional remove from reality)
sustain language: nevertheless, language must
not violate the bit, event, percept,

fact—the concrete—otherwise the separation that means
the death of language shows:

                                        ("Essay on Poetics")

The fruits of this consciousness most brutally surface in *Tape for the Turn of the Year* whose experience must have fed Ammons' crucial third volume of poems, *Corsons Inlet* (1965):

> only the lively use of
>   language lives:
>   can live
>   on dead words
>   & falsehood: the
> truths poetry creates
>   die with
>   their language:
>   stir any old
> language up,
> feel the fire in it &
> its truths come true
>   again:
>   the resource, the
> creation, and the end of
>   poetry is
>   language:

This second passage seems to go farther than the first. Language not only dies when too far from "the concrete," but its life depends, perhaps more directly, on the superficial energy of use: it dies and survives within itself. This kind of basic thinking does not prevent Ammons from sometimes hoping the opposite: that language can transcend language—a tautology which underlies the very strain of poetry—its unresolved struggle and hard music. Ammons still rages against the stolen ambition, the one ambition worthy of a poem—that is, become the voice of nature, let the Not-Me, forever alien from the verbal sphere, speak.

Ammons tries everything yet he knows what he is doing. Three recent and very fine testimonies to consciousness—"Cascadilla Falls," "Center," and "This Bright Day"—transform the context of the argument out of an argument and into song, be it heavy song. Yes, perhaps, even into transcendence: the reader almost forgets that he is reading. Ammons tries everything to the extent of constructing and complicating a cosmic system that would surely obscure the doubleness inherent in each word. How distracting, clever. Except the poet had to tinker with his system everywhere he went until at last in his backyard he could make it work. If there's any chance at all of "unnaturalizing" nature and attempting to make it "us," it's in our backyard. But not only does Ammons' backyard grow dense with artifacts and actual facts, the poems also increase their concealment. All sorts of language and situations are introduced; the level of language (the very "line" of poetry) is pried open to let anything in: "I've been/looking for a level/of language/that could take in all/kinds of matter/& move easily with light or heavy burden:" (*Tape*). In "Summer Session" alone, a cousin to *Tape*, zigzags of ironical, lyrical, moralistic, and journalistic language mix and blend until every detail upholds the single life of the poem: 1) Ammons' own brand of philosophy, his "gay science"; 2) a blow-by-blow account of certain daily activities including necessary sex; 3) markers to tell you where you are in the poem; 4) fatherly, priestly, or friendly advice; 5) definitions and variations on what he's trying to do in poems; 6) cosmic shots altered with intimate scenes; beauty beside beast; 7) word play (a few obviously outrageous puns); 8) sheer Rabelaisian accumulation. The "small and easy" poems can inhibit him, but the long polyphonic mazes, monsters of courage and indulgence, sound like Ammons at his happiest, even in despair.

Before confronting Ammons' "system," I'd like to return to "Cascadilla Falls," "Center," and "This Bright Day," three alternative reactions to a growing consciousness of self-differentiation. Ammons writes a combined poetry of mystification, acceptance, and grief—sometimes, though rarely, limiting himself to one of the three states of mind. Consciousness wins out in all three cases over mystification but with different emotional responses: a shrug before the inevitable and some sadness ("Cascadilla Falls"); a removed indifference ("Center"); and grief ("This Bright Day"). The system would help explain these poems, would enrich them, but I don't want to rely on it yet.

In "Cascadilla Falls," Ammons leaps immediately into the cosmic vision of everything-related.

> I went down by Cascadilla
> Falls this
> evening, the
> stream below the falls,
> and picked up a
> handsized stone
> kidney-shaped, testicular, and

thought all its motions into it,
the 800 mph earth spin,
the 190-million-mile yearly
displacement around the sun,
the overriding
grand
haul

of the galaxy with the 30,000
mph of where
the sun's going:
thought all the interweaving
motions
into myself: dropped

the stone to dead rest:
the stream from other motions
broke
rushing over it:
shelterless,
I turned

to the sky and stood still:
Oh
I do
not know where I am going
that I can live my life
by this single creek.

The first two objects, stream and stone, which appear by a trick of enjambment separated from their dependence on language because torn away from their articles, enter the order of astronomy. The numerical precision of great speeds and distance establishes a kind of authority and sense of control vis-à-vis the poet's materials; it also adds to the atmosphere of awe and to the surprise of the paradoxical closing: "This *single* creek." Ammons' "scientistic" language, an identifiable trait of his diction, is perhaps no more unusual than Dante's specialized star-gazing and, in fact, indicates a nostalgia for a Unity or something like the "Love that moves the sun and the other stars" (*Paradiso*). The stone is manlike: kidney and testicle. Here Ammons slips into his gravest temptation: if everything is a body part—rocks or even words, "clauses (tissues), sentences (organs), verses (organ systems), poems (living worlds)" ("Essay on Poetics")—the universe can literally make love. Poems with poems maybe, or rocks with rocks; but isn't the rest *verboten*? When the poet steps into this cosmic scheme, the "overriding/grand haul," wonder (praise or terror?) overtakes him. Is it reassuring or devastating to tumble through space? At any rate, the stone is abruptly dropped from the hand: "to dead rest." The rock returns to itself; it is and always has been dead. The stream, like the "air's glass jail" in an earlier poem "Gravelly Run," "seals" the stone in its own entity. Now the stone only revolves "in crystal" (Stevens, "Notes Toward a Supreme Fiction"). The "I" in its own entity of loneliness stands still—where is all the past motion?—and utters a mysteriously true sentence: "Oh/I do/not know where I am going/that I can live my life/by this single creek." Implied is a simultaneous going and stasis (like the illusion of stillness one has turning on earth) and some mildly proud resignation—after all he *can* live his life. The single creek, like the backyard, contains all the imagage and wordage he'll ever need, so much futile wealth since his language may never possess the stream itself, much less the galaxy.

"Center" tries the mystification of "Cascadilla Falls" in reverse: instead of following the stone's ripples to the edge of the universe, the poet watches bird, bush, stream, and road collapse into some invisible "center." The procedure of reversals is one of Ammons' trademarks: a going-out, a coming-in, a piling-up, a digging-down (see "The Arc Inside and Out"). It's "good bth cmng & gng" or "gng in & cmng out" (*Tape*), as Ammons spoofs Frost. Both directions attempt the same destruction of difference. The world created in "Center" as it progresses is eery, not unlike Stevens' "The Palm at the End of the Mind" or "The Snowman." The locus of the poem has penetrated so deeply into a nucleus as to have found a void, an entropy—"wasteful song"—where there's nothing like human care or therapy—"improvident"—where one is lost between echoes: "green/green."

> A bird fills up the
> streamside bush
> with wasteful song,
> capsizes waterfall,
> mill run, and
> superhighway
> to
> song's improvident
> center
> lost in the green
> bush green
> answering bush:
> wind varies:
> the noon sun casts
> mesh refractions
> on the stream's amber

> bottom
> and nothing at all gets,
> nothing gets
> caught at all.

The final sentence has a spare beauty. Clearly at the end no more general correspondence will emerge besides that of bush to bush. With help from other Ammons poems, one can further elaborate this final impression: language is often referred to as a net or finger ("Motion"): "we/agree upon/this (the poem) as a net to/cast on what/is." The words of the poem become the "uninterfering means on paper" ("Poetics"); Ammons' later poems in their wide stanzas are supposed to function as "lattices" to let "the world breeze unobstructed through" ("Essay on Poetics"). Every now and then he acknowledges a yearning to catch the "breeze" materialized for a second into a vision: a fish.

> hauled in, the net is
>   a window of fish.
> gathered into thin, starving air,
>   the ocean, sucking, returned whole
> to itself, separation complete,
>
> fish from sea, tiger
>   from jungle, vision from experience.
>   ("Concentrations")

In the earlier poem, "Concentrations," the poet definitely hopes to rescue something substantial from the meeting of vision and experience; the "tiger from jungle" insertion—reminiscent of Henry James' short story—alerts us to the distance and diversity Ammons would cover with his casting, but the phrase, completing some perfect syntactical triad, seems, in this case, oddly out of place. The extent of the poet's catch at the end of "Center" is, however, rhetorically more convincing; the double negative, as in "The Snow Man," insists in its own sober way. The last sentence stutters so that "at all" intensifies "nothing" in the first phrase and then puts it weight on "caught" in the revision. A change of sense is suggested as if, at first, the net of words set out to get something and failed, and then, dangling unaggressively in the stream, still stopped nothing. The "I" being absent from the poem also removes all hint of perspective: the poem simply says this is the way it is.

"This Bright Day" covers a greater emotional range than the previous two poems discussed. The first line pretends to embark on an ecstatic performance similar to "The City Limits," a poem generally agreed to be one of Ammons' best. But by the last line of "This Bright

Day" the litany of praise has turned to lamentation. Sound and word
repetition, enjambment, and the inimitable Ammons colon ease the
transition from exuberant joy to sorrow:

> Earth, earth!
> day, this bright day
> again—once more
> showers of dry spruce gold,
> the poppy flopped broad open and delicate
> from its pod—once more,
> all this again: I've had many
> days here with these stones and leaves:
> like the sky, I've taken on a color
> and am still:
> the grief of leaves,
> summer worms, huge blackant
> queens bulging
> from weatherboarding, all that
> will pass
> away from me that I will pass into,
> none of the grief
> cuts less now than ever—only I
> have learned the
> sky, the day sky, the blue
> obliteration of radiance:
> the night sky,
> pregnant, lively,
> tumultuous, vast—the grief
> again in a higher scale
> of leaves and poppies:
> space, space—
> and a grief of things.

At first, no happier greeting could be offered to morning: the ah's and oh's
ring out of dazzling words—poppy, flopped, pod, and gold, open—and call
attention to the carefully placed echoes of "once more," "day," and
"again." The poet appears to rejoice in a beneficent eternal return. Then
a slight jolt comes with the second "I" and the enigmatic: "like the sky,
I've taken on a color/and am still." These lines depend on positioning to
heighten significant ambiguity. "Like the sky" seems natural after "stones
and leaves" but the "I" linking himself up Whitman-like again to the
universe is a step farther than even ebullient appreciation. The "I" has
"taken on a color"—become substantive, material, has covered over the
"White Self," the ghost that continually wanted out of the world in the
early poems. The subsequent "I am still" can support two very different

interpretations: 1) the empirical "I" also returns "once more," surviving with the rest of the earth; or 2) the other "I," the original ghost, still exists. As much as the poet tries to dissolve his ego into the natural environment, something remains resilient. The colon permits a fascinating confusion; the reader cannot help but hear: "and am still the grief of leaves." There is and is not a full stop at the colon. The autonomous "I" can only define itself in terms of loss: I am the loss of leaves; I am what has given up the leaves and stones. Even physical death does not bridge the gap: the "I" always seems to be filling a slot or space just behind "things." What is striking about this poem is the confession that, despite some victories of the imagination, he hasn't changed; he hasn't "improved," his grief is still as real. What has changed is self-consciousness: "only I/have learned the" as if this were some consolation. Although I become skeptical of the almost automatic hanging articles in Ammons' linebreaks, I rationalize this one with a suitably farfetched interpretation; I almost hear "I have not learned rock, I have only learned the The" reminiscent of both Stevens ("The Well-Dressed Man With a Beard") and Dugan ("Wall, Cave and Pillar Statements after Asôka"). What else has the poet learned? And is he the only one to learn? In reply Ammons sets up a delicate dialectic of sky: he has seen 1) what radiance can be seen, the modified One of day, a toned-down transcendency; he has seen 2) the almost infinite movement of night: births, deaths, flights, flowing. But grief is also associated with this knowledge, and one gets the feeling that the poet is mourning not simply the cyclical death of things but his own death to things, to everything that is not the white of absolute radiance. In fact complete self-differentiation and, thus, identity would burst forth in the paradoxical statement: I am the loss of things; I am no-thing. If the poet is like the sky, he is originally white but must appear on this earth in colors; he is originally that old "White Self" burning somewhere outside the earth's atmosphere:

> Find me diffuse, leached colorless,
> gray as an inner image with no clothes
> along the shallows of windrows: find
>
> me wasted by hills,
> conversion mountain blue in sight
> offering its ritual cone of white:
>
> so look for my white self, age clear,
> time cleaned: there is the mountain:
> even now by blue
>
> ghost may be
> singing on that height of snow.
> ("Look for My White Self")

And if the young poet once maintained that he was already "wasted" just as the later Ammons repeats that he's a "spent seer," it doesn't mean that he won't rise again stronger. To be spent upon achievement is natural—not only in sexual terms—but in transcendental terms. To step out "into the open," to leave the world implies losing everything, giving everything up, stripping to the soul. Victor Hugo in his most ambitious poetic failure, *Dieu*, where the poet steps out into the blue to become God, knew that he had to "perdre terre"—not just lose his footing, but relinquish the whole earth.

THE SYSTEM: VISION BY THE BACKDOOR

The number of transformations, of snake segments the self goes through in Ammons' poetry, is so great that there may be no such thing as nakedness. At first I thought the White Self of the early poems gave away the deepest impulses of a poet who hadn't had time yet to camouflage his clandestine activities of transcendence. But as he hints much later (he makes a habit in his later "essays" of cutting you off at any pass of solution), there in the flapping sheets of ghostdom spiraling above the earth he was his most elaborate of personalities:

> everyday (somedays, twice) I remember who I am and I
> metamorphose away through several distracting transformations
> till I get myself out in biddable shape on comfortable
>
> ground, and then the shows, the transactions, carry
> traces of such brilliant energy of invention that I am
> half willing to admire my new self, thrust into its
>
> lofty double helices, so winding:
>
> ("Hibernaculum")

Since all we have are various spinning selves anyway, perhaps the system we choose to hide in is as close as anyone will get to us and is, in its mechanisms, terribly honest. Ammons would probably not call his imaginative construct a system: just an "Uh, Philosophy," a "Direction," a "Project," a "Put-Down Come On," a "Translating." However, Ammons' titles alone invite abstraction. Consider the difference between his titles and those of recent poems written by other poets: "Strato in Plaster" (Merrill), "The Story of Our Lives" (Strand), and "Variations on a Text by Vallejo" (Justice). These three titles suggest that poems are born of literary and/or personal experience.

Ammons' titles suggest that poems are born of contemplation.

"Experience" enters his poem in its largest sense as the apprehension of phenomena. Although Ammons is very close in cadence and form to early Williams, titles show the two poets' distinct orientations. Williams will call his poem about rain "Rain"; not Ammons, who calls his "Mediation" or "Translating." The mere outlines of a project reveal a particular impulse for writing. Is the system a tool for discovery or mock-discovery? With "direction," don't you know what you will find? Do words basically fill slots, fit "nuts and bolts" ("Even"), or do they illuminate on their own? And is there any difference, any value to be placed on one view over the other? Having some overall project certainly alleviates the primary anxiety of the poet—new beginnings with each white page: "something/about direction/lets us loose/into ease/ and slow grace" ("Anxiety"). Individual beginnings and endings are not as crucial since they are only a semi-solution in the ongoing enterprise. And, of course, the eternal problem of subject is solved.

To talk of Ammons' ongoing project one must become familiar with certain key words and word clusters. Flowing from a movable *center*, Ammons' Emersonian or Dickinsonian *circles*, his *arcs*, contract and ex-pand, going out as far as *peripheries* where *order* begins to disintegrate into *entropy*. The energy and challenge of the whole depend upon the *saliences*, *unassimilable facts*, *extremes* that demand complete revision of any provi-sional *unity* while undergoing themselves a *moderating* influence. In "The Arc Inside and Out," this living organism—a possible replica of the universe, the mind, our lives, the poem, language (?)—reaches its fullest expression, only to be rejected as false in the end:

> suasion, large, fully-informed, restful
>
> scape, turning back in on itself, its
> periphery enclosing our system with
> its bright dot and allowing in nonparlant
>
> quantities at the edge void, void, and
> void.

The filling out of this vision took time. And although I have been speaking about Ammons' poems synchronically, as if his earliest themes still flourish, a chronological approach can sometimes show the logic behind significant stages of development. Harold Bloom devotes three careful and moving essays to Ammons' poetry, concentrating on three periods of the canon and their central poems: 1) before and after "Corsons Inlet" and "Saliences"; 2) the small poems of *Upland* (1970) and *Briefings* (1971), especially "The City Limits"; and 3) the longer "essay" poems.

For Bloom, "Corsons Inlet" and "Saliences" are a breaking-point in the evolution of Ammons' work and provoke the crucial insights that guide later poems. The poet of "Corsons Inlet" admits that he "perceives nothing completely." The preconceived lines of his mind loosen, curve, and merge into transitions, blurrings, "eddies of meaning," so that the only outcome possible is "order held/in constant change." With this discovery, Ammons renounces two paths that his poetry has taken up to then: 1) he reduces the amount of credence he will accord the Transcendental Oversoul and 2) he wrenches himself away from the tempting union with Particulars, with a Fate or "Beautiful Necessity" that would swallow up hope, mind, and control. Bloom honors the keen disappointment that would necessarily follow from a lost quest while praising the autonomy of mind and imagination that such loss allows. A certain section of "Saliences" testifies to the mind's coming to power, and Bloom introduces these lines by linking their content with the workings of Coleridge's secondary imagination: "Holding himself as he must, firmly apart from still-longed-for unity, he finds himself now in an astonishing equilibrium with the particulars, containing them in his own mind by reimagining them there":

> in
> the hollow,
> where a runlet
> makes in
> at full tide and fills a bowl,
> extravagance of pink periwinkle
> along the grassy edge,
> and a blue, bunchy weed, deep blue,
> *deep into the mind the dark blue*
> *constant:* [my italics]

The knowledge described in "Saliences" frees Ammons, according to Bloom, and ushers in the lyrical resurgence of *Briefings* and *Upland*. But ultimately the poet runs the danger of enclosing himself in his rings only to break out during temporary bursts of epiphany. The hypothesis of "astonishing equilibrium" is terribly tenuous as both Bloom and Ammons know. A juxtaposition of deep blue weed and dark blue constant of mind does not necessarily connote a relationship, an interpenetration. Certainly the first half of the 1961–1965 grouping of the *Collected Poems* struggles to establish some third alternative to the previously strict dialectic of Unity and Particulars which were considered first mutually inclusive ("Hymn I"), and later mutually exclusive ("Guide"). The new alternative would be a delicate balance between form and change, order and motion. Temporality enters Ammons' work for the first time as a serious force, more than enters the work—obsesses it.

An imitative language is what lends the most support to Ammons' subtle interconnecting realities, to his new alternative vision of perpetual change. The overall landscaping of Ammons' poems is immediately striking, and the care devoted to the lay of the language applies on a small as well as large scale. With motion as the guiding principle of his poems—a wind that would no longer dash to pieces but keep the order reordering—the poet could use to advantage former techniques and develop new ones: certain syntactical and narrative practices, particular grammatical and rhetorical preferences, out of which emerges an identifiable view of language. Sentences in poems-of-process must be doubling back all the time, qualifying, contradicting. "Though" and "but" become necessary links in phrasing:

> certain things and habits
> recognizable as
> having lasted through the night:
> though what change in
> a day's doing!
> ("Saliences")

The poet must be alert to any tendencies for rest and sweep the words up again. Synonyms, parenthetical expressions, present participles, and the colon all help maintain the illusion of many things happening at once; this is Emerson's and early Ammons' One and Many propelled into millions of motions—running, winding, falling, bending, shaping. The colon allows for a long, sinuous poem to be secure as one sentence and yet contain a myriad of relatively separate parts. A period closes a box; a colon initiates a swerve. The narrator too is relieved of a heavy responsibility; he no longer need be omniscient. His eye had previously pretended total vision (like Hugo's "grand oeil fixe ouvert sur le grand tout"—perhaps more tasteful than the "transparent eyeball"); now if he misses what the egret spears, it's ok. The narrator is expected to change like the swallows; he and everything else comply under a universal metonymic order: while they are separate parts, each represents the whole. This does not mean that he *is*, like Whitman, the whole and parts. Even so, the blatant metaphorical connections that bring together such entities as mind, universe, plants, animals, language, and "reality," make me nervous. I'm not relaxed in such an obviously referential and devious language: it reveals meaning by obscuring basic distinctions. In "Corsons Inlet" the repeated use of metaphor created by the *of* prepositional phrase leaves no mystery about the "meaning" of the poet's images: "geography of my work," "sayings [. . .] like the inlet's cutting edge," "sandy paths of remembrance," "wandering of mirroring mind," "old dunes/of mind." Every event seems to become a symbol or lesson for understanding a larger principle. When on a windy day a grackle can't fly or sit, Ammons claims "it's just like reality" ("Windy Trees"). A part rarely stands on its own without being moved into the center of the universe, which gives rise to a frequent formula for a short poem: an A B Á sonata or A B synthesis A/B. The universe usually opens the scene, a particular wanders on and struts in detail, then joins with the universe which lingers after, fading out at the end in a lesson.

THE SHORELESS TIDE

The universe with its
universal principles
was out exact with concision—

but toying, idling—
again this morning: that
is, the lemon-yellow

lime-veined sugar maple
leaves were as in a
morning tide, full but

slow with the slowness
of huge presences, nicking
off the branches and

coming down points up, stem-end
first, centered and weighted,
but spiraling nicely,

a dance perfectly
abundant: I got excited,
the universe concentrated

on the small scope of
a fall, as if to
expend reserves of

spectacle on the doomed so
we might, I thought, consider
some well beyond all loss.

These short poems are like a series of the same still life in different colors, arrangements, with different objects done by a painter whose style on each canvas would never fool us.

This metonymic poetry of motion is always surrounded by transcen-
dencies pushing to get in, if by the backdoor, the old faithful Particulars
and Unity. "February Beach," less recognized than "Corsons Inlet" and
"Saliences" whose heels it follows on, seems to run both poems backwards, to undo every bit of good or harm they achieved. The poem opens
in a grey transcendency of winter where fog rises over "the hard deep
marriage/of sand and ice," where the wind is not variable but "low, even,"
and the sound of the ocean breakers merge. All is a cold oneness waiting
for a thaw. But the thaw doesn't replay the situation in "Corsons Inlet";
transitions, blurrings, mergings are no longer possible: only in ice were
they possible. Now each thing moves under its glass again: the saliences
become resiliences. On which does the poet stake the claim of truth?
Obviously neither:

> here with these chances
> taken here to take these chances: land winds will
> rise, feed
> back the sands, humble the breakers: today's
> high unrelenting cry will relent:
> the waves will lap with broken, separate,
> quiet sounds:
> let the thaw that will come, come: the dissolved
> · reorganizes
> to resiliences.

So motion has been squeezed out again by the stark undifferentiation of
winter and the imprisoned individuals of spring. The tenuous balance at
the end of Purgatory (see "The Bridge") can give you a moment's pleasure
in the earthly paradise before canceling itself out, leaving the darkness of
Hell behind and pure transparence ahead.

Ammons' early passion for black vision and some shimmering grays
and silvers gives way to semi-white, moonlike apparitions, soft pastels,
safer radiance. I have grown quite fond of some of the earlier walks out
into "the great black unwasting silence" ("Rack"); "the black so round
and deep" ("Consignee"); "the unseasonal undifferentiated empty stark"
("Hymn I") though I still don't know how to take them. Surely Ammons
was earnest but the posture he assumed was undergirded (not -mined) with
humor and surely he knew this. Surely there's irony involved. "Levitation"
and "Touching Down," later poems, have to be parodies of his earlier
danglings in air. Here's this guy having a vision with a crick in his neck
bent uncomfortably in the upward currents of wind. The early ambitious
poem "Doxology" enacts a levitation and, though it is a truly remarkable
"song of myself," when I get to the frog, I can restrain my smile no longer:

> Silent as light in dismal transit
> through the void, I, evanescent,
> sibilant among my parts,
> fearing the eclipse of a possible glance
> and not glancing, shut-eyed,
> crouch froglike upon my brain,
> hover and keep dark,
> fervor opposed by dread,
> activity numbed by its mixed result,
> till some awaited drop falls
> upon the mound and chaos
> perfects the eternity of my silence.

The humor reminds me of a later more sinister poem I actually break out laughing in, "The King of Ice." Ice, an ambivalent vision in murky white, has descended like a frigid migraine over the regal temples. It's Ammons disguised as Stevens, the Emperor of Ice Cream, telling Frost where to go and enlisting Shelley's historical help. The King stiffens as the "intolerable," the ice-vice presses during this war of nerves and he waits for "the thing to slip or for"

> my attention to fix, somewhere on
> the inner glacier, on polar bears
> in disconcerting romp: I figure
> the intolerable not to be dealt with
> just set aside: I am going to

> wait: look at these interesting
> stitches in my robes, I say:
> I've already settled my affairs of state;
> that is, I'll take the cold when it comes,
> but I will never believe in ice.

No Imagination rises out of the Abyss, no one hails the terrible Mount Blanc or Auroras of Autumn; this Ionesco-Pirandello-like King waits— heating up his mind to make the intolerable melt faster?

The most humane and personal of all Ammons' poems, a kind of down-home Wordsworthian elegy, celebrates Nelly Myers and the "bright, clear days" of his past, but even here a consciousness of the present must have its ironic say:

> the bright, clear days when she was with me
> and when we were together
> (without caring that we were together).

Ammons is, however, an expert at getting away with semi-radiances: therein lies a saving grace. "The City Limits" transforms the "dread" of the pale void into praise, and the balance between each object's own light and the mind's lamp is regained though both must stay partially hidden even in extreme generosity: "air or vacuum, snow or shale, squid or wolf, rose or lichen,/each is accepted into as much light as it will take" This abundant half-light reappears in "Love Song" as "the light along your lips." During the day the blinding white is softened by pale shades of green and blue ("The Yucca Moth" and "Winter Scene"). Nevertheless, the round dark still seems to wait behind each flickering, ready to return. In "Jungle Knot" the moon-illumined anaconda fights back with hidden coils. In "Hardweed Path Going," a sort of silver apocalypse is slowed down so we can see the awful loss. Sparkle, a suitably ironic name for Ammons' favorite hog, transfigures gruesomely before his youthful eyes:

> Bleed out, Sparkle, the moon-chilled bleaches
> of your body hanging upside-down
> hardening through the mind and night of the first freeze.

The bleak unity and captivating particulars keep working their way in. Even a definition of "Epiphany" where one might expect a New Jerusalem gets finally wrapped up in the old familiar images: the glass prison is back and hard death.

> such is the
> invisible, hard as glass, . . .
> being without body, energy
> without image:
> how they will be dealt
> hard realizations, opaque as death.

("They": those discovering the invisible for the first time.) If the equilibrium of shapely motion seems lost, the poetry isn't. Ammons preaches golden moderation but surely his ironic self cultivates extremes. I'm not even sure that a poetry of balance and motion can be sustained. No-Order sounded over and over with enough insistence eventually takes on an Order of its own—what happens in Nietzsche. Change does not wear well "as a word too much repeated falls out of being" ("So I said I am Ezra"). In "Corsons Inlet," doesn't the constant motion become a constant, the permanent again swallow up all efforts at being provisional?

> the possibility of rule as the sum of rulelessness . . .
> so that I make
> no form
> formlessness:

If Ammons has learned anything, it's the complexity of his quest. Equilibrium is more than reimagining the object in the mind. The constant of
the mind moves around in a landscape which is still and moving; and the
poem using a language that changes and is the same must render the
staying metamorphoses of both mind and land in its own motions and
itself "be reproduced whole, all its shapeliness intact" ("Essay on Poetics"). This is a quest to end all quests.

THE IRONIC QUEST

But Ammons is still trying. He runs into his gravest problems, it seems, when
he attempts to portray the rare conglomeration of events and entities he is
after by one all-inclusive object. No object can sustain such depth of slippery
significance. The apple almost works. A symbol of man's fall and mortality,
a fruit that bruises easily, a word that makes the mouth water, a kind of
heart, if the apple can be tossed rolling into language, if its curves and
descents are preserved, perhaps such vision will be lasting?

> and came home dissatisfied there
> had been no
> direct reply (from the wind)
> but rubbed with my soul an
> apple to eat
> till it shone.
>
> ("Grassy Sound")

> Everything begins at the tip-end, the dying-out,
> of mind . . .
>
> come: though the world ends and cannot
> end,
> the apple falls sharp
> to the heart starved with time.
>
> ("Peak")

But in the final poem of the *Collected Poems* the apple must give way to an
object loaded with literary history—the sun:

> neither way to go's to stay, stay
> here, the apple an apple with its own hue
> or streak, the drink of water, the drink.
>
> the falling into sleep, restfully ever the
> falling into sleep, dream, dream, and
> every morning the sun comes, the sun.
>
> ("The Arc Inside and Out")

Though these are graceful lines and the repetition is effective at suggesting motion, return, and autonomy—the apple as apple—are these lines finally not too reminiscent of Stevens, Whitman—Dante?

> chè la mia vista, venendo sincera,
> e più e più intrava per lo raggio
> dell'alta luce che da sè è vera
> [. . .] chè quasi tutta cessa
> mia visïone, ed ancor mi distilla
> nel core il dolce che nacque da essa.
> Così la neve al sol si disigilla;
> così al vento nelle foglie levi
> si perdea la sentenza di Sibilla.

"for my sight, becoming pure, was entering more and more through the beam of the lofty light which in itself is true. [. . .] for my vision almost wholly fades, and still there drops within my heart the sweetness that was born of it. Thus the snow loses its imprint in the sun; thus in the wind on the light leaves the Sibyl's oracle was lost."
(*Paradiso*, Canto XXXIII, ed. and trans. John D. Sinclair)

The falling off of Dante's vision, as well as the vision itself, brings many Ammons passages rushing to mind—the slow heavy rain drops he lingers over, the piling and receding snows, the leaves lifted showing their white: "the wind/underleaf white against/ the tree" ("Motion"). In many ways, Dante and Ammons share the same ambition—not to write the longest white transcendency in existence; it should be noted anyway that the action of *Paradiso* can take place in a moment's epiphany. No, their common motivation is expressed in a word that has recently entered the Ammons canon: suasions. The word, set off by a colon, closes a new poem "Narrows" published in *The Chicago Review*. At first the word sounded like salience to me, or swervings; the word had motion. But it is also a salience broken out into slightly more stability, a moment's resting place above the clanking of change, but not an epiphany. The word also combines etymologically the two paradoxical qualities that Dante achieved in *Paradiso* and that Stevens, according to Jarrell, found in poetry: will fused with enjoyment. Suasion includes both moral persuasion and plea-sure (*hedere*) and connotes a softness, a suaveness. What better sign for ego integration is there? "Essay on Poetics" names "suasions" as a kind of bridge . . . or swing . . . from the mechanized catalogues of human life and thought to a revised paradise.

> I am seeking the
> mechanisms physical, physiological, epistemological, electrical,

chemical, esthetic, social, religious by which many, kept
discrete as many, expresses itself into the
manageable rafters of salience, lofts to comprehension, breaks

out in hard, highly informed suasions, the "gathering
in the sky" so to speak, the trove of mind, tested
experience, the only place there is to stay, where the saints

are known to share accord and wine, and magical humor floats
upon the ambient sorrow:

This is almost the sinuous path of some quest or initiation. After the
outleapings from social and scientific schema, one arrives at hard yet
agreeable moral conclusions, a better way to live: "tested experience."
Humorous saints toast there, fully mindful of their losses and grief.

The splits that resolve at times in a smooth summary can always
pull apart again and exaggerate themselves. The only way I can describe
this final movement in Ammons' poetry is irony. Irony to define a
doubleness of consciousness fits; irony in language too—Ammons can
laugh at himself "levitating" or falling on his face, like Baudelaire's sage in
The Essence of Laughter. But there are times in Ammons when it would be
sacrilegious to laugh—actually this is true too for Baudelaire.

Somehow Ammons would like to effect change, would like to act
with his words. And yet irony crouches even in Ammons' highest ambition. He's got to feel silly every now and then crusading from his backyard; his mission turns into slapstick, resignation, or tyrannical pronouncements. This goes beyond the well-meant imperatives of many of his
poems: "keep/free to these events,/bend to these/changing weathers." The
man doing-the-best-he-can fragments into saint, seer or sibyl behind
whom are preacher, showman, shyster who are distantly related to the
farmboy, mountaineer, word mechanic, salesman, domestic husband, green
thumb, birdwatcher behind whom plots a madman who wants to take over
the earth. And this same man, this "misfit"—can we trust him?—comments
on all his selves with irony: Dante has usually got a Chaplin mimicking him.
"I can't reconcile the one with the many either—except in the fuzzy land
of radiant talk" ("Hibernaculum"). "It was just another show: as the mystic
said, it's/all one to me" ("Essay on Poetics"). After this, how can you
speak seriously about the yearning for the transcendental One in Ammons?
You know he's back there chuckling at you, while you fail. And yet . . .
there was and is that yearning. And more. The ambition to persuade
through words goes farther; he still wants words to be action, to be a thing
and things to speak. The constant referential use of language reveals a
hope that mind, universe, and words do overlap and interact. When he

dreams of the poem as stone, sex, or stream, he's both joking and dead serious. He would still like to write a mountain:

> mean the telling's unmediated:
> the present allows the reading of much
>
> old material: but none of it need be read:
> it says itself (and
> said itself) so to speak perfectly in itself.
> ("If Anything Will Level with
> You Water Will")

Perhaps this sheds some light on the famous Ammons talking mountain— like Blake's, or Shelley's or, for me, like in old mountain tales I read as a kid whar the horse, cow, or hill tole the ole woman which-a-way her purse went. He not only would like wind and mountains to speak, he'd like everything to live in his poems, literally. A rather frenetic endeavor results. If he can't find the One word that catches every motion and goes beyond them like the apple, sun, or suasions, then he'll have to say All words.

> I'll have to say everything
> to take on the roundness and withdrawal of the deep dark:
> less than total is a bucketful of radiant toys.
> ("Cut the Grass")

The toys are ok but the final epic battle is between Poet and Deep Dark and he'll need a background, a whole cosmos behind him. The way to enlist the cosmos is from his backyard, in his chaise longue, pulling all science in, all knowledge, all things. Those strange technical terms— *foraminiferal millennia, microvilli sporangi*—are magic words that bring unnamable, invisible worlds into the dictionary which someday will cover everything, a compendium of the universe. Ammons laughs at his hungry maw in the mirror and yet dances in front of it just to see, ironically, how he looks:

> for to go with a maw at
> the world as if to chew it up and spit
> it out again as one's own is to trifle with terrible
> affairs: I think I will leave out China.
> ("Hibernaculum")

All the time he is dancing and gathering up words afraid one will elude him, he knows that the faster and more prolific he gets the farther he strays from the impossible goal: "In naming have we divided what/unnaming will not undivide?" ("Two Motions"). In an ironic quest, you cannot win for losing. The gap of irony has widened from the ambiguous early poems to the wry passages of "Hibernaculum" which means that the digs at himself could be deeper, painful and yet the leaping saliences higher. And perhaps climbing out of the first you find you have achieved the second. Appearing is being or at least becoming:

> the head is my sphere:
> I'll look significant as I deal with
> mere wires of light, ghosts of
> cells, working there.

For when the curtain is drawn back, the Wizard of Oz is a little man with levers, and when the next curtain is drawn, the man with levers is the Wizard of Oz and when the next. . . .

HAROLD BLOOM

The Breaking
of the Vessels

Paul Valéry, in defining an artist as someone who compelled others to create in response to *his* creation, went on to speak of "creative misunderstanding" as being the artistic mode of interpretation. If there is any validity to my own belief that canon-formation, the general acceptance of a poet into a tradition, is itself necessarily the strongest mode of creative misunderstanding, then there would be a particular value in examining a poet whose work is in the actual, contemporary, on-going process of being raised high into the hierarchy of poetic tradition. No contemporary poet, in America, is likelier to become a classic than A. R. Ammons, and so I intend here to re-visit some of his major poems, in that kind of re-reading I am trying to teach myself, in which one tries, however vainly, to guard against or compensate for the strong mis-readings that are created by the rigors of canon-formation.

Ammons is a dangerous poet to read in the context of hierarchy, because hierarchy is one of his overt and obsessive concerns, particularly in his new, long poem, "Sphere: The Form of a Motion," which may be his most remarkable achievement to date. "Hierarchy" as a word goes back to the Greeks, where it meant the "rule of a priest," but our dictionaries define it as a body of persons or entities graded by authority, by rank or, surely most crucially, by capacity. Ammons once told an interviewer that, in his view, poetic influence is only a sub-branch of the

---

From *Figures of Capable Imagination.* Copyright © 1976 by Harold Bloom. Seabury Press.

larger subject of hierarchy, and I suspect that for Ammons, as for Milton's Satan, hierarchy actually serves as what Satan called "quickening power," or what Nietzsche called the Will to Power. Nietzsche thought that the Will to Power, in an artist, resulted in the willful misinterpretation of all reality, which I find a refreshing de-mystification of what the publicists of poetry always assert to be the true relationship between poetry and reality. Yeats, a fierce Nietzschean when most himself, was merely fibbing when he said that art was but a vision of reality. Ammons fibs a lot about art also, but when most himself Ammons is a fierce Emersonian, and a fierce Emersonian is about as dangerous a visionary misinterpreter of "reality" as you can find. Ammons, like Whitman, has inherited from Emerson a wild ambition for the poet, which involves some very dark hierarchical obsessions, as in "Sphere: The Form of a Motion":

> . . . the gods have come and gone
> (or we have made them come and go) so long among us that
> they have communicated something of the sky to us making us
>
> feel that at the division of the roads our true way, too,
> is to the sky where with unborn gods we may know no
> further death and need no further visitations: what may have
>
> changed is that in the future we can have the force to keep
> the changes secular: the one:many problem, set theory, and
> symbolic signifier, the pyramid, the pantheon (of gods and
>
> men), the pecking order, baboon troop, old man of the tribe,
> the hierarchy of family, hamlet, military, church, corporation,
> civil service, of wealth, talent—everywhere the scramble for
>
> place, power, privilege, safety, honor, the representative
> notch above the undistinguished numbers: second is as good
> as last: pyramidal hierarchies and solitary persons: the
>
> hierarchies having to do with knowledge and law, the solitaries
> with magic, conjuration, enchantment: the loser or apostate
> turns on the structure and melts it with vision, with
>
> summoning, clean, verbal burning: or the man at the top may
> turn the hierarchy down and walk off in a private direction:
> meanwhile, back at the hierarchy, the chippers and filers
>
> hone rocks to skid together . . .

The passage, like most of "Sphere," is extravagantly pell-mell, and by its implications substitutes "hierarchy," as a trope, for mental order of any kind, for those intellectual demarcations that Ammons is always telling us have no kin in nature, where the hierarchies flow together, where there are no sharp lines. Of the multitude of intense struggles that never abandon the poetry of Ammons, the most violent is the war between two visions of the mind, one that believes it can take nature up into itself, and the other that believes nature can never be adequate to it. Even the first of these visions has a transcendental strain in it, but the second is almost unmatched in our century in its exaltation and high sorrow. I say "almost" because of Hart Crane, a poet who also stemmed from Whitman, as Ammons does, but who seems not to have affected Ammons. But only Crane rivals the extraordinary poignance of prophetic self-presentation that Ammons sometimes allows himself, as here in the dedicatory verses to "Sphere":

> I went to the summit and stood in the high nakedness:
> the wind tore about this
> way and that in confusion and its speech could not
> get through to me nor could I address it:
> still I said as if to the alien in myself
>   I do not speak to the wind now:
> for having been brought this far by nature I have been
> brought out of nature
> and nothing here shows me the image of myself:

What was the mode of his speech when he still addressed the wind? I go back to the earliest Ammons, to the ephebe who walked "the bleached and broken fields" near the North Carolina shore, listening to the wind yet not being inspirited by it, but rather punished into song: "the wind whipped my throat." He "swayed as if the wind were taking me away," but knew already that: "unlike wind/that dies and/never dies I said/I must go on/consigned to/form that will not/let me loose/except to death." Except for an occasional chat with a mountain, the young Ammons seems to have relied upon the wind for most of his conversational company. The most poignant of these early encounters is called "The Wide Land":

> Having split up the chaparral
> blasting my sight
> the wind said
>   You know I'm
>   the result of
> forces beyond my control
> I don't hold it against you
> I said
> It's all right I understand

> Those pressure bowls and cones
> the wind said
> are giants in their continental gaits
> I know I said I know
> they're blind giants
> Actually the wind said I'm
>   if anything beneficial
>   resolving extremes
> filling up lows with highs
> No I said you don't have
> to explain
> It's just the way things are
>
> Blind in the wide land I
> turned and risked my feet
> to loose stones and sudden
>
> alterations of height

The wind is apologetic because of its particular relation to Ammons, being his guide, yet here the guide is blinding its seer. We can say that the wind, throughout his poetry, serves as Virgil to Ammons' Dante. As the emblem of the composite precursor, the wind subsumes those aspects of the Emersonian-Whitmanian tradition that most deeply have found and touched Ammons. Emerson said: "We cannot write the order of the variable winds," and Whitman sang of "the impalpable breezes that set in upon me" as he confronted the ebbing of his own poethood. Ammons, always affectionate towards the wind, confronts it more directly than any poet since Shelley, as here in the early "Joshua Tree":

> unlike wind
> that dies and
> never dies I said
> I must go on
>   consigned to
> form that will not
> let me loose
>   except to death
>   till some
>   syllable's rain
> anoints my tongue
> and makes it sing
>   to strangers:

This is not yet what Ammons now calls "the form of a motion." In one of the early Ezra-poems, "The Wind Coming Down From," the wind identifying with the Emersonian law of Compensation: "pushed, pushing/

not air or motion/but the motion of air." "Nothing is got for nothing" is Emerson's motto, and is the Law of Compensation for Ammons also. Excerpts from Emerson's essay, "Compensation," are the proper context for Ammons' encounters with the wind:

> . . . An inevitable dualism bisects nature, so that each thing is a half, and suggests another thing to make it whole. . . .
>
>   Whilst the world is thus dual, so is every one of its parts. . . .
>
>   The same dualism underlies the nature and condition of man. Every excess causes a defect; every defect an excess. . . . For every thing you have missed, you have gained something else; and for every thing you gain, you lose something. . . . Or do men desire the more substantial and permanent grandeur of genius? Neither has this an immunity. . . . With every influx of light comes new danger. Has he light? He must bear witness to the light, and always outrun that sympathy which gives him such keen satisfaction, by his fidelity to new revelations of the incessant soul. . . .

It is this obsession with the *Ananke* of Compensation that seems to have motivated the greatest experience of Ammons' life and poetry, the savage will-to-transcendence that marked him with an ecstasy he had to abandon, all too quickly, in order for life and poetry to go on. I don't find it possible to over-praise those poems in which Ammons violently first found and first lost himself: "Hymn," "Gravelly Run," "Bourn," "Mansion," "Prodigal," "Guide," "Terrain," "Bridge," "Raft," ending in the double culminations of this phase, "Corsons Inlet" and "Saliences." In these dozen or so poems, Ammons tried the impossible task, beyond a limit of art, in which language seeks its own end to the one:many problem. Whitman wisely took this impossibility as a given of his art, and began *Song of Myself* as though the great experience of union were accomplished already, and subsequently could be celebrated. But the young Ammons was a purer and wilder Emersonian, akin really to the young Thoreau or to Jones Very, and so attempted the incredible. He gave himself up to the wind of Compensation, as here in "Mansion":

> So it came time
>   for me to cede myself
> and I chose
> the wind
>   to be delivered to
>
> The wind was glad
>   and said it needed all
> the body
> it could get
>   to show its motions with

The magnificent compensation comes in one of Ammons' masterpieces, "Guide," and here I want to subject this poem to a full-scale
antithetical critique, for this is one of those texts in which Ammons
clarifies the way in which a poem is for him as much an act of breaking as
of making, as much a blinding as a seeing. "Guide" is a revisionist poem
in relation to Ammons' American tradition, and its meaning needs to be
developed in the interplay between it and major precursor texts in Emerson and Whitman. The dialectic of revisionism, as I have explained
elsewhere, is perfectly applicable to Ammons. His characteristic poem
moves back and forth from tropes, defenses, images of limitation to those
of representation, and always through an extraordinary agility in rhetorical
and psychic *substitution*. For Ammons, as for all revisionists since the
Gnostics and Kabbalists, every act of creation is also a catastrophe, a
breaking-of-the-vessels, to use the great image of the Lurianic Kabbalah.
Ammons' way of saying this is admirably instanced in the poem "Guide":

> You cannot come to unity and remain material:
> in that perception is no perceiver:
>   when you arrive
> you have gone too far:
>   at the Source you are in the mouth of Death:
>
> you cannot
>   turn around in
> the Absolute: there are no entrances or exits
>   no precipitations of forms
> to use like tongs against the formless:
>   no freedom to choose:
>
> to be
>   you have to stop not-being and break
> off from *is* to *flowing* and
>   this is the sin you weep and praise:
> origin is your original sin:
>   the return you long for will ease your guilt
> and you will have your longing:
>
>   the wind that is my guide said this: it
> should know having
>   given up everything to eternal being but
> direction:
>
> how I said can I be glad and sad: but a man goes
>   from one foot to the other:
> wisdom wisdom:
>   to be glad and sad at once is also unity

and death:
> wisdom wisdom: a peachblossom blooms on a particular
tree on a particular day:
> unity cannot do anything in particular:

are these the thoughts you want me to think I said but
> the wind was gone and there was no more knowledge then.

Breaking off from *is* to *flowing* is the Ammonsian Breaking-of-the-Vessels. I find that Ammons reminds me (without, I think, his knowing anything, overtly, about Kabbalah) of the origin or original sin of the image of the vessels breaking. The Kabbalists say that it was the strength of the Divine Light, the influx of transcendental power, that broke the vessels that ought to have received the radiance. In his private experience, which hardly benefits by being termed "mysticism," the young Ammons seems to have taught himself this paradox of all belated creativity.

Ammons begins "Guide" with his own version of a dialectic of images of presence and absence. Neither unity nor materiality is present, and a rhetorical irony offers us a perception without a perceiver, an arrival that has gone a station too far, and then by synecdoche is converted into a Source that is Death's mouth, every origin suddenly being seen as a mutilated part of the whole unity that is Death.

With the negative image of a reified Absolute, without direction or openings, the language of the poem moves into the psychic defenses of undoing and isolation, but only in order to recoil from this limitation so as to mount up into a daemonic Sublime, itself based upon a repression of this poet's deepest longings. With this, the wind ceases to speak, and the poem moves into a psychic area that alternates sublimating metaphor with a sad, final projection of the wind, in which the possibility of future knowledge is lost.

In Ammons, the Breaking of the Vessels is what another great poem, "Prodigal," calls "the mental/blaze and gleam,/the mind in both motions building and tearing down." But the wind in "Guide," though it represents Compensation, is less balanced and hopeful than the Emersonian law of our nature and of all nature. What does it mean to have "given up everything to eternal being but/direction," which is to say, what would it mean if we were speaking of the poet and not of the wind? The answer is not just that "unity cannot do anything in particular" except presumably move in one direction at a time, but is more largely involved in this poem's transumptive stance at its close. Transumption, as I've indicated in other contexts, is a trope upon a trope that undoes time. Here, it undoes the future, which is projected with the wind, leaving Ammons with no present moment, but alone with a past ecstasy, a guide evidently no longer a guide.

In one of his most visionary poems, "Bridge," Ammons achieved a momentary tone of acceptance in regard to his central dilemma:

> when the spirit comes to the bridge of consciousness
> and climbs higher and higher
>   toward the peak no one reaches live
> but where ascension
>   and descension meet
> completing the idea of a bridge
>
> think where the body is,
>   that going too deep
>
> it may lose touch,
>   wander a ghost in hell
>   sing irretrievably in gloom,
> and think
>
> how the spirit silvery with vision may
> break loose in high wind
>
>   and go off weightless
>
> body never to rise or spirit fall again to unity . . .

But the costs of such acceptance are too high, even for Ammons. His version of the High Romantic quest for oblivion, his equivalent of Shelley's "Alastor," is the darkly beautiful poem, "Raft," where he surrenders even direction and goes with the tide, only at last to be rescued again, however equivocally, by the wind. Motion for motion, I think it fair to say that Ammons was losing his battle against himself until he wrote his most famous poem, "Corsons Inlet," and its more remarkable sequel, "Saliences." One of his most distinguished and sympathetic critics, Geoffrey Hartman, insists that Ammons, as opposed to Wordsworth, is trapped perpetually in the difficulty of nature-poetry, which is the "loss of self and voice to nature." I think myself that Hartman beautifully and canonically misreads when he says of Ammons that "he subdues himself totally to *love of perception*, refusing all higher adventure." For Hartman, even the later Ammons of the long poems, including *Hibernaculum* and presumably even "Sphere," is giving us "a massively playful nature-thinking" in which adequate form is partly evaded. The danger, as again Hartman wisely observes, is that a longer poem by Ammons can seem "all periphery and no center." The dangers of pastoral, on this critical view, become constant in Ammons. Every poetic phrase becomes casual rather than causal, and the poem becomes less an instrument against entropy, and more a part of entropy itself. Ammons of course defends his procedure by comparing the energy of his poems to that of nature, so that the movement of a poem becomes more sexual in its rhythm and less compensatory. Yet Hartman, despite his admiration for Ammons, implies a very dangerous critique; the Ammonsian poem begins to show rather more in common with nature's entropy than with nature's energy.

I myself would say that both Hartman and Ammons are strong mis-readers of Ammons, for at least from "Saliences" on he does not write nature-poetry, and indeed I would go back to origins and say truly that he never did write nature-poetry. What Ammons calls "nature," whether he celebrates it or says goodbye to it, is no more natural than Emerson's Nature was, or Whitman's either. Unfortunately Ammons wants it both ways, as Emerson did, and so he indulges himself in such wasted postures of the spirit as section 38 of "Sphere," where the hard-pressed writers of New York City (who have troubles enough) are urged out into the woods to watch the redwing. But this is a quirkiness that we have to accept, reading Ammons. He seems to need it, because he cannot bear always to concede the truth, which is that he is as foreign in nature as if he had landed, a visitor. His image, as he admits, is of desire or the will-to-power, what he calls *longing*, and such an image can never be fulfilled by or in nature. Ammons, like Wordsworth, and like Whitman, was and is a poet of the Romantic Sublime.

The best account of the Romantic Sublime is by Thomas Weiskel, who emphasizes transcendence as being central:

> The essential claim of the Sublime is that men can, in feeling and in speech, transcend the human. . . . An "humanistic Sublime" is an oxymoron. Yet . . . the Sublime revives as God withdraws. . . . The Romantic Sublime was an attempt to revise the meaning of transcendence precisely as the traditional apparatus of sublimation . . . was failing to be exercised or understood.

Let us trace the Sublime backwards in Ammons, from "Sphere" to the early Ezra-chants that began his work. In "Sphere" there is no daemonic Sublime, as there is in earlier Ammons, but we are given instead a curiously discursive Sublime:

> > . . . so to look to the
> moment of consciousness as to find there, beyond all the
> individual costs and horrors, perplexing pains and seizures,
>
> joy's surviving radiance: I ask because I am terrified of my
> arrogance and do not know and do not know if the point in the
> mind can be established to last beyond the falling away
>
> of the world and the dreams of the world . . .

This is very much the poetry of our moment, of an economy and a culture undergoing catastrophe. As a seer, Ammons shies away from prophecy, but "Sphere: The Form of a Motion" allows itself to end in a difficult joy:

> to float the orb or suggest the orb is floating: and, with the
> mind thereto attached, to float free: the orb floats, a bluegreen
> wonder: so to touch the structures as to free them into rafts
>
> that reveal the tide: many rafts to ride and the tides make a
> place to go: let's go and regard the structures, the six-starred
> easter lily, the beans feeling up the stakes: we're gliding: we
>
> *are* gliding: ask the astronomer, if you don't believe it: but
> motion as a summary of time and space is gliding us: for a while,
> we may ride such forces: then, we must get off: but now this
> beats any amusement park by the shore: our Ferris wheel, what a
> wheel: our roller coaster, what mathematics of stoop and climb: sew
> my name on my cap: we're clear: we're ourselves: we're sailing.

Partly this is a transumption of the earlier poem, "Raft," as Ammons attempts to carry his past alive into his own future. Partly it is a fine desperation, again too appropriate to the present moment. But mostly it is a revision of Whitman, who haunts all of "Sphere," and whose presence is pervasive in the last third of the poem. Here is Whitman, in the last section of *Song of Myself*, clear, himself and sailing:

> The last scud of days holds back for me,
> It flings my likeness after the rest and true as any on the shadow'd wilds,
> It coaxes me to the vapor and the dusk.
>
> I depart as air, I shake my white locks at the runaway sun,
> I effuse my flesh in eddies, and drift it in lacy jags.

Whitman projects and so casts away the past, and introjects and so identifies himself with the future, at the price of the present moment. So, in the poem's final lines, the floating Walt is no place in no time, but we must quest for him:

> Failing to fetch me at first keep encouraged,
> Missing me one place search another,
> I stop somewhere waiting for you.

Part of Ammons' meaning is his loss of this Sublime sense that as the bard he is up ahead of us somewhere, waiting for us like Whitman. No, he says, he is sailing *with* us, floating along, and he also is going to lose his cap. His poem has no center, because *he* is its center, as Walt was earlier, but the Emersonian self once wavered a touch less than now, though it was always rather unstable. There is an illuminating comment by a great allegorist, Angus Fletcher:

> For what is a center, in human terms? Surely the body, and surely within the body some part of the body regarded as *its* center, whether head, heart or loins. By giving so much value to such a frail temple the critic has been forced to measure the bleakness of the hostile world of nature. Nothing could be more striking than those obsessively emptied scenes represented by so many of the quotations in this book. Shelley is the master of the bleak Antonioni vista, but there are sanddunes and deserts here from Whitman, from Stevens, and above all from . . . Ammons. Ammons particularly emerges as the poet of earth's intransigent geometrical control over men. *Corsons Inlet* and the other Ammons poems are sublime in their emptiness and their adherence to the magic of pure line, absolute boundary and border.

A sublime emptiness: this parallels Hartman's praise of Ammons at his best, when the poet addresses "the empty place that threatens his power of speech." Certainly Fletcher and Hartman are correct in finding that Ammons attains the Sublime in a context of the void. His power touches the heights in one passage of *Hibernaculum* that comes near to the Stevens of "The Auroras of Autumn" as a major example of the American Sublime, in our age:

> . . . to lean belief the lean word comes,
> each scope adjusted to the plausible: to the heart
> emptied of, by elimination, the world, comes the small
>
> cry domesticating the night: if the night is to be
> habitable, if dawn is to come out of it, if day is ever
> to grow brilliant on delivered populations, the word
>
> must have its way by the brook, lie out cold all night
> along the snow limb, spell by yearning's wilted weed till
> the wilted weed rises, know the patience and smallness
>
> of stones: I address the empty place where the god
> that has been deposed lived: it is the godhead: the
> yearnings that have been addressed to it bear antiquity's
>
> sanction: for the god is ever re-created as
> emptiness, till force and ritual fill up and strangle
> his life, and then he must be born empty again:

Though the patterning of images here depends upon a sexual reductiveness (since for Ammons the center is loins, not head or heart), the larger reduction comes from Ammons' characteristic metonymic defense of isolation, his version of *kenosis*. One sees now why his earlier guide was the wind, not because of its traditional identity with spirit, but because it was already a metonymy for the lean word, and then for the empty word. Whitman's word located all directions in Whitman himself, a location inherited by Stevens Hoon, when that Paterian grandly said: "I was myself the compass of that sea." Ammons' word began by locating direction only in the wind, a metonymic limitation that prepared for a perpetually possible Sublime representation, for all those daemonic and repressive hyperboles through which the young Ammons touched the Sublime.

Moving backward from *Hibernaculum*, I want now to center upon three lyrics by Ammons, all of them justly famous: "Plunder," "Peak," and "Moment," the first later Ammons, the other two middle, and all of them poems about the precariousness and the expense of the Ammonsian Sublime. "Plunder" is so complete a lyric that very nearly the whole of Ammons is in it:

> I have appropriated the windy twittering of aspen leaves
> into language, stealing something from reality like a
> silverness: drop-scapes of ice from peak sheers:
>
> much of the rise in brooks over slow-rolled glacial stones:
> the loop of reeds over the shallow's edge when birds
> feed on the rafts of algae: I have taken right out of the
>
> air the clear streaks of bird music and held them in my
> head like shifts of sculpture glint: I have sent language
> through the mud roils of a raccoon's paws like a net,
>
> netting the roils: made my own uses of a downwind's
> urgency on a downward stream: held with a large scape
> of numbness the black distance upstream to the mountains
>
> flashing and bursting: meanwhile, everything else, frog,
> fish, bear, gnat has turned in its provinces and made off
> with its uses: my mind's indicted by all I've taken.

The poem's crucial word is "indicted" which does not so much mean "accused" or "charged" here as it does "proclaimed" or even perhaps "dictated," both of them significations held back in the pre-history of the word. Ammons accuses himself of a misprision of nature, a mis-taking or mis-apprehending by all the tropes of limitation: dialectical irony of presence and absence, metonymic reduction, metaphoric displacement. What this lyric powerfully refuses is the full burden of representation; it excludes tropes of representation, and so willfully negates the Sublime.

"Plunder," as a word, goes back to the Middle Dutch for household goods or clothes, and thus Ammons indicts his mind for having been a thieving guest of the natural world, betraying hospitality. Nature proclaims the poet's mind as its despoiler, and Ammons, despite his pride, manifests anxiety as to the dictation involved. Yet whatever kind of a poem we want to call this, it is no version of pastoral, for implicitly the poet tells us that nature was never his home.

Contrast this to Ammons, briefly but poignantly caught up in the Sublime, in the perfectly entitled "Peak":

> Everything begins at the tip-end, the dying-out
>   of mind:
> the dazed eyes set and light
> dissolves actual trees:
>
>   the world beyond: tongueless,
> unexampled
> burns dimension out of shape,
> opacity out of stone:
>
> come: though the world ends and cannot
> end,
>   the apple falls sharp
> to the heart starved with time.

This brief lyric, one of Ammons' most astonishing artistries, is both a total, Sublime epiphany, and a complete, revisionist act of misprision in relation to the American tradition of Romantic sublimity. It does all that a short poem can do, as a complete pattern of images, both as a structure of tropes and as a network of psychic defenses against the burden of anteriority. "Peak" begins with a dialectic of presence and absence, things present and mind absent, conveyed through the rhetorical trope of irony, since Ammons says "everything" and means "nothing." This is his *clinamen* or reaction-formation against Emersonian perception, against the dark and solipsistic adage: "That which we are, that only can we see." The poetic compensation for this initial contraction or withdrawal of meaning begins with the synecdoche of "the world beyond" replacing "actual trees." The antithetical completion of Emerson represents psychically a turning of Ammons against himself, a fresh realization that *his* poetic self is at last only part of a mutilated whole.

With the metonymy of "tongueless" for that world, Ammons goes on to a *kenosis*, an ebbing-away of the poetic self that is defensively an undoing, emptying out the imagery by moving from examples to the "unexampled," burning shape away. Yet, with almost incredible economy, the characteristic Sublime representation of Emersonian tradition, the repressive force Emerson called "transparency," is immediately invoked as opacity is burned out of stone, so that even stone becomes transparent. "Come," the poem tells us, urging us to enter its final movement with it, where the external world re-enters with the dualizing perspectivism of an apocalyptic metaphor. This sublimation or *askesis* is a fearful one for Ammons to suffer, whether as visionary or as naturalist, but is miraculously and all-but-immediately restituted by the poem's closing transumption: "the apple falls sharp/to the heart starved with time." Time, necessarily meaning past time, has been introjected here, and there seems no more future than there is a present at this peak-moment. Yet the moment *is* a moment of vision or of what Emerson called Influx or Reason. The apple falls sharp because the angle of vision is sharp, and momentarily the axis of vision is indeed one with the axis of things. In just fifty words, Ammons has extended an intolerably wealthy tradition, and compelled anteriority to yield him some room. There are not many poets, in any generation, who can edge a mountain of meaning over, even if just a notch, by the use of fifty very plain words.

As I am exhibiting Ammons in his most drastic mode of economy, I turn now to an even more remarkable act of poetic compression, "Moment," where Ammons needs only about twenty-five words:

> He turned and
> stood
>
> in the moment's
> height,
>
> exhilaration
> sucking him up,
>
> shuddering and
> lifting
>
> him
> jaw and bone
>
> and he said
> what
>
> destruction am I
> blessed by?

Rather than comment on this, I want to juxtapose it to one of the greatest of entries in Emerson's vast journal, this one being March 24, 1838, one of the seeds of the essay "Self-Reliance":

In the highest moments, we are a vision. There is nothing that can be called gratitude nor properly joy. The soul is raised over passion. It seeth nothing so much as Identity. It is a Perceiving that Truth and Right ARE. Hence it becomes a perfect Peace out of the knowing that all things will go well. Vast spaces of nature, the Atlantic Ocean, the South Sea; vast intervals of time, years, centuries, are annihilated to it; this which I think and feel underlay that former state of life and circumstances, as it does underlie my present, and will always all circumstance, and what is called life and what is called death.

Ammons speaks of an exhilaration that is a destruction, and of a blessing that might as well be a wound. Emerson too speaks of a heightening that is an annihilation, but characteristically he emphasizes only the gain of the exalted moment, and not its compensating loss. For Ammons, the transcendental moment is a Purgatory, and not the Edenic state it was for Emerson. Yet even this distinction is only part of a complex difference that Ammons' quest for autonomy has enforced. Here, in the clarity and maturity of *Sphere*, sections 32–33, is Ammons tolling up the cost of a purgatorial wisdom:

> poor assessments, it's hard to draw a line, the careful,
> arrogant, arbitrary imposition, the divider that blocks off
> and sets apart, the arising of difference and distinction:
>
> the discrete a bolus of slowed flux, a locus of depressed
> reaction rates, a boned and fibered replication: slowed
> but not stopped (heightened within its slows): on the instant
>
> of cessation, disintegration's bacteria flare: bloom, puff,
> and blow with change: much energy devoted to staving off
> insweeps of alteration: to slow, defer, to chew up change
>
> into the materials of slowing: until the body, increasingly
> owed, is paid: take the mind's radiant works, the ground
> changes under them: they lift off into distraction: one
>
> needs clarities to know what one is baffled by, the small
> left- and righthandedness: suppose one saw the nonsupportive
> clearly: how could the mind, lit up and possessed, find
>
> energy for salvation's befuddlement: to confront nothingness
> the best baffler, is to disengage monsters and prevent
> lofty identifications: to be saved is here, local and mortal:
>
> everything else is a glassworks of flight: a crystal
> hankering after the unlikely: futures on the next illusion:
> order is the boat we step into for the crossing: when we

step out, nothingness welcomes us: inspiration spends through:
by the snowroad the boulder floats afire: fir-bark,
skittering under a startled squirrel, falls in flames

This is wisdom, and it is also defeat. I do not mean personal defeat, nor do I mean poetic defeat, but a purely transcendental surrender, akin to Wordsworth's in the last stanza of the "Intimations" Ode, or to Whitman's in "As I Ebb'd," or Stevens' in *The Rock*. Ammons has got to learn to be a different kind of poet than he was, and he is still in the process of learning that this different kind will return him to origins again, though with a more exacting music than he set out to bring into being. The canon of American poetry will read him more deeply into his tradition than he cares to read himself, but this characteristic misreading need not be deplored, as it too is part of the poetic process. Let us return him to origins by going back to one of the early Whitmanian chants that began his poetry nearly a quarter of a century ago. This is chant 27 of the "Ommateum" poems, excluded by Ammons from the *Collected Poems* (as well as the *Selected* volume), yet it is a poem I, as one reader, cannot get out of my memory:

> I should have stayed longer idle
> and done reverence
> to it
> > waterfalls
> > humbling in silent slide
> the precipice of my effrontery
> > poured libations of arms
> like waterwheels
> toward the ground but
> knowing the fate of sunset things
> I grew desperate and entertained it
> > with sudden sprints
> > somersaults
> and cartwheels figuring eight
>
> It would not stay
> > Ring of cloud I said
> high pale ringcloud
> ellipsis of evening moment's miracle
> where will I go looking for your return
> and rushing to the rim
> I looked down into the deep dissolution
>
> I should have held still
> before it
> > and been mute

> cancelled by an oak's trunk
> and done honors unseen
> and taken the beauty sparingly
> as one who fears to move and
> shatter vision from his eyes

Patricia Parker, in what I judge to be the best essay yet written upon the poetry of Ammons, observes the curious centrality of this rejected poem in the geometry of the Ammonsian heterocosm:

> . . . it takes us, both in image and concern, all the way forward [in Ammons]. . . . The poet who knows the fate of sunset things and from the western rim looks down into the deep dissolution is, of course, simply reminding us of the obvious visual extensions of the first sentence of Emerson's remarkable essay Circles—"the eye is the first circle; the horizon which it forms is the second."

I think that Ammons is warning us now, in "Sphere," against "rushing to the rim," out of his prophetic fear that to know us, and himself, is to find oneself "knowing the fate of sunset things." By one of the ironies of canon-formation, a self-proclaimed "spent seer" finds himself in the unsought position of opposing a transcendental stance, that he himself has forsaken, to his own and our conscious belatedness. The necessity of misreading will make of Ammons what he ceased to be when he was a young man, a monist attempting to hold mind and nature together in a single vision. Ammons, as a man, must be rueful about so misprized a critical destiny, but as a poet he prophesied it, darkly, in the closing lines of his first volume:

> Sometimes the price of my content
> consumes its purchase
> and martyrs' cries, echoing my peace,
> rise sinuously like smoke
> out of my ashen soul.

But I will not end on such a tone, for this great poet demands more. Though for him "the apple falls sharp/to the heart starved with time," for him also the last word is more central. Like Whitman, he ends with the sun, and with the fruit of existence uniquely radiant at each fresh encounter. Here are the lines that he chose to end his Collected Poems:

> . . . neither way to go's to stay, stay
> here, the apple an apple with its own hue
> or streak, the drink of water, the drink,
>
> the falling into sleep, restfully ever the
> falling into sleep, dream, dream, and
> every morning the sun comes, the sun.

DENIS DONOGHUE

Ammons and the
Lesser Celandine

Near the end of *Sphere*, a long poem
in 155 sections, A. R. Ammons writes to the reader:

> I don't know about you,
> but I'm sick of good poems, all those little rondures
> splendidly brought off, painted gourds on a shelf: give me

> the dumb, debilitated, nasty, and massive, if that's the
> alternative: touch the universe anywhere you touch it
> everywhere.

So he touches the universe anywhere, catch as catch can, according to a
preference already made in "Corsons Inlet" halfway through the *Collected
Poems*:

> I see narrow orders, limited tightness, but will
> not run to that easy victory:
> still around the looser, wider forces work:
> I will try
> to fasten into order enlarging grasps of disorder, widening
> scope

Ammons does not admit that many long poems are merely many short
poems strung together or that one victory is just as hard-won as another.
Like other American poets, he feels an urge to go after the big one, the
long poem, shooting the rapids, the *Deliverance* syndrome. Anything
Whitman, Pound, Williams, and Stevens can do, Ammons can do too,

---

From *Parnassus* 3 (Spring/Summer 1975). Copyright © 1975 by Poetry in Review Foundation.

more or less, better or worse. But in fact his best poems thus far have been little rondures splendidly brought off, painted gourds now on the shelf of the *Collected Poems*. My anthology (unpublished) has about ten such rondures, "Dark Song," "Loft," "Kind," "February Beach," "Gravelly Run," "The Eternal City," "Corsons Inlet," "Expressions of Sea Level," "Laser," and "Eyesight." The idea of the long poem is fascinating, often more powerful in principle than in particle, but it has not been demonstrated that Ammons has a native gift for the big one, or anything more than a yen for it.

Conceding to the artist his donnée, I report that Ammons is sick of short, tight poems, and wants to write poetry rather than poems, a poetry capable of accommodating the flats and the peaks, prosaic stuff as well as the surges. He said as much in *Tape for the Turn of the Year*, and even more explicitly in "Hibernaculum," a pretty long poem, 112 sections, three stanzas each, three lines to a stanza, and about fifteen syllables to a line. The same stanza, grouped in fours not threes, is the device of *Sphere*, and the formal source in each case appears to be Stevens' *Notes toward a Supreme Fiction*. Ammons starts by catching the universe wherever he can, usually with a weather report, the day is cold or hot, the temperature is so-and-so, the forecast is rain or sleet or snow. Once in motion, he moves flexibly between chance, whim, and choice, giving the poem his head. "Strings of nucleations please me more than representative details"; this means, I assume, that he doesn't look for a significant detail but takes what the weather happens to give, at least to start with. He trusts to luck; or rather, he trusts his own knack of recognizing when he is in luck. One talent this poet has (among other talents, that is): he can get himself going with a very small push, anything will do, a bird hopping on the garden gate, rain or the lack of rain. The formula is given in section 75 of *Sphere*:

> having
> been chastened to the irreducible, I have found the
> irreducible bountiful: the daffodil nods to spring's zephyr.

And Ammons nods to the daffodil; so they're all in business.

As to themes and tropes, Ammons specializes in the big metaphysical questions, the One and the Many, permanence and change:

> poetry has
> one subject, impermanence,
> which it presents
> with as much permanence as
> possible.

Division and unity, light and darkness, chaos and order:

> how much disorder must I learn to tolerate
>   to find materials
>   for the new house of my sight!

On the back shelves he has a stock of subordinate themes: what the mind can do and what it can't, the nature of light, motion, variety, process, abundance. His current interest is in the form of a motion, a concern first announced in an early poem, "A Symmetry of Thought," in which the mental object is invoked in diverse appelations and this sentence:

> coming into matter
> spirit fallen
> trades eternity
> for temporal form:
> is a symmetry of motion,
> can always find its way
> back to oblivion.

If you, spirit fallen, are going to trade eternity for temporal form, you ought to bid for a form as long as possible, make your whole life a long poem, make a long poem your whole life. Call the bits and pieces of life *nucleations*, and string them together.

     Ammons has described his procedure in "Poetics" and "Essay on Poetics":

> not so much looking for the shape
> as being available
> to any shape that may be
> summoning itself
> through me
> from the self not mine but ours.

Otherwise put:

>   the way I think is
> I think what I see: the designs are there: I use
> words to draw them out.

What he sees is usually whatever is happening in his garden or along the beach or in the local bird sanctuary: weather, birds, fish, clouds, land-scapes, trees, horizons. That makes a start. Call it Nature, however ambiguously. To get the poetry moving Ammons ruminates by recourse to meteorology, botany, geology; such things interest him, and help him toward the surges. Then there is Man, who comes into this poetry mostly in the role of perceiver, he is the one who brings the sundry of the world to order. In *Sphere* Ammons writes:

     each of us stands in the peak and center
of perception.

There is Man, there is Nature (the visible part of it), and there is the
relation between them, asserted in *Sphere* and elsewhere:

>   a leaf cannot
> appear on or fall from the branch except via the total
> involvement of the universe: you and I cannot walk the street
> or rise to the occasion except via the sum total of effect
> and possibility of the universe: we are not half-in and
>
> half-out of the universe but unmendably integral: when we
> move, something yields to us and accepts our steps.

Ammons wants to be "at ease with my findings," and he is prepared if
necessary to lose the self "to the victory of stones and trees." But it is
never necessary to run to that defeat:

> while the leaf may not answer one's questions, it waves, a
> nice language, expressive and complete.

Waving back, Ammons is gratified to live in such a waving world.
    When all goes well, Ammons takes off into consciousness, a mo-
mentary thrill:

>   so to look to the
> moment of consciousness as to find there, beyond all the
> individual costs and horrors, perplexing pains and seizures,
> joy's surviving radiance.

In "Requiem":

> No creation equals a moment's consciousness.
> No cymbal cones and crashes peaks so.
> No white shark stabs so.

And in *Tape:*

>   intellections are
>   scaffolds, trellises
> we wish some vine of
>   feeling would take to
> & possess
> completely.

But that's another day's work, feeling is the rub.
    Given these preoccupations, Ammons takes unto himself an ena-
bling set of figures, mostly reducible to two, wind and mountain. He has
other trademarks, notably an addiction to the following words: periphery,

salience, loft, suasion, remnant (adjective rather than noun), curvature, meld, and flotation. But he is chiefly a wind-and-mountain man. In the early poems the speaker is rarely a person, finite, historical, but more often a spirit, mostly a spirit of place, *genius loci.* The poetic act is deemed to be an entrance, an intrusion upon the natural scene if it goes wrong, a dance or a symmetry of motion if it goes right. The mountain has the quality of being simply there, reality inescapable but inviting, not yet waving but with the promise of a wave. Wind is the poetic spirit, "the wind that is my guide." There is an early poem called "In the Wind My Rescue Is," as though the wind were consciousness itself, which it is— companionable guide, walking-mate, a good man for a long hike through the woods. Like consciousness, the wind "leaves no two moments on the dunes the same," provokes new "saliences of feature." Wind is the creative principle, making a virtue (variety) out of necessity (change); it is imagi- nation, the correspondent breeze. "Saliences" is a hymn to the wind and (the same thing) to imagination. Ammons shows wind and mountain together, animation running both ways, in "Virtu," and in "Reversal" mountain rebukes poet for his arrogance, taking the harm out of the rebuke by saying:

> the wind in your days
> accounts for this arrogance.

Otherwise put: a sense of your imaginative powers, rushing through you like a wind, makes you rise above yourself. The mountain, apart from the wind, is a sad thing, a changeless prospect, an unalterable view: given half a chance, however, it attracts voices and furnishes replies. If it were utterly impregnable, Ammons could not deal with it, speak to it: "Firm ground is not available ground." Wind makes mountain available, imagi- nation asks reality to wave. Ammons does not claim that these ingratia- tions are easily achieved, but he is honest, true to his word: "no humbling of reality to precept." He respects the given for being different.

    This is well enough. Ammons approaches an ethic by way of an aesthetic; or he makes aesthetic forces do some ethical work, silently. The burdens of "Hibernaculum" include that one: to derive a way of life from a way of looking at objects. But Ammons is not hard on himself, he is too readily charmed by his own image: if things get rough, he wanders away down the beach. He treats the present moment as the gist of history, the present man (poet, *ipse*) as the gist of humanity, the present place as the gist of everywhere: so this triple-thinker can at one glance evade the responsibility of history, circumvent the claims of other people, and derive from the satisfactions of living in Ithaca, New York, the felicity of not having to bother with the horrors of living in the slums of New York, New York. Santayana has a sharp definition of the barbarian as "the man who regards his passions as their own excuse for being." No, that is too sharp for Ammons, but it points to the limitations in his art. He protests that he is concerned with Nature, including human nature, but he rarely makes me feel that he cares much about any human nature but his own. His poetry is rural in the sense that you can walk for miles in it without meeting anyone; so the dramatic sense of life never appears. Ammons could write his poetry if there were nothing in the world but mountains, winds, weather, birds, fish, sand dunes, beaches, and a poet accustomed to living in his art alone. What he can do with those things is impressive, but most of it leaves me unmoved; the true vine of feeling rarely climbs upon his trellises. I am touched, moved, by Yeats' "Among Schoolchildren," Frost's "Fire and Ice," Eliot's "Marina," Williams' "To Daphne and Virginia," Empson's "Aubade." Or, since it is a question of *Sphere* as a long poem, I am moved by *Leaves of Grass, Paterson, Notes toward a Supreme Fiction,* and *Four Quartets.* I can remember nothing of *Sphere* but incidental felicities and (as a general impression) the degeneration of feeling in routines and postures: this poet is not setting his chisel to the hardest stone. Nothing in the poem convinces me that Ammons has anything comparable, so far as language is evidence, to the capacity of feeling which the finest work of Eliot, Yeats, Stevens, and (with some degree of reservation) Williams possesses. By these standards, much of *Sphere* is facile, the kind of poetry about which it is easy not to care. I put in evidence the end of the poem, where it surges:

> we're gliding: we
> *are* gliding: ask the astronomer, if you don't believe it: but
> motion as a summary of time and space is gliding us: for a while,
> we may ride such forces: then we must get off: but now this
> beats any amusement park by the shore: our Ferris wheel, what a
> wheel: our roller coaster, what mathematics of stoop and climb: sew
> my name on my cap: we're clear: we're ourselves: we're sailing.

I can't help it, the achieved poems seem to me not the big ones but the little rondures splendidly brought off. I remember, and care for, "Dark Song," not a typical Ammons but a poem which sounds as though it insisted upon being written and the poet conceded the point:

> Sorrow how high it is
> that no wall holds it
> back: deep

it is that no dam undermines
it: wide that it
comes on as up a strand

multiple and relentless:
the young that are
beautiful must die; the

old, departing,
can confer
nothing.

R. W. FLINT

The Natural Man

When one thinks of men and women who in despite of the critics will be called nature poets merely because they write in and about small towns or open country, one has to regret a gradual loss of fated action, or the illusion thereof—rituals in which custom helps us join. Hardy's melancholia and Frost's bearishness are comforting, somehow right for the imagined possibilities. A citified readership expects to slow down, knows it must in order to see or to understand anything. But there is another kind of nature poetry, rooted in times when most towns were small and many highly intellectual poets were rusticated for one reason or another, that has returned during this century in often rather baffling, footloose guise. Its shaping ritual is the walk, the climb, the trip, and the voyage, actions lending themselves all too easily to a vaporous abstraction.

A. R. Ammons began his career as the latter sort in full eclectic spate. The plot of his best poems of the Fifties and early Sixties before he started teaching at Cornell was largely a swift, sometimes brilliantly executed play of disjointed perceptions fleshing out a very private psychodrama. Charming and appealing digressions there were, to which I'll return. But the dominant voice seemed to have been sired on *The Duino Elegies* by an Emerson, a Dickinson transsexed, a Hopkins, Dylan Thomas, or Roethke—all the intoxicated solipsists of an age that requires such minds to fabricate their own plots, to expect little aid from tradition. Recently, though, with admirable recklessness and uneven results, he has been remaking himself closer to the Frost or Hardy model. Joining the academy just when its boom times were passing, assuming its by now well

From *Parnassus* 4 (Spring/Summer 1976). Copyright © 1976 by Poetry in Review Foundation.

known and often dramatized responsibilities, he gave his existence a new visibility not unlike Frost's out there "north of Boston," a life gently freighted with old solemnities, not too far and not too near.

So much for the gains. Now the difficulties. Readers of his newest long poems, "Extremes and Moderations," "Essay on Poetics," "Hibernaculum," and especially *Sphere: The Form of a Motion*—a rambling, confiding, button-holing poem of 155 12-line sections—will know what they are. In *Sphere* Mr. Ammons makes a grand broken field run and a curious performance it is. To dodge about and reach a point not already plotted for him by one or more of the imposing exegetes lured to his earlier work by its obvious need for exegesis required some fancy footwork. You can think of Ammons as a sort of country-and-southern Prometheus nailed down on Cayuga Heights (above Ithaca!) by the Zeus of respectability, tormented by the eagle of higher criticism in the shape of Harold Bloom. Or, what seems more likely, you can detect in all his recent work clear notes of irreverence mixed with affection and amusement toward the gaudier theories of his friends.

One thinks of another southern Galahad, Jimmy Carter, and soon drops the thought. Poet and politician do display an ease with Rotarian banalities; both shoulder a burden of sometimes overpowering charm. But the Ammons humor, though moderately adept in certain raunchy country-club comic routines, ranges far wider and deeper than Mr. Carter's as presently revealed. He remains in spite of everything a naturally, incurably, honorably private man.

A comparison with James Dickey is much more to the point. Neither poet would have attracted attention so soon had he not been expert in matching means to ends, at picking out of the air just the right look and sound for his talents. Dickey hove on the scene doing several things remarkably well; the dry, controlled aesthetic piety of "In the Lupanar at Pompeii," the exalted Dylan Thomas synaesthesia of "Dover: Believing in Kings," the eerie twilight incandescence of "The Owl King." After which came "Cherrylog Road" and other quasi-narrative lyrics that people think of as essential Dickey. But still later, at about the same moment in his career that Ammons had reached in "Essay on Poetics" and "Hibernaculum," rebellion surfaced; against facility, against aesthetic piety, and sometimes, in his essays, against the arts altogether. Like the Ammons of *Sphere* he seemed ready to join the philistine opposition as far as his lively professional conscience would allow, to look back on his energetic early cult of naiveté from as remote a vantage point as possible.

Ammons is cooler, more reflective, absorptive, and self-contained than Dickey ever was and in him the Southeast may be making one last convulsive effort to put its message across; namely, that throughout its now expiring century of gothic, baroque, and neo-classical flamboyance it was secretly nurturing a middleness, an ordinary absolute center-cut Americanness, second to none. Faulkner's Ratliff and Horace Benbow suggested as much, so did the Faulknerian humor; but the message was ambiguous. *Sphere*, however, is not; it's an amiable but firm rejection of any highstrung ideologue's project for Ammons' apotheosis either as a sainted solitary or as a panurgic prophet of spiritual democracy. One must salute him for braving the pitfalls of such an operation—occasional forcings of tone, unwitting smugness, sententiousness, cuteness, *blague*. Denis Donoghue thinks he has isolated the problem by conceiving it to be formal, by accusing the poet of surrendering to an American mania for mere size, for imagining that a few dozen short poems strung end to end might make a qualitative leap into grandeur. But the fact that Ammons is keenly aware of such objections, has worked them into the poem, seems to indicate that he had no choice. The American atmosphere forced him into the optative mood—maybe these topics and digressions *would* make the orbicular leap, maybe if the poet's heart were pure enough a trip around his head *would* emerge as a mystic sphere. No choice in any case but to try.

Let me suppose for the rest of this review that a kind of intractable confusion may be the real entelechy, the formal and final end, of Dickey and Ammons who began so suavely and self-assured. And that we should make of it what we can and not.waste time advising them to return and seek their lost innocence. Harold Bloom, always generous when his feelings are stirred, is prepared to call Ammons "great" but at the price of sternly reproving him for swerving from the path of Whitmanlike prophecy that his Emersonian instincts, again according to Bloom, fatally marked out for him. "Ammons has got to learn to be a different kind of poet than he was, and he is still in the process of learning that this different kind will return him to origins again, though with a more exacting music than he set out to bring into being." And why should he do this? Because he had early discovered a way to be transcendental and modern at the same time, by identifying the true American Sublime as the Void, by projecting the lyric pain of this discovery in a new species of Counter-Sublime. Like a man always seen going beautifully downhill. Which, Bloom finds, is quite in keeping with the "disastrous" times and makes Ammons the very latest of his cherished late-comers. The poems he chooses as the most telling expression of such counter-prophecy—"Corsons Inlet," "Saliences," "Gravelly Run," "Guide," "Bridge," "Peak," and the lovely passage in "Hibernaculum" that begins ". . . to lean belief the lean word comes,/ each scope adjusted to the plausible:"—are the right poems for his thesis.

Still, one must pause to ask if in his zeal to consecrate only this high-tragical, philosophical Ammons Bloom may not be reserving too much drama to himself and making it too neat. There are facetious or whimsical notes in all but a very few poems that set us on our guard. Also many fine poems that don't cast so much as a glance at these elevations. Maybe Bloom should ask himself whether, if Emerson is the fountainhead of our poetry, we ought not to read as Emersonically as the sage's descendants write, with the same hospitality toward wide swings of mood and purpose, with the same dexterity in matching tone to technique, form to theme. (In formal variety Emerson's own poetry is as "romantically" unstable as Byron's. Sometimes he sounds like Plotinus arranged for a German village band, sometimes, as in the beautiful "Threnody" on the death of his son, like a pure-bred Metaphysical.)

My guess would be that it is neither Emerson or Whitman (certainly not Whitman) that Ammons is currently undermining but a too portentous Idol of the Tribe called Poetry which, in some of its current academic investitures—subtlety piled on subtlety like the shawls of an Eastern princess—has become a real spook. Bloom is a great potentate who having been given an eloquent nightingale sends it out to be gilded and fitted with a clock-work larynx.

As a matter of fact, Ammons' poems had already begun to group themselves into thematic clusters a good while before he began writing long poems in earnest. To my mind it's the interplay between these clusters that gives Ammons his chief vitality. I find no formal or other reason not to like a "Nelly Myers" about an old family friend almost as much as one of the fine-spun lyric meditations that sound like a Neo-Platonic Buckminster Fuller soaked in Emily Dickinson. Or a "Nucleus" about his trip to Montreal to buy a factory; or the drily affecting "Belief" on the death of J. F. K. Or an entertaining "Silver" and "Mule Song" about a mule, a "Coon Song" about a raccoon trapped by dogs. To Bloom's list of best poems Donoghue is right to add "February Beach" and the exquisite "Eyesight."

> It was May before my
> attention came
> to spring and
>
> my word I said
> to the southern slopes
> I've
>
> missed it, it
> came and went before
> I got right to see:

> don't worry, said the mountain,
> try the later northern slopes
> or if
>
> you can climb, climb
> into spring: but
> said the mountain
>
> it's not that way
> with all things, some
> that go are gone.

Even Bloom acknowledges that this poet was never a naive visionary. Rather, a rueful, sportive, lyrical civil engineer, a musical geo-physician. Who would want to scuttle his prose sense of this transmogrifier of our prosiest disciplines, when he offers so novel a mixture of the contemplative and the suburban-saturnine, makes of "Extremes and Moderations" a pungent ecological fable, turns aside to tell us how to drain a swamp or dig a well, how to pick pears so the branches won't jerk the best ones out of reach, who above all is one of the most accomplished celebrators of the seasonal backyard drama since the great Alfred Lawn Tennyson himself? Rarely dropping his role as *homme moyen américain* Ammons can flourish a vocabulary of "saliences" and "suasions," motions, forces, and forms in mountain, wind, brook, and tree, with no missionary intent to substitute his vocabulary for ours. If he shaped his normally elegant style from examples of Williams, Marianne Moore, Dickinson, Cummings, Dickey, Roethke, or Merwin, he also aspires to their modesty.

Transplanted from the relative solitude of North Carolina to the goldfish prominence of Cornell, he issued a lowbrow poetics to balance the high, a Leopold Bloom to enliven the Harold.

> I believe in fun:
> "superior amusement" is a little shitty: fun is nice: I believe in it:
> I have no faith in the scoffers: they are party-poopers who are
>
> afraid they ought to believe in history or logical positivism and
> don't have any real desire to do so: they are scarcely worth a
> haircut: . . .
>
> I want, like Whitman, to found
> a federation of loveship, not of queers but of poets, where
> there's a difference: that is, come on and be a poet, queer
> or straight, adman or cowboy, librarian or dope fiend,
>
> housewife or hussy (I see in one of the monthlies an astronaut
> is writing poems—that's what I mean, guys): now, first of
> all, the way to write poems is just to start: . . .

> sing your hangups and humiliations loose into song's
> disengagements (which, by the way, connect, you know, when
> they come back round the other way): O comrades! of the
>
> seemly seeming—soon it will all be real! soon we will know
> idle raptures (after work) leaning into love: soon all our
> hearts will be quopping in concert: . . .
>
> (from Sphere)

I'm a librarian, or was, and can't quarrel with this. But neither can I help asking if it *really* plays in New Haven. ". . . we're going to climb," he also announces in *Sphere*, "up the low belly of this sow century, through the seventies,/ eighties, right on upward to the attachments, the anterior/ or posterior fixation, anything better than the swung pregnancies/ of these evil years. . . ."

Diversifications features 65 new poems, most quite short, and two showpieces, "Three Travelogues" and the 19-page "Pray Without Ceasing." Its general effect is of the usual charm, of compactness, assurance, good-humored summary and mild second thoughts. Most of the poems seem thrown off in the intervals of harder work. "Transcendence," the opener, once more rejects all well meant summonses to self-immolation.

> Just because the transcendental,
> having digested all change into
> a staying, promises foreverness,
>
> it's still no place to go, nothing
> having survived there into life:
> and here, this lost way, these
>
> illusory hollyhocks and garages,
> this is no place to settle: but
> here is the grief, at least,
>
> constant, that things and loves
> go, and here the love that
> never comes except as permanence.

Mr. Donoghue would welcome that embracement of grief, something he finds too often missing in Ammons. But note the "at least"; his euphoria is by no means exhausted. "Three Travelogues" is another handsome syncretic exercise in auto-intoxication out in the boondocks, pregnant with phrases like "a white-sailed cloud's blue hull of rain." In "Ballad" he neatly inverts his normal tree poem; wanting to "know the unity in all things and the difference/ between one thing and another" the poet goes to the willow and discovers that all the willow wants to know is "how to get rid of the wateroak," in the rasping tones of an under-secretary of the Interior Dept. at six of a Friday afternoon.

Other poems toy with grief. "Guilt's been circling/ my head all morning/ waiting for the crime/ to be defined . . ." Or

> I refuse the breakage:
> I hold on
> to the insoluble knots
> I've circled for years
> turning in contradictory
> wildness, as
> safe with center as
> jugs and stars: what
> I can't become keeps me
> to its image: what
> can't be reconciled is
> home steady at work.
>   ("Imago")

It's too early to say much about "Pray Without Ceasing," a phantasmagoria or verbal happening wherein passages of characteristic eloquence or quiet elegance are answered by tormented newsreel episodes from the Vietnam war, with frantic doodling, demented witticisms, and grim premonitions. My shaky opinion is that he had very little new to say about the poem's ostensible subject, or else put thought aside and ruffed like a grouse, spread like a peacock or cobra. The time of mutation is not yet, not for him, not for us.

ROBERT PINSKY

Ammons

From the beginning, some of the most exciting, overwhelming moments in the modernist tradition have come when a poet breaks through into the kind of prose freedom and prose inclusiveness which I have tried to suggest with words like "discourse" and "discursive." The freedom and scope of speech may convey the idea better than those of prose, if by speech we mean not its idiom, but its way of moving, inquiring, expanding. This generosity of movement, in modern poetry, is peculiarly affecting. I have in mind a range of passages in which the dull plains of description or the exactions of the "image" are not abandoned, but transcended: the poet claims the right to make an interesting remark or to speak of profundities, with all of the liberty given to the newspaper editorial, a conversation, a philosopher, or any speaker whatever.

Because of the philosophical and emotional background of modernist techniques, because of the techniques themselves, and because the anti-verbal prejudice is transcended, such passages are exhilarating: the breezy lines of Williams when he seems to build his poem upon an interesting remark ("It's the anarchy of poverty/ delights me"); Eliot's dark, abstract set-speech on History in *Gerontion;* the autobiographical, passionate moralizing of Canto LXXXIII ("Here error is all in the not done,/ all in the diffidence that faltered"). All of these are especially moving to us because the language has emerged through the underlying confines of description, mastering description and going beyond it to words as a means of life.

A fine example of what I mean, and for many readers perhaps a supreme example, is Stevens' "Sunday Morning." Earlier, I have discussed "The Snow Man" as a superb poem posing the terms of the nominalist-realist dilemma: the words, ideas, and feelings which might seem real to a human observer are "not there" in a landscape; yet except for those nominal words, ideas, and feelings we have no way of observing the flow of particulars or "nothing" which *is* there. If "The Snow Man" demonstrates how profoundly that philosophical quandary can be felt, "Sunday Morning" demonstrates how deeply we respond to a transcendence of the quandary.

The poem's remarkable blending of sensory detail and intellectual definition, natural image and abstract term, has often been pointed out by critics, especially in regard to the last sections. Consider, too, the third section, which gives a kind of lightning-summary of the anthropological history of religion:

> Jove in the clouds had his inhuman birth.
> No mother suckled him, no sweet land gave
> Large-mannered motions to his mythy mind.
> He moved among us, as a muttering king,
> Magnificent, would move among his hinds,
> Until our blood, commingling, virginal,
> With heaven, brought such requital to desire
> The very hinds discerned it, in a star.
> Shall our blood fail? Or shall it come to be
> The blood of paradise? And shall the earth
> Seem all of paradise that we shall know?
> The sky will be much friendlier then than now,
> A part of labor and a part of pain,
> And next in glory to enduring love,
> Not this dividing and indifferent blue.

This is the history, not only of religion's past, but of its future, too. And one reason it moves us so, I think, is that we feel the poet's language expanding to the full reach of its grand style, to a breadth of predication, as it pushes upward from the solidness of a created natural world of sky, weather, birds. That movement toward intellectual speculation, Stevens convinces us, in some way parallels the historical motion he dares to summarize: an idea of god as remote from earth and the human mind changes to an idea of god as partly human—and, finally, to an idea of divinity which does not "fail" while becoming wholly human and of the earth. Poetry itself, we feel as we read "Sunday Morning," can move from mythology to metaphorical imagery to, finally, a sublimely direct relationship between experience and words. Stevens overcomes our doubts of such a relationship by force: the force of his Wordsworthian grand style, and of his piercing natural images.

I have referred to an "anti-verbal prejudice." Although earlier sections of this book help justify the use of such a phrase, this is a suitable point for offering some evidence that such a prejudice exists, and that it is also possible to find related ideas like "the effacement of the poet," and in far from negligible writing. The first example is from critical prose, an essay on "The New Surrealism":

> The poem proceeds by needle-thrusts of imagery. . . . There is a kind of anonymity in the tone, as if the images emerged without a voice, from out of the language itself. This is a touchstone of the pure surrealist text, which avoids giving any sense of personality, since what is being written belongs to the flow of pure chance, not to the needs and feelings of a "self." . . . the poet may be telling us that his poems are written by nobody; that they come from no place, and mean nothing.

I feel that the title of the essay, and its subject, are important to mention, because the poems in question are in some ways a new departure, by fairly young writers; and the ideas of anonymity and non-predication are matters I have tried to trace back as far as the "Ode to a Nightingale." In the quotation, the phrase "from out of the language itself" might seem to contradict the idea of an anti-verbal bias; however, "language" in the quotation is not a means for predicating concepts or making statements about experience. Rather, the word is used as part of a reification (to use a fancy word) of language itself; the "language itself" is there only to "mean nothing." At least according to the theory defined by this prose quotation, the "New Surrealism," whatever else it does, does not attack the barriers between consciousness and nature which Stevens seems to force through.

My second and more complex example, which leads back eventually to the ambitions of "Sunday Morning," is from A. R. Ammons' poem "Motion," which begins:

> The word is
> not the thing:
> is
> a construction of,
> a tag for,
> the thing: the
> word in no way resembles
> the thing, except
> as sound
> resembles,

> as in *whirr*,
> sound:
> the relation
> between what this
> as words
> is
> and what is
> is tenuous: we
> agree upon
> this as the net to
> cast on what
> is: the finger
> to point with: the
> method of
> distinguishing,
> defining, limiting:

Here, language is not utterly reified; it is understood as being, largely, a defining and distinguishing gesture of the mind, isolating parts of reality. But insofar as it is such a defining gesture, "the word" in this poem has no reality, is no part of "what is." That, by definition, is the nominalist view of language; as general categories, words are arbitrary and unreal, however convenient. The poem suggests that words can be a part of "what is"—or rather can manage to *resemble* "what is"—only to the extent that they are particulars: that is, in their sound. "Motion" goes on to extend this idea logically from words to poems as a whole:

> poems
> are fingers, methods,
> nets,
> not what is or was:
> but the music
> in poems
> is different,
> points to nothing,
> traps no
> realities, takes
> no game, but
> by the motion of
> its motion
> resembles
> what, moving, is—
> the wind
> underleaf white against
> the tree.

The poem is extraordinary in that it presents a view of language which is lucid, rigorously thought out, and hard to disagree with. (Although Ammons has elaborated this position in later poems, I believe that he has not fundamentally changed it.) To that extent the poem succeeds in discoursing, without the suasion of a grand style, about its materials, forcefully arguing—the word seems just—that the words of a poem have two distinct aspects; and, the aspect which defines or captures reality is precisely the one which fails to "resemble" reality, which is particular and fluid.

To summarize: Stevens in "Sunday Morning" imagines a kind of harmony or rapprochement between the conceptions created by the human mind and the particulars of the world, and he makes a poetic style which makes such a divine partnership credible, by the way it mingles the senses and the sense of the mind. Ammons in "Motion" presents the division as absolute and so, implicitly, more problematical for the poet, since the parts of his medium which most "trap" reality are least like it, and vice versa.

The division of essential nature between words and reality is an especially difficult issue for this particular poet, who has a bent toward abstraction, toward authenticating abstraction as an activity, and toward keeping his predicating, assertive self in the poem. All of those inclinations conflict with the impersonal, yielding method and conception reflected by Ammons' poem "Poetics," which ends with these lines, logically consistent with the ideas of "Motion":

> not so much looking for the shape
> as being available
> to any shape that may be
> summoning itself
> through me
> from the self not mine but ours.

This passivity and self-effacement also underlie Ammons' well-known poem "Corsons Inlet," which begins on the page after "Motion" in the *Collected Poems*. Together, I think that these poems help explain the strange, unmistakable style of Ammons. His work is based upon a clear, concentrated meditation of the problem which I have made central to this book. The result is a difficult marriage of poetics or epistemology with natural description: the fluid landscape and the poet's repeated definition of his own role in relation to that flux. The style which strives to resolve these demands is strained in various directions, with an oddly garrulous reliance upon claims and disclaimers. The concluding stanzas of "Corsons

Inlet," for example, comprise an awkwardly argumentative, definitive, self-conscious protest against argument, definitiveness and unwillingness "to go along, to accept/ the becoming/ thought":

> orders as summaries, as outcomes of actions override
> or in some way result, not predictably (seeing me gain
> the top of a dune,
> the swallows
> could take flight—some other fields of bayberry
> could enter fall
> berryless) and there is serenity:
>
> no arranged terror: no forcing of image, plan,
> or thought:
> no propaganda, no humbling of reality to precept:
>
> terror pervades but is not arranged, all possibilities
> of escape open: no route shut, except in
> the sudden loss of all routes:
>
> I see narrow orders, limited tightness, but will
> not run to that easy victory:
> still around the looser, wider forces work:
> I will try
> to fasten into order enlarging grasps of disorder, widening
> scope, but enjoying the freedom that
> Scope eludes my grasp, that there is no finality of vision,
> that I have perceived nothing completely,
> that tomorrow a new walk is a new walk.

The strained, nearly pinched quality of the idiom ("still around," "there is serenity," "widening scope") goes oddly with the self-praise or self-admonishment in the language of literary criticism: "I . . . will not run to that easy victory" or "finality of vision." In the presence of so much strain, it is hard to credit either the joy or the capitalization of "Scope" in the phrase "enjoying the freedom that / Scope eludes my grasp"; and the phrase is, along with the rest of the final five lines, contingent upon the line "I will try." This tentative, doubting quality—an "enlarging" and difficult resolve simply to "try"—characterizes Ammons' most memorable work, strangely as it does conflict with the assertive, proscriptive tone of "no forcing," "will not run," and "there is no finality": a largely negative definitiveness. Ammons' more prophetic, Romantically affirmative poems are both fewer and less convincing—like "The City Limits," in which the abundance of natural "radiance" falls on the accepting earth around one until:

>   the dark
> work of the deepest cells is of a tune with May bushes
> and fear lit by the breadth of such calmly turns to praise.

If fear ever turns "calmly" to anything, being "of a tune with May bushes"
is a lamely rhetorical motive for such turning, especially given the sinister,
cancerous implications of "the dark work of the deepest cells." Moreover,
it is the "breadth" of the natural world itself, and its radiance, which
kindle fear. In "Corsons Inlet," the "grasps of disorder" as a goal, the
pervasive terror, and the unpredictable, uncontrolled appearance of serenity carry more conviction than the "praise" of "The City Limits." The
reason, I think, is that in "Corsons Inlet" Ammons' voice conveys the
difficulty and tentativeness of its own role in the world, a role within
which neither praise nor vision can come with finality or for long.

Perhaps more than any other contemporary poet, Ammons displays
a consistent, explicit, intelligent taking up of the themes and problems I
have tried to present as central to the modernist tradition. He takes up
the implications of the great poetic subject I have exemplified by citing
the "Ode to a Nightingale," "The Most of It," "The Term," and "The
Snow Man"; it is even possible to argue that he brings to that subject a
discursive style. So it is essential for me to explain why I find something
dull and strained in his work, for all its accomplishments. Underlying that
particular question is the larger question of how gravely limiting the
traditional problem at stake must be for contemporary poetry.

The problem can be summarized as a need to find language for
presenting the role of a conscious soul in an unconscious world; the terms,
of course, vary historically and from individual to individual. "Sunday
Morning" suggests that for a human being "divinity must live within
herself," finding correspondences in the natural world for internal passions—

>   unsubdued
> Elations when the forest blooms; gusty
> Emotions on wet roads on autumn nights;
> All pleasures and all pains, remembering
> The bough of summer and the winter branch.

The unconscious natural world provides "destined" comparisons, figures of
speech, terms or "measures" for the conscious soul and its actions. Through
a blank-verse style which is a sort of rich distillation of Wordsworth's,
Stevens makes this arrangement seem rich and promising, a spiritual
correspondence dwelling in the poetic mind. The style is grand, and
indeed implies a grandly hieratic role for the poet and his language, which
becomes a religious medium.

The characteristic manner of Ammons seems at moments similarly grand, but with odd catches or mutterings, an undertone of uncertainty and misgiving which becomes explicit in the following poem:

PLUNDER

I have appropriated the windy twittering of aspen leaves
into language, stealing something from reality like a
silverness: drop-scapes of ice from peak sheers:

much of the rise in brooks over slow-rolled glacial stones:
the loop of reeds over the shallow's edge when birds
feed on the rafts of algae: I have taken right out of the

air the clear streaks of bird music and held them in my
head like shifts of sculptured glint: I have sent language
through the mud roils of a racoon's paws like a net,

netting the roils: made my own use of a downwind's
urgency on a downward stream: held with a large scape
of numbness the black distance upstream to the mountains

flashing and bursting: meanwhile, everything else, frog,
fish, bear, gnat has turned in its provinces and made off
with its uses: my mind's indicted by all I've taken.

A poem like this depends upon great sharpness of physical detail, and "Plunder" is convincingly vivid in many of its natural images, particularly in the second stanza: the loop of the reeds, the algae in abundant rafts. But this adept descriptive writing, which is part of the poem's subject, is halted or made jagged by what seems a deliberate flatting: the limping phrases "like a / silverness," "like shifts of sculptured glint" and "held with a large scape / of numbness." These mumbled similes and "-nesses" act as protestations of how difficult and oblique a process this plundering-by-language is, for the poet. On the one hand, there is the assertion of bardic power, and on the other hand, the poet doubts the integrity of what he does when he tries to find likenesses for the glitter of reality. The doubt is literal, it is implicit in the halted style, and it is explicit in the conclusion of the poem: the "appropriating" and "stealing" which seem to indicate the poet's authority and subtlety in the first stanza become literal transgressions by the last line.

As a result, the tone and scope of "Plunder" are peculiar; it appears that personally, the poet praises himself, while philosophically, he throws literal, grave misgivings upon what he has done with his mind and his language. However, I think that the repeated presence of the note of bardic assertion in Ammons' work is no mere disorganization or accident of personality. That sometimes combative, intrusive presence is, as I have pointed out, somewhat paradoxical in view of the "yielding" advocated in "Corsons Inlet," the "self not mine." Yet it is an inevitable presence given the assumptions and bases of these poems.

That is, Ammons believes in abstraction, he has no desire to sink into pure description or to be a nature poet, and yet he also believes deeply that the mind and its essential tool—the net or method of words— are indicted by the flux of reality. And so, between the alternatives of description and what might be called Romantic epistemology—an obsessive re-definition of the poet's relationship to natural reality—we also have the mediating presence of bardic self-assertion. The bardic note, in a way, is not an emotion itself, but rather a way of holding together other, conflicting emotions. To some extent, it performs the same role as the mellowly oracular grand style of "Sunday Morning."

Thus, Stevens discourses about the largest of abstract questions while evoking the natural world, and all the time implies—but never states—a central role for the poet as a spiritual model. Ammons, conversely, must discourse explicitly about the role of the poet in order to make his way, by apology and explanation, toward philosophical questions and the natural world. "Corsons Inlet" is largely an account of the walks on which the poet discovers the sources, and the limits, of his poems; this procedure, and what might seem a boastful or self-obsessed personal mode, are in fact corollaries of Romantic epistemology: the perpetual mending and inspection of the net of language.

The limits of such material and such a style are severe; the poet cannot in good faith go very far from natural phenomena, and his own relation to reality. These limitations are reflected stylistically in the movement and diction of a poem like "Plunder." In diction, the ambivalence appears in semi-ironic reclamations of Romantic vocabulary: "twittering," "flashing and bursting," "provinces." In movement from part to part, the strings of repeated colons suggest a conflict between the stationary or simultaneous and the developing or sequential; each part explains every other part, with a minimum of the consecutive structuring in which part rests on part as in a building or a tree. This closeless structure is the contrary of Stevens' elaborately organized periods, and the contrary of the kind of progress I mean by the word discursive. Ammons makes very much the same point himself, using the similar word "disquisition":

> (disquisition is sesquipedalian pedestrianism, tidying up
> the loose bits, but altogether misssing the import of the impetus):
> a center's absolute, if relative: but every point in spacetimematter's
>
> a center: reality is abob with centers: indeed, there is
> nothing but centers:
>
> ("Essay On Poetics")

Entirely as I disagree with this passage, insofar as it calls for a kind of poetry, or decries one, I think that it sets the terms of the matter accurately. The passage itself illustrates the awkwardness with which Ammons must approach the chore of disquisition: the strained jocularity of the wordplays and chattiness, the impatient alliterations, the slightly false slang and breeziness, all express a certain embarrassment with the task at hand. The more congenial style and material of "Plunder" represent an honorable and masterful kind of poetry, moving within its narrow spectrum. But the human limits—the *social* limits, the conversational limits—of Romantic epistemology suggest a diminishing of poetry's scope, if not a dead end. The limits and pressures I have described produce the style which, reading Ammons, I find myself calling "dull," pinched, hard to read with absorption despite my other response of admiration.

FREDERICK BUELL

"To Be Quiet in the Hands of the Marvelous"

Those who first became acquainted with the work of A. R. Ammons by reading his more recent poetry have probably been surprised by looking back to the early poems reprinted in his *Collected Poems: 1951–71*. A large number of the poems dated between the years 1951 and 1955 (the date when his first volume of poetry, *Ommateum*, was published) do not seem to be characteristic of his mature work. Ammons has set these poems in a grim, at times overtly Gothic, world of death, shame, grief, and unexplained loss, and he has centered them around gestures of mysterious impotence or failure. Even where the poems' speakers move toward self-extinction, the result is neither peace nor catharsis, but a state of sensibility that is hauntingly difficult to describe. For want of a better phrase, I would call it a state of incomplete suffocation. An example is the conclusion of the volume's best-known poem, "So I Said I Am Ezra":

> I moved my feet and turning from the wind
>   that ripped sheets of sand
>   from the beach and threw them
>   like seamists across the dunes
> swayed as if the wind were taking me away
> and said
>   I am Ezra
> As a word too much repeated
> falls out of being
> so I Ezra went out into the night

From *The Iowa Review* 8 (Winter 1977). Copyright © 1977 by the University of Iowa.

> like a drift of sand
> and splashed among the windy oats
> that clutch the dunes
> of unremembered seas

Ezra's "fall out of being" is not a metaphysical fulfillment. It is not a loss of self to a cosmos, to a larger order. Ezra falls out of being into a partly psychological, partly mythical limbo; this place does not bring peace, but the sense of suffocation and unexplained turbulence that is expressed in the way the oats "clutch" the "dunes of unremembered seas." The poem's Ezra, a reference to a hunchback playmate of Ammons' youth and also ironically suggestive of Ezra the biblical scribe, cannot assert his name against the visionary indifference of the wind and ocean.

The landscape that haunts these early poems is less Ammons' native rural South than it is the ancient Near East. It is the landscape of Sumerian mythology, to which these poems abound in reference. Its God is unapproachable, and its earth is one of dust, sand, wind, and desert. One feels that the landscape is burdened with a timelessness that is stifling to the creatures of time; in it, apocalyptic transformation, though yearned for, is inconceivable. The landscape thus blends imperceptibly into the domain of the Queen of Darkness of the Gilgamesh epic, the realm from which "none who enters ever returns . . . the road from where there is no coming back." As Enkidu's dream reveals, the underworld is a place of suffocation where men endure forever, retaining selfhood but not their vitality, their connection with Being. In the Gilgamesh epic, moreover, no one can escape death, neither the hero Gilgamesh, two-thirds a god, nor the "priests of the incantation and ecstasy"; Ammons' early poems abound in examples of failed heroes and seers.

Ammons' lyric voice in his early poetry is that of a seer who has no social or individual characteristics but is instead a presence of more than ordinary awareness and longing. The seer, moreover, is one who has lost or never securely had a saving message or special revelation; one could say that he is the creation of a Christian sensibility which had lost its faith in the "good news" of the New Testament and had delved back into the eschatological pessimism of the older Jews and Sumerians. The poems begin as the seer enters their largely mythic landscapes, unlocated in place and historical time. They begin with statements that have biblical and visionary overtones, such as "I went out to the sun," "Turning from the waterhole I said Oh," "I came in a dark woods upon / an ineffaceable difference," or "I came upon a plateau." The seer then moves through the mysteriously, often whimsically, often ominously changing landscape into encounters with gods or phantasmagora that are intentionally and suggestively indefinite. Though magically capable of extraordinary movement ("So I left and walked up into the air"), the seer is curiously unfree, damned to failure in an indeterminate quest ("How shall I / coming from these fields / water the fields of the earth / and I said Oh, / and fell down in the dust"), or to protracted wanderings, or to a quest for failure that ends without attainment of self-annihilation:

> Peeling off my being I plunged into
> the well . . .
> went on deeper
> finding patched innertubes beer cans
> and black roothairs along the way
> but went on deeper
> till darkness snuffed the shafts of light
> against the well's side
>   night kissing
> the last bubbles from my lips

These journeys and encounters are filled with a pressure that one feels would have been a hunger for apocalyptic transformation if time and the possibility of meaningful change had not already effectively ceased. Of that hunger, there remains only in the poems the consciousness of there having been a great longing. In the well, as in Enkidu's dream, vitality is lost, while consciousness remains.

Though Eliot's poetry is one of the proximate sources for these poems, they are far more turbulent with their unsatisfied desire than "The Waste Land" and related poems. Behind Ammons' early work looms a desire too large and sometimes too corrupted by indefinite sin or decay to be able to find in nature an image for itself or to be able to make, going beyond nature, objects for itself. The longing behind the poems' incomplete failures is so strong that, when one comes across the poem "This Black Rich Country," one reads it as a result of a nearly heroic endeavor. It begins with the line "Dispossess me of belief"; in renouncing the absoluteness of his longing and in attempting to claim for himself a world of ordinary mortality, the poet, who is now as much a man as he is a seer, appeals to an unnamed force to

> leave me this black rich country,
> uncertainty, labor, fear: do not
> steal the rewards of my mortality.

It is one of the first poems to end with a period rather than a timeless suspension, and it searches for what, in light of the earlier poems, are achievements. It would find uncertainty, rather than a limbo in which all possibilities are suffocatingly voided, though unstilled; it would have labor rather than an impotent longing without means to realize itself; and it would experience fear rather than a state of sensibility that seems to be alienated from all merely human emotions.

Ammons' early work thus seems to lie far afield from the poetry that leads immediately up to "Corsons Inlet" and then into his major long poems; it seems to have little to do with Ammons' reputation as an Emersonian "nature poet." Though the distance between the absoluteness of the early poems and the speculative liveliness of the later work is great, the change is by no means arbitrary. Ammons' achievement has been to relativize and multiply the absolute for the sake of imaginative survival and the promise of a nearly unlimited intellectual growth. He abandons the seer of the early poems for an astonishing variety of inventions of voices and personae, the variety of which becomes clear only as one surveys a large number of poems. Ammons humanizes the seer and gives him specific identities. Though Ammons compromises thereby the absoluteness of his visionary quest, though he absorbs more of the imperfect properties and knowledges of time, he is imaginatively freer within these limitations. He has consciously humbled himself to accept an object, imperfect earthly nature, for his now controlled but always resurgent longings.

In doing this, Ammons begins to expand his work in two directions. He brings it closer to the American commonplace, and he opens it to a broad eclecticism of knowledge and wisdom. He enters, in short, the mainstream of American visionary poetry. The poetry after *Ommateum* gradually reveals the extent of and the principal sources for Ammons' spiritual eclecticism. Behind the bulk of it (the only major exception being perhaps *Tape for the Turn of the Year*) lies a varied use of Greek thought, the Ionian nature philosophy that is the point of origin of Western science, and a personalized use of ideas and terminology that comes from Eastern thought, ultimately Laotse, named by Ammons as his "philosophical source in its most complete version." Most of Ammons' mature writings—in idea and strategy—are made up of his interweaving of these separate sources, and their union is like the union of compensatory opposites. Ammons' juxtaposition of intellectual speculations with his references to emptiness or the void, his virtuosic capacity to give precise though fluid form to idea and perception coupled with his repeated attainment, within the rapid flow of his verse, of moments of stillness or serenity reveal how he has united his two very different sources. These moments of sudden rest in his verse, moreover, free idea and perception from logic and referential knowledge; by them the mind is stilled and refreshed so that it is ready for renewed speculation and perception. The use of these sources, then, provides controlling ideas for the poetry as well as resources of mood and mode. Ammons' use, for example, of the colon as a structural device is a stylistic derivation from these polarities. Perhaps the best summary of how the two sources help constitute Ammons' vision would be to say that the one is the basis for his active knowledge and the other is the wisdom that enables him to engage in the activity of knowledge.

Ammons' creation of a nature with which he could initiate a richly provisional expressive relationship was a conscious reaction against the direction of his early poetry. Ammons' mature poetry is not a rebellion against a corpse-cold Unitarianism. As Ammons' early poems would indicate, his religious background was, if anything, too hot, too passionately apocalyptic to be dealt with directly. To naturalize his imagination was thus a saving achievement, as "This Black Rich Country" would indicate, and the provisional accords with nature in Ammons' work should be seen as an accomplishment that is often most sublime when it is most humble, brilliantly equivocating, and overtly comic.

Most immediately striking in the poetry dated in the *Collected Poems* between 1956 and 1966 is the great variety of voices and lyric selves that Ammons has created. Sly or serious inquirer, chanter, celebrant, country skeptic, diarist, observer, reasoner: the speakers range in utterance from the formal, hortatory, or celebrative Whitmanian chanter of songs to the wry, ironic doubter of prophecy. Ammons often addresses the reader directly, rupturing the absoluteness of the early lyrics. Sometimes, he will address the reader's soul with Whitmanian urgency, and sometimes he will appeal to the reader's interests and sympathies in a breezily chatty manner. Equally various are the terms that he employs in these poems for metaphysical speculation and for definition of the nature of temporal process. He writes of, reasons about, or chants the one, unity, the overall, the underlying, the void, the changeless, and the divine in different poems, and he uses terms like motion, order, entropy, accident, mechanism, and weaving and unweaving to present in different poems the processes of nature in time.

It would be incorrect, I think, to call these poems mere experiments in voice and idea, though they do establish many of the modes for the longer, more encyclopaedic poems to come. (One could even say they require Ammons to attempt the longer poems as acts of self-integration.) Their variety comes instead from a pragmatic and organic impulse: to develop a mode of expression that is suited to the different subject or mood presented. Some modes and wisdoms are peripheral. Ammons' direct appeal to the Christian mystery of the incarnation in "Christmas

Eve" is unusual, although the mode and tonality of the poem are crucial for the wonderful book *Tape for the Turn of the Year*; Ammons' regression into an amniotic unity in "Sphere" is most unusual; and his weaving and unweaving of self in "Muse" is unusual in the Whitmanian cadences of the first half and the immediacy and directness with which this theme is handled. In general, the overt recreations of Whitman's style do not endure in Ammons' work, although it abounds in wonderfully indirect echoes of him.

Ammons' main interest, as it emerges from the variety of his middle poems, is in the realm of the changing in nature and its accessibility to the mind. Ammons discovers two complementary approaches to this theme. The most familiar is Ammons' remarkable ability to rationalize process into flowing order and to make it intelligible by means of the Ionian concepts of the one and the many. This is a realm of intellection at which Ammons is an unparalleled master. Ammons presents his "one" as ungraspable, not to be fully thought or experienced; he sees experience of it as a destruction of self. The world short of the one is the human realm. In it, Ammons exercises the full play of his mind; he brings the world of multiplicity into changing orders by means of an intellectual resourcefulness which is as fluid and undogmatic as natural process. It is not logical reasoning, but an underlying motion in the mind which parallels, precariously, the motions of things. Ammons experiences that motion in the mind in the act of poetry, and he images it as the wind:

> but the music
> in poems
> is different,
> points to nothing,
> traps no
> realities, takes
> no game, but
> by the motion of
> its motion
> resembles
> what, moving, is—
> the wind
> underleaf, white against
> the tree.

To try for totality is a destruction; it ends the motion that informs nature and the creative mind.

The less familiar strain in Ammons' poetry is a mode that is not of motion and the mind, but of an underlying receptivity in both the cosmos and man. Ammons sees this receptivity as something prior to identity or self; it is his version of Taoist emptiness or void. In the cosmos, the void contains process, and, in the person, the void is a cultivation of inner stillness and receptivity. Ammons arrives at a statement of it at the end of the fine poem "Terrain," a poem about the soul:

> it is an area of poise, really, held from tipping,
>   dark wild water, fierce eels, countercurrents:
> a habitat, precise ecology of forms
>   mutually to some extent
> tolerable, not entirely self-destroying; a crust afloat:
>   a scum, foam to the deep and other-natured:
> but deeper than depth, too: a vacancy and swirl:
>
> it may be spherical, light and knowledge merely
>   the iris and opening
> to the dark methods of its sight: how it comes and
>   goes, ruptures and heals,
> whirls and stands still: the moon comes: terrain.

Ammons' essay, "A Poem Is A Walk," which is, according to Harold Bloom, "infuriatingly Emersonian," is perhaps not so dark once this strain in his work is recognized. A poem, as Bloom quotes Ammons,

> is a motion to no-motion, to the still point of contemplation and deep realization. Its knowledges are all negative and, therefore, more positive than any knowledge.

Ammons argues that the poem, as well as the self and cosmos, has an inner stillness and vacancy. It is a wholeness accessible even where the mind in motion fails to attain the one, rebuffed by the provisionality of its orders. It is the stillness against which the provisionality of motion has meaning and form. Ammons makes explicit the fact that these two modes coexist as parallels in his imagination in his poem "Two Motions."

The justifiably well-known poem "Corsons Inlet" integrates rather than juxtaposes, as does "Two Motions," these modes of imagination. The poet's active mind is no longer animated into motion by an external wind, but is completely in his possession, and it is fused with the full acceptance that "Overall is beyond me," an acceptance that, fully realized, yields "serenity." The poem is a walk and thus a mixture of the active and the passive, not a voyage or a nonvoyage, the opposing terms of "Two Motions." The fact that it is a casual walk, yet a walk for meditative discovery, locates it somewhere between the uniqueness and goal-directedness of a quest and a passive vacancy of receptivity to its surroundings. In a walk, one loiters and absorbs as much as one attempts to get anywhere; in a repeated, daily walk, this passive absorbtiveness is emphasized. Ammons' controlling idea in the poem is active. It is the mind's ever recrudescent and expanding capacity to "fasten into order enlarging grasps of disorder," to combat increasing entropy. He finds, however, rest in an insight that is related to the passive or receptive elements in the walk:

> there is no finality of vision,
> that I have perceived nothing completely,
> that tomorrow a new walk is a new walk.

Ammons thus reveals how the activity of mind and the receptive stillness of wisdom are necessarily related to each other. When they are integrated with each other, the poet can achieve a fuller and fuller (though forever incomplete) naturalization of his imagination and human- ization of nature. The motions of the poet's mind can become more and more a part of and supplement to nature's active motions. They neither need be merely "wind," the appearance for moments in the human mind of something essentially nonhuman, nor need they attain a finality or auton- omy that would be threatening and unnatural in its conclusiveness. They need neither be too natural in origin to include human consciousness nor too human and conscious to find a place in natural process. With the resources of intellection and wisdom, Ammons can locate himself within the mid-world of natural process, the realm of time and change. He can root himself precariously within the flowing. In this context, his use of the colon, a staple now of his poetic syntax and to remain so, becomes luminous. In Emerson's prose style, each sentence often seems to be a unique origin, and an essay is at best a cumulative series of original insights and at worst a collection of mutually repellent particles. Ammons' poetry, by contrast, accents continuation in process as much as it does surprise and involvement in natural fate or law as much as it does freedom. Ammons mitigates and brings into a balance terms that are paradoxical polarities in Emerson's thought. Indeed, in "Corsons Inlet," Ammons modifies the terms "law" or "fate" in order to make them responsive to his scientific understanding of natural process, which he sees as neither a total discontinuity of original self-recreations nor something bound by adamantine law or fate. Nature is, like the poet's mind, a process of mingled order and disorder, cause and accident, event and probability.

The "freedom" of "Corsons Inlet" is the unfinished quality of nature and of vision. The poem balances subtlety in order with a maxi- mum of possibility, and this balance of order and possibility allows the experience of freedom. The price for the freedom Ammons attains is risk:

the risk of possibility, the risk that the accident of death will shatter time, and the risk of order, the risk that the imagination will quail before an apparent rigidity of order, the tight food-chain of death.

In its celebration of provisionality, "Corsons Inlet" is a self-conscious summary of Ammons' work to that point. In it, Ammons attempts to rationalize his diversity of thought and voice. In firmly establishing a mid-world of imaginative existence within temporal process, and in its attainment of inner and outer coherence within the changing, the poem looks forward to the impressive developments of Ammons' later work, particularly the *Tape for the Turn of the Year*, the long poems that appear in the *Collected Poems*, "Essay on Poetics," "Extremes and Moderations," and "Hibernaculum," and the book-length poem *Sphere*.

In *Tape for the Turn of the Year*, Ammons takes the wisdom of "Corsons Inlet" as far into the American commonplace as one could wish. A long, skinny poem, written on an adding machine tape that Ammons found at a home and garden supply store, it extends through several hundred pages and a five-week period of time his achievement of freedom within time, his precarious balance of continuum and surprise.

Ammons bases his *Tape* upon an affectionate parody of the *Odyssey*. He relocates the epic story to a diary-like account of his passage through a little over a month's time, and he breaks the voyage of Odysseus up into a series of internal and external side-trips or forays and encounters with daily eventualities or accidents. Like Odysseus, Ammons has a destination, a home he seeks; this is one of the main themes of the poem. With wonderfully disguised slyness, Ammons seeks another Ithaca, as he is waiting to hear about a job offer from Cornell University, Ithaca, New York. The theme of homecoming itself is, however, far more complex. The opening sections of the poem announce it as a story of "how / a man comes home / from haunted / lands and transformations" to an "acceptance of his place / and time." The poem thus becomes, in theme and in overall form, the attainment of a way of "going along with this / world as it is." Ammons' resources are those of "Corsons Inlet," active intellection and receptive wisdom; the goal of his quest can also be put in the terms of "Corsons Inlet" as the continuing and ever unfinished attainment of a partial humanization of nature and naturalization of the imagination. Ammons attempts continuously to deal with the question he raises at the end of the poem:

> have our minds taken us too
> far, out of nature, out of
> complete acceptance?

The home sought is thus finally not a fixed residence. It is a home in motion; Ammons realizes that

> those who rely on any shore
> foolishly haven't faced
> it that
> only the stream is
>   reliable:

Indeed, "home is every minute." Ammons includes in the poem a number of wonderfully vivid and clear remembrances of his boyhood in the South; they are too finely realized for nostalgia, for he recollects them with the insight that there is no way home in going back. Ammons thus distinguishes himself from a yearning for paradises lost. He also distinguishes himself in *Tape* from a yearning for paradises to be regained, making it clear that his conception of time retains the irreversibility but not the teleological goal of Christian history.

These Miltonic echoes Ammons intends; he also explicitly echoes Wordsworth's "Prospectus." His high quest is not to justify the ways of God to man nor to effect a marriage, with apocalyptic overtones, between the mind of man and the external world, but to come to an acceptance of changing place and time, a reconciliation he describes as a "going along with this / world as it is." This reconciliation is never so complete nor final as a marriage. Instead, it involves a blend of continuous activity of wit and intellect with a large draught of acceptance, abandonment to being swept along, and it necessitates a poem that is as arbitrary in beginning and ending as is the *Tape*, a going along with a section of the poet's time. Ammons' sense of transience is even more extreme in this poem than Emerson's was in his essay "Circles," itself a resistance of apocalyptic marriage with nature. Rather than draw larger and larger circles of awareness about himself, each one an attainment which is dissipated by a return to time and which necessitates a further self-recovery, Ammons attempts to ride a "moment- / to-moment crest." He attempts, in short, to ride rather than to circumscribe. The wisdom of "Corsons Inlet" has become now a possession of daily life, not the sublime assertion of a recognition attained at the end of a meditative walk. Ammons tests that assertion to see if it will be capable of sustaining an ordinary man in the disorder and homeliness of daily life in a house in inland New Jersey (a location now removed from the ocean margin).

The *Tape* is thus set in the mid-world of "Corsons Inlet," a world whose visibility and clarity of form is rooted in the active knowledge of Greek philosophy and receptive wisdom of Taoism. Something that is specific to the *Tape*, however, is an expansion of Ammons' religious and philosophical eclectisism. More than in any other poem, save perhaps the most recent long poem, *Sphere*, Ammons suspends this mid-world in darkness, a darkness out of which the clarity of fact emerges with the same attained sweetness as invests the "natural light" attained at the end of the atypical poem "Bridge." In writing that the

> eternal
> significance is of some
> significance to me: I
> just don't know how: but
> temporal significance is
> a world I can partly make,
> loss & gain:

Ammons surrounds the processes of time with something larger, something unknown and unknowable in terms of inner need and external knowledge; though the "Overall" is still beyond him, it is very much in the poem, if only in the background of the New Jersey winter nights, a natural darkness. This darkness, however, may at times suggest something more than nature to "the terror-ridden / homeless man / wandering through / a universe of horror"; this homeless wandering man always haunts the background of the poem, even though Ammons seeks to be the "man at ease / in a universe of light," saying

> let's tend our
> feelings &
> leave the Lord
> His problems
> (if any): He
> got us this far on His own:
> & millions have come
> and gone in joy
> (predominantly):

Though Ammons leaves the Lord on his own and only comically gives Him personal identity, and though one could not call even the moment Ammons speaks of the Lord devotional in intention, his acceptance of uncertainty is Judeo-Christian in overtone. The atmosphere of the Christmas setting for the *Tape* determines to a certain extent its tone and substance. Between the obedience of Abraham, submitting to an unknowable will, and the regeneration of Pauline faith, a death and rebirth to a new world, the poet of the *Tape* is to be found. Of course, Ammons follows neither of these paths. He retains his limited freedoms and whimsy and he tries to stay within time as mere ongoing. But that Ammons' middle road is flanked by these Judeo-Christian paths is clear from his credo, the *Tape*'s central moment, spoken after a description of an afternoon church service in which "the deacons went down / the aisles & gave light to / each row / & the light poured / down the rows & / the singing started":

> though the forces
> have different names
> in different places &
> times, they are
> real forces which we
> don't understand:
>   I can either believe
>   in them or doubt them &
>   I believe:
> I believe that man is
> small
> & of short duration in the
> great, incomprehensible,
> & eternal: I believe
> it's necessary to do
> good
> as we best can define it:
> I believe we must
> discover & accept the
>   terms
>   that best testify:
> I'm on the side of
> whatever the reasons are
>   we are here:
>
>   we do the best we can
> & it's not enough:

The terms of this poem are finally a nonintellectual humility and limited hope, not entropy and order and serenity, an acceptance of the void. The credo's humility indicates what lies beneath the poem's rich play of the mind, and the highly conditional hope—whether it comes from choice, faith, or the delightfully comic rendering of the American desire to be on "the right side of things"—underlies the poem's quest for acceptance from within time. Just as it is the humble and always hopeful fabric of daily American life that sustains this poem as its imaginative setting, it is humility and provisional hope that sustains the speaker.

Ammons thus deprecates his speculative ideas to the nonintellectuality of Christian humility and hope and to the routines of daily life they inform. It would, moreover, be doing an injustice to the *Tape*, both in its own right and in its position as forerunner to the more difficult and intellectually brilliant later long poems, to omit a notation of the poem's range of thought. Ammons attempts in this poem to take account of the whole range of man's knowledge: he deals with questions aesthetical, epistemological, metaphysical, religious, psychological, sociological, social, sexual, and scientific. The *Tape* previsions the later poems' attempts to find models that include and unify all these realms. I shall discuss this point later at some length in connection with the "Essay on Poetics"; here I only wish to note that the *Tape* is the herald of the later poems' intellectual cosmoses. In the *Tape*, Ammons does not yet assert ideas as ideals, saying "ideas are human products, / temporal & full of process"; he modifies this description slightly but significantly in the later long poems. In the *Tape*, Ammons undercuts ideas by juxtaposing them to the fabric of daily life, a poetic resource which provides much of the entertainment as well as wisdom of the poem. Ammons will, while on a flight of thought, frequently interrupt himself with a parenthesis "(just went to take a leak: / jay on the back lawn, / hopping, looking around, / turning leaves)" or refer back to a past speculative flight in a way that is comic but not completely deflating "(I had / lunch after / 'who cannot love')."

The *Tape* is Ammons' essential poem of America. Whereas some of the poems prior to "Corsons Inlet" echo Whitman's mode directly and with remarkable success, the *Tape* is both highly personalized and rich in indirect echoes. Ammons writes it as a song of myself, a self, however, empiricized and provincialized. Though the poet remains the representative man and the poem is a poem of America, the poet and poem attain this status through their provinciality and smallness or homeliness of delineation. When Ammons uses the word "we," his tone is familial and sharing, something appropriate to a poem about a quest for home and to a poem that is rich with the Christmas winter atmosphere. He seeks to temper the external adversity of the weather, the long dark winter nights of ice, and the nearness of an inscrutable mystery by recreating the internal hearth warmth of family event and shared daily eventualities. These voices and attitudes are a barbaric yawp, a genuine one for our day. Ammons is a rebel against the "literary" in catching the humble, casual, and provincial in American speech and event; a sympathetic portrayal of an American Christmas, an event regarded by the merely literary as the fountainhead of *kitsch*, is a remarkable achievement in a Whitmanian vein.

Ammons' long poems since *Tape for the Turn of the Year*—the major ones are "Essay on Poetics," "Extremes and Moderations," "Hiber-naculum," and the book-length poem *Sphere: The Form of a Motion* and a comparatively minor, but sheerly delightful one is "Summer Session" —make use of the continuous form of the *Tape*, but alter its import and effect in a number of ways. I shall focus on "Essay on Poetics" as represen-tative of the major long poems and content myself mainly with references to the others, for, even taking "Essay on Poetics" alone, I am all too conscious that justice cannot be done to its richness in a brief survey of Ammons' whole body of work.

The speaker of the "Essay" has a somewhat different identity than had the speaker of *Tape*. No longer primarily identifiable as a provincial American, he emerges more vividly as an ironic Stevensian and mock-Victorian essayist-comedian. The essayist writes in a language of proposi-tions, a language that is not as various as that of the *Tape*, though its variety of thought and expression is stunning. The language of the "Essay" relies heavily upon the resources of connective syntax, as its propositions, thoughts, and aphorisms are connected not only by the continuation of the colon and the surge of continuation of thought, but also by a host of connectives that modify or qualify the direction of the thought, such as "indeed," "still," "but," etc. (This is a language that the essayist himself calls attention to at one "point of provisional summation" in the poem). The effect of the poem's freedom with connectives is to multiply its thought rather than to restrict it. Like the *Tape*, the "Essay" is always in motion, but this motion is far more rapid and sustained than that of the *Tape*, and it quickens still more in the other long poems, less tied to the meandering mood of an essay.

The "Essay" has a quotidian setting, for it is written during the "natural suspension" of a snowstorm, and it refers often to the weather and the look of the land outdoors. In contrast to the setting for the *Tape*, the snowstorm is a "natural suspension," in which the poet distances himself slightly from his normal life in order to write a poetic essay, not a diary. Thought has gained a slightly greater degree of primacy and even autonomy. Though, as in the *Tape*, Ammons hews a "middle way," it is now a middle way of thought rather than experience, a way cut between an "artificial linearity" and "nonsense."

Ammons' change in mode signifies an important development away from the *Tape*; it is a slight push away from his former attempt to naturalize the imagination and toward an attempt to assert the autono-mous freedom of the imagination. Ammons explicitly avoids a complete liberation from nature, however; the distinction is an important and subtle one. At one point, early in the poem, Ammons writes "what this is about," the " 'gathering / in the sky' so to speak, the trove of mind, tested / experience, the only place to stay . . . the holy bundle of / the elements of civilization, the Sumerians said." This "gathering in the sky" is akin to the Heavenly City and the ungrasped Overall of Ammons' earlier poems, though it is now no longer a destruction. It is "impossibly difficult"; it is an ideal that guides human action, inaccessible, nonexistent in a literal sense, but nevertheless an ideal to be striven for. That Ammons feels an immense risk of loss and a profound pathos in his quest now for something slightly out of nature is clear from the moving dedicatory poem (for Harold Bloom) that begins the book *Sphere*. In it, Ammons returns to the mood and Sumerian setting of his earliest poetry as he covertly identifies himself with Enkidu, who was removed from nature and humanized at the cost of his ability to converse directly and live in harmony with it. Ammons concludes his magnificent lament with the lines:

> this place has provided firm implication and answering
>   but where here is the image for *longing*:
> so I touched the rocks, their interesting crusts:
> I flaked the bark of stunt-fir:
> I looked into space and into the sun
> and nothing answered my word *longing*:
>   goodbye, I said, goodbye, nature so grand and
> reticent, your tongues are healed up into their own
> element
> and as you have shut up you have shut me out: I am
> as foreign here as if I had landed, a visitor:
> so I went back down and gathered mud
> and with my hands made an image for *longing*:
>   I took this image to the summit: first
> I set it here, on the top rock, but it completed
> nothing: then I set it there among the tiny firs
> but it would not fit:
> so I returned to the city and built a house to set
> the image in
> and men came into my house and said
>   that is an image for *longing*
> and nothing will ever be the same again

The "Essay" and the other long poems in the *Collected Poems* do not, however, seek to attain or give themselves up to such finality. Instead, Ammons carefully draws in them the line between naturalization and apocalyptic freedom of the imagination; he makes the distinction clear in two passages in "Hibernaculum." The first explicitly resists apocalypse:

some think mind will continue
growing out of nature until possessed of its own self
second-nature it will bespeak its own change, turn with
or against the loam out of which it grew: I'm pessimistic:

for my little faith, such as it is, is that mind and
nature grew out of a common node and so must obey common
motions. . . . :

The second passage, however, sets itself against the apparent naturalism of
the previous one:

the mind's
one: it pre-existed, I think: even before it was

mind it was mind plausible: it was the earth: when
it is fully born, it will be another earth, just like
the earth, but visionary, earth luminous with sight:

These are not oppositions, finally. Though the second passage echoes the
new heaven and earth of *Revelation*, it is a new earth exactly like the old,
and the progress toward it is not a second birth but a continuation of the
first. Whereas Emerson wrote of extremes, the poetic recreation of a
second world and the complete naturalization of the mind, Ammons
precariously edges against and holds together both possibilities.

"Essays on Poetics" is a poem that quite obviously is about poetry.
It is, however, also an encyclopaedic poem, as was the *Tape*, and it
attempts what the *Tape* avoided, an integration of the different realms of
knowledge that it draws on. Ammons builds a model of the ideal poem
which serves as the "symbolical representation of the ideal organization,
whether / the cell, the body politic, the business, the religious / group, the
university, computer, or whatever." "Ideal" means a level of abstraction from
nature and not what constitutes nature; as an ideal, it is something
nonexistent but which guides human striving.

To understand just how poetry forms a model for the ideal organization necessitates some reference to the controlling image for the "Essay," an image that comes from the field of cybernetics. Ammons' new
form of conceptualization and thus partial humanization of nature involves
transforming nature into information bits: this transformation means first
an act of abstraction and second a kinetic act of relation of the parts.
Ammons reworks the model of order and entropy he used in "Corsons
Inlet" into the model of cybernetics. It is a cooler and a higher-speed
model, and this determines a change in the tone of the verse. Interpreting
physical processes now in terms of conceptual processes, rather than in

terms of "laws of nature" which are prior to and perhaps antagonistic to those that govern mental processes, Ammons has made a subtle change in both the mode and the vision of his poetry. His abstraction of reality into information-bits is precarious, and "language must / not violate the bit, event, percept, / fact—the concrete—otherwise the separation that means / the death of language shows"; how precarious this is, and how impotent we are to control the processes consciously, is illustrated by Ammons' meditation on the word "true." The word "true," related etymologically to "tree" and therefore the elm tree of the essay, itself physically composed of more "bits" than the mind can handle, is shown to contain greater resonance and rootage of meaning than a logical mind can comprehend. Not in logic then, but only in poetry, a medium capable of dealing with greater complexity in motion, is abstraction possible. To accomplish this end, poetry has, for one thing, the capacity for illusion, as it can heighten "by dismissing reality." Once the bits are abstracted, they are immediately, as a part of that abstraction, brought into relational motion: both speed in motion and intellectual virtuosity are essential, as one can see from Ammons' stunning printout of variations on William Carlos Williams' "no ideas but in things." If Ammons should stop on any word, "language gives way; / melting through, and reality's cold murky waters / accept the failure." Just as computers in action retain information by rapid electronic circulation of it, so Ammons' verse retains its meaning in its mobility.

Ammons' cybernetic model of poetry as bits thrown into motion is based on an ideal of organization. He gradually feeds into his poems bits of different information (ideas, themes) and then, in the course of the poem's high-speed motion, he produces different clusterings or core-tanglings of the bits. These core-tanglings are Ammons' new approach to the familiar one: many problem, and they form a model for societies, businesses—whatever—as well as for computers and for poetry. The ideal is a maximum of unity without distortion or suppression of any of the bits. Poetry is the highest model: it has resources beyond those of computers. It has forms of order that are more than merely an increase of the motion's speed:

> nothing defined can
>
> be still: the verbal moves, depends there, or sinks into unfocused
> irreality; ah, but when the mind is brought to silence, the
> non-verbal, and the still, it's whole again to see how motion goes:

We are back again in Greece and China in the long poems in *Collected Poems*, the themes of which are intellection and the quieting or giving up that represents wisdom. A familiar technique of the "Essay" and of the later poems generally is something that echoes classic American silent films. Ammons will multiply information, pour more into the poem than a rational analysis is capable of, will then, if an explosion of nonsense is not the result, recover himself with a gesture of giving up that returns the mind, suddenly, to integration. After multiplying the considerations that make it impossible to ever determine the location of the elm in his backyard, let alone say anything about its inner structure, Ammons falls back into a wonderful self-recovery that also recovers the wholeness of the elm:

> I am just going to take it for granted
> that the tree is in my backyard:
> it's necessary to be quiet in the hands of the marvelous:

A. R. AMMONS

Event: Corrective: Cure

POETRY MISCELLANY: In "Pray With-out Ceasing," you talk about "tensions sprung free / into event." And "Saliences" talks about the "one event that / creates present time / in the multi-variable / scope." The "event" and "eventuality" figure prominently in "Essay on Poetics," too. It seems to me this is a useful way to begin responding to your poems—they have the character of "events"—they use "events" as opposed to concepts or abstract ideas. Even words like "sua-sion," "salience," "periphery" must be described in terms of "events" from which they emerge. In fact, on one level "events" are modes of emergence of meaning, experience, perception, aren't they? Could you begin to "weave" some further descriptions of the nature of events?

A. R. AMMONS: Not only is the finished poem about an event, but the making of it is an event as well. I am probably externalizing a sense of forces and events from an interior recognition of things that are happen-ing; probably externalizing them onto the environment and then onto analogous situations in the environment. The emergence of the poem is often unexpected, though the poet may be under durance of heavy tension—those interior forces. There's a certain undefined anxiety before the poet recognizes that two or three things come together in the mind that create an unexpected conjunction which is integrated and expressive at the same time. The poet consequently feels the release of himself into this "event."

Another reason the "event" is interesting to me is that it can be so manifold. We can talk about sand on the beach, a flock of swallows flying

From *Acts of Mind: Conversations with Contemporary Poets*, by Richard Jackson. Copyright © 1983 by The University of Alabama Press.

in so many directions and yet seeming to assume a single shape. The result of this manifold dimension is that an "event" has the capacity to criticize given mental forms, conventional thinking, any kind of narrowness, any sort of insistence on the truth of a particular point of view. The event in its power and unexpectedness is more material to be considered against the too narrow symmetry of a previous definition. What I try to do in my poems, essentially, is to resist my own obsessions and others', to dissolve those obsessions to some extent, and to replace them with a more complex, easy-going, tolerant mental scope. I appreciate the tiny event that in its many-sidedness can be so staggering as to dissolve bigger forces.

POETRY MISCELLANY: The notion of "event" might also be related to your feeling for the moment, the now. This raises the larger issue of time. In "One: Many" you talk about how you "tried to summarize / a moment's events," which becomes an enormous if not impossible task. One thing always leads to another. There is always a pressure from within the moment to expand—as in *Sphere,* where you talk about the "moment of consciousness" which is a participation with what moves past and through a moment, and this leads to radiations and expansions in subsequent sections. In section 67 you say, "the purpose of the motion of a poem is to bring the focused, / awakened mind to no-motion, to a still contemplation of the whole motion" of the poem. So the moment seems to contain both motion and rest, many and one. Hegel describes this coalescence as one between the action of a whirl and the consciousness of a repose. The moment sometimes becomes for you like a peak of a triangle or mountain with time spreading down its sides as in *Sphere* 47–48. The event of the moment is a "riding horseback between / the obscure beginning and the unformulated conclusion." The poet seems often, as Heidegger says, in this state of "betweenness."

A. R. AMMONS: An event can only occur in time. If you have certain subconscious or subterranean forces or energies, they, after their coalescence or occurrence as an event, become recognizable and knowable as forces. My poem, "Clarity," which begins, "After the event the rockslide / realized," is about this. So, though I don't have a theory of time, I would think about time as the procedural necessity of an event.

The most interesting thing about a poem is that the motion occurs through time to a still point, from the verbal to the nonverbal level. The most interesting motion to me is the coincidental, peripheral event, the simple, minute particular that leads to something inevitable; that is, you see some peripheral connection leading to something more central, becoming more binding until the poem completes itself in an inevitable place. This whole motion suggests something as demanding in its rigor as a traditional form. So, from my own point of view, I like to be between the local periphery where no fact is excluded and some point where certain timings can begin a train of necessity toward a realization of itself. This is the way that I have tried lately to alert the deeper symmetries of the self. I try to recognize certain events on the surface mind, or the periphery so to speak, of our perception. Then the process of making connections can begin that reveals what Coleridge calls an undercurrent of feeling which is not at all coincidental, but is staged within us permanently in its quality.

POETRY MISCELLANY: In "Hibernaculum," you describe a possible hell as "the meaninglessness of stringing out / events in unrelated, undirected sequences." I think you have been suggesting that when we move from random series to the orderly sequence of the poem a certain stillness emerges. In the context of this movement, and of the narrative nature of the poems, I think of Tzevtan Todorov's definition of narrative as something that "puts time into motion and suspends it."

A. R. AMMONS: Yes, I think we use the word "narrative" in too limited a way. That is, any qualitative progression is also a narrative. I like to have the narrative of the surface, the actions and events that are described, but in reading the poem one should realize that a deeper narrative has taken place. That narrative is made up of the shifts in one's feelings and sensibilities about things.

However, a poem doesn't exist only in motion, in time. It seems to me that when you know the poem intimately you know it radially and complete. You have a nonlinear perception of the whole thing. If you have a single dancer on the stage, she exists in one body and does one thing at a time as she dances across that stage. At the end you recognize that certain figures have been repeated, that there has been a certain narrative. Something has occurred that is more than any single event and which memory recalls. The same is true of the poem. Once you know the poem intimately, why then you come to a still contemplation of its component parts, and of its vacant center perhaps. At that point, it seems to me you can deepen your awareness of things yourself *without* the help of the poet. He has brought you to this still point, and now you have your own resources. It is here that words can become the cure of words, motion the cure of motion. That is to say, when the verbal construct creates a place that is nonverbal, then the very verbal construct has been criticized by itself. This is appropriate in that it heals the division in ourselves between thing and word.

POETRY MISCELLANY: This relation between language and things, the verbal and the nonverbal, is very complex. Language, you say in

"Essay on Poetics," and other places, can reduce the world. I think of Wordsworth's "Note" to "The Thorn" where he talks about the proximity of words and things. In "I'm Unwilling," you say, "things / keep nudging me / to siddle with / them into / words."

A. R. AMMONS. At some point in our development words and things were indistinguishable, and words had power over things. That is no longer, I think, feasible, except as a primitive impulse or desire.

Perhaps it is not only a dichotomy between words and things, but also between us and ourselves. There are certain resources in ourselves that are nonverbal, and only at a certain level, as we said before, do they start to become represented as words: I think that some of this internal energy remains latent and we want to believe in a validity that the sound system of the poem might have.

Though words and things exist in different realms, the motion of the poem imitates the motion of reality, mirrors the motion of things. Perhaps that is as close as we can get to a correspondence between this system of language we have invented and use and the system of reality that is so profound.

POETRY MISCELLANY: You talked a few minutes ago about the function of the poet diminishing as one comes to know the poem. What, exactly, is the function of the poet? What are his responsibilities?

A. R. AMMONS: That is something that has troubled me all my life. My poems have not dealt directly with definable issues of my time. Only recently have I begun to realize how I operate. I feel myself to be so peripheral that I don't address groups but look for the single person in his room. He's the person I try to mean something to. I don't address an already defined stratum of society or a particular cause. Poetry has never seemed to me to be the best instrument for communication of a practical kind. In this respect, I think of the hermit lark, a shy bird with an unlocatable, indescribable sound. I identify with that in myself and in the poets I read, too. There is a one-to-one correspondence, a relationship between poet and reader whose undercurrent may radiate outward to affect the way other individuals perceive things.

POETRY MISCELLANY: One interesting aspect of this is the notion of the "Anthology." You say in section 16 of *Sphere* that "the anthology is the moving, changing definition of the / imaginative life of the people, the repository and source." What, specifically, makes a poem part of this anthology, of what Foucault calls the "archive"?

A. R. AMMONS: I think a poem must be entertaining, and it seems to me that the dialectic of one and many that we have been discussing in several ways is likely to produce this entertainment. That is, it is likely to produce the tissue, the weaving in a poem sufficiently complex so that the thinking mind can dwell upon it and find it enjoyable as an artifact that mirrors the mind and its world. I don't think a poem that is propaganda or speaks to a specific issue is capable of entertaining the many-sidedness of one's assent to and exception from realities. I think we want a poem sufficiently complex so that we are willing to invest in it a dwelling of our time because it corrects our narrowness, our smallness. I think that the people gradually approve of those poems that have this truth or openness toward things and will make these poems part of their imaginative reality.

POETRY MISCELLANY: I think you have struck the balance between the philosophical or unified statement and the multisided, unordered periphery very carefully in your poems. It is that balance between the repose and the whirl, stillness and motion, too. What has always struck me about your work is that there is always a potentially dichotomous vision that threatens to burst apart the world the poems operate in, but that the poems nevertheless achieve the "wholeness" you hold so valuable.

A. R. AMMONS: You erase all possibility of wholeness if you eliminate one side of the dichotomy. When you have an enlargement of vision, it is to provide a landscape in which to see the particular, the differences among things and not just their sameness, their unity.

POETRY MISCELLANY: This notion of difference is an important one for you. Your description of it in "The Account" as an almost imperceptible trace is close to how Derrida describes it: "Something finer / than perception, a difference / so opposite to ground it will / have no mass, indifferent to mass." And in "The Flaw" it is a difference from sameness that defines a whole world. Of course, that is only half the problem—the other half is how differences are related, or as you say in "Essay on Poetics," a "preservation of / distinction in a seeming oneness." In *Sphere*, section 117, you say, "the poem insists on / differences, on every fragment of difference till the fragments / cease to be fragmentary and wash together in a high flotation / interpenetrating much like the possibility of the world." The fragments, together but distinct, are to form, to "declare a common reality past declaration." So the problem is that "something / thin & high / cuts through whatever is / and makes no difference of difference." Could you talk about the play between difference and indifference, about the "reality past declaration" that emerges from this play?

A. R. AMMONS: This has been a concern of mine since the 1950s when I used it in conjunction with a sense of risk and possibility. Possibility occupies the same world for me as event and coincidence. That is, it is because of chance that one doesn't have to conform to given structures—possibility is open. In this context, I think of difference as an enrichment. In the poem, "Possibility Along a Line of Difference," there is a flat, western terrain. A river goes through the terrain, but from your perspective you can't see it, can't see the difference ahead. The invisible difference creates a terrifying enrichment because there is no longer simply the flatness or evenness of the ground but a dramatic change. All these other actions have become possible, terrifying and beautiful, because of that gully washing through the terrain. The difference then would be to retreat from the high unities and amassings into the minute particular, the single event, the perceivable correction that criticizes the unifying tendency of sameness.

POETRY MISCELLANY: I think of this poem, like your others, as being in a conversational mood. A poet like Ignatow has an interrogative mood, Pack a suppositional mood. There is a sense of continual dialogue with readers, listeners, the self, even the world (whereas in some poems you have a conversation with things in the world—a feather, a mountain). It is a dialogue mode, I suppose, a mode of exchange, dialectic. Heidegger recounts a favorite phrase, from Rilke, I think: "Since we have been a conversation."

A. R. AMMONS: I think that this is a variation of the "one:many" notion. That is to say, the dialogue would be between the ambivalences of the one:many situation and represented by a dialectics of two voices: Voice, then, in its largest possibility, would tend toward the summary, and tone and variety of effect would tend toward the periphery, toward difference. Voice would then be the bridge between these two sets of possibilities. I am bothered by certain courses where students are taught to concentrate on voice and tone in a narrow sense: what happens is that the poet begins to identify in himself something he calls voice but which is really becoming only a mannerism. But voice philosophically, as we mean it here, is a resolved action of many voices, a large sameness in the Coleridgean sense of a unifying sameness in difference.

As far as the actual conversations with things in the poems go, obviously I didn't believe that mountains talk. But I did believe that when you stand in front of a mountain, you have a certain impression of majesty; what you have in the poems, then, is what majesty or height might say. In those poems, I'm often the little figure who comes up to ask what it is all about.

POETRY MISCELLANY: Isn't that dialogue mode related to your use of colons and more recently to the parallel columns in *Snow Poems*? I mean, these techniques certainly allow the poem to have motion in time, to be open-ended, to chart out certain directions, but they also provide the stillness you described earlier, doubling back, a return, an exchange or dialogue, a reversibility.

A. R. AMMONS: Yes, I think they are related. The double columns in *Snow Poems* have unnerved some people, I suppose. They are intended to be playful; they can be read one at a time, but with an awareness of the other column, the other perspective. Once the center of a poem is found and established in the way we talked about earlier, then the poem is both closed and open, and it will have a dialectical form.

POETRY MISCELLANY: This notion of vacancy has become increasingly important recently, though its roots go far back. In "Hibernaculum," you talk about two kinds of "nothing"—one beyond, outside, and the other at the center, inside. In *Snow Poems* you talk about a state where all will be "an illustration of, allegory of, nothing." For you, it seems a state that enables continual beginning. It is related to the absence at the center of things in *Snow Poems*, "an empty-centered space." A basic absence is that of the self as in "The Hieroglyphic Gathered"—

> the central self unattended,
> unworn while the untouchable
> other, far and away, calls forth
> the bark, the slaver, the slobber,
> scenting: to pull up stakes!

Could you elaborate on this nothing, absence, the silent self as opposed to the verbal other?

A. R. AMMONS: It seems to me that in both amassing and excluding you come to nothing. I wrote about this aspect in "The Arc Inside and Out." If you amass all your perceptions, the sum becomes undeliverable as a verbal construct. You have to break things down. But when you begin to break things down, you eventually come to an equally nonverbal inside, an equal nothingness. It seems to me, then, that language is an area of knowledge of contact with things; beyond that is the nonverbal, and within that is the nonverbal. That frightens some people, perhaps because silence is associated with death. But life can also be silent, and as we were saying earlier, it seems to me that the cure for words and the divisions of words resides in both that amassing of exteriors and that breaking down toward the unconscious interior. That seems to be a sort of healing, a place to begin anew. It is really the source of the erotic in poetry—some things move at a level without definition before they move into definition, are refreshing, inform our lives, and give us energy.

HUGH LUKE

Gestures of Shape, Motions of Form

In a loose world though
    something can be started—
a root touch water,
    a tip break sand—

Mounds from that can rise
    on held mounds,
a gesture of building, keeping,
    a trapping
into shape.

—A. R. AMMONS, "Dunes"

As a student and teacher of litera-
ture, my central interest since beginning graduate studies almost twenty
years ago has been with the English Romantic poets. The poems of
William Blake and Percy Bysshe Shelley and John Keats and William
Wordsworth have in enduring ways given shape to my understanding of
human experience, have served for me (if I may use that phrase of
Matthew Arnold's, so often wrongly understood) as a criticism of life.
Reading poems by Shelley, say, or Blake, I have never had the sense that
they were foreign, or dated, or used up; if an occasional allusion or turn of
phrase did from time to time briefly stir an awareness that they were one
ocean and almost two centuries distant, that fact seemed merely to enlarge
their vitality: they still seemed more alive than Allan Tate, or Yvor

From *Pebble* 18, 19, 20. Copyright © 1979 by Greg Kuzma.

Winters; more native than Ezra Pound or T. S. Eliot (reading *The Cantos* or *The Wasteland* has always made me feel that I was travelling in foreign lands, talking with an accent, and having trouble breathing).

For the past three years, however—or perhaps almost four years, now—much of the time which I have spent reading and thinking about literature has been spent with poems by contemporary American poets. I began this reading in preparation for an upper-level course which I had somewhat presumptuously offered to give (I did, after all, own a couple of anthologies, had from time to time looked through the little magazines, and had off and on for a dozen years read manuscript submissions for *Prairie Schooner*); I have continued because I found, and do find, unexpected riches there.

Those riches are, I think, extraordinary. I can find little doubt in my mind that the poetry of our own time, our own country in its present moment, may be compared without disadvantage to that of any other age or any other culture. It will hold its own. (I do not, of course, wish to be misunderstood: there can also be little doubt that most of the verse written today, including much that has been widely praised, is superficial, sloppy, and ephemeral, and will last little longer than tomorrow morning's *Lincoln Star:* not long enough, that is, to sustain a second cup of coffee, and perhaps not all of a first. And I believe that William Blake wrote truly when he said that all true poets are finally equal, and do not stand in competition.)

Any attempt to explore in a full way the evidence for this statement would lead inevitably to a manuscript of book length, or longer. To discuss even briefly the work of those true poets now living and writing in America, now in the fullness of their power and with a visible magnitude of accomplishment already on the record, would go well beyond the limits of a single essay. It would be easy to list a score or more of such poets ranging in age from the early thirties to the roomy neighborhood of fifty, but such lists (I am reminded) are invidious, and I shall forbear. I should like, rather, to concentrate in these pages on just one of those poets: a poet whose work I have in recent months found myself returning to with increasing frequency, and whose poems have continued to grow and to illuminate themselves (and the world I live in) in a remarkable way.

II

A. R. Ammons was born in North Carolina in 1926, and is now Professor of English at Cornell University, where he has been since 1964. Before that time, he worked for a dozen years for a firm which manufactured biological glass; he was executive vice-president of that firm when Cornell offered him an instructorship. His first volume of poems, *Ommateum* ("compound eye"), was published in 1955, his second in 1964, his eleventh in October of 1975. The present total of eleven volumes includes a *Selected Poems* (1968) and a *Collected Poems: 1951–1971* (1972). It also includes two book-length poems: *Tape for the Turn of the Year* (1965: "a long, thin poem," Ammons described it; originally typed on a roll of adding-machine tape, it is long—two hundred and five pages—but even though its lines are short the poem is far from thin; it should have been included in the *Collected Poems*, but wasn't); and *Sphere: The Form of a Motion* (1974).

The *Collected Poems* won the National Book Award for 1973; *Sphere: The Form of a Motion* won the Bollingen Prize for 1975. Within the recent past Ammons has received major reviews in such journals as *The Yale Review, Poetry, The Southern Review,* and *Hudson Review.* An entire issue of *Diacritics* was recently devoted to Ammons and his poems. He has also occupied pages in *People* and *Time* and (perhaps therefore) has been attacked in *Commentary.* All of this seems to me clearly to suggest that Ammons's poetry has begun to assume a place in what he himself, in *Sphere,* has described as "the anthology": that organic body of "good sayings . . . , images, poems, stories," which is "the moving, changing definition of the imaginative life of the people, the repository and source, genetic."

My own first acquaintance with this poet began when I saw his name in an anthology—Mark Strand's *Contemporary American Poets,* perhaps, or it may well have been the more recent *Norton Anthology of Modern Poetry*—when I read his name over a poem called "Corsons Inlet." After long months, I still recall the experience of reading the poem through for the first time: "I went for a walk over the dunes again this morning," it begins; "rounded naked headland" (the recurring "naked pool" which invests one of those high lyric areas of Wordsworth's *Prelude* came to mind, unbidden) "I allow myself eddies of meaning . . . organizations of grass . . . white sandy paths of remembrance in the overall wandering of mirroring mind. . . ."

With a kind of leisurely intensity, the lines—not sharp lines, neither here in the verse nor, as Ammons insistently tells us, here in nature—moved on, and grew, and have for me continued to grow:

> so I am willing to go along, to accept
> the becoming
> thought, to stake off no beginnings or ends, establish
> no walls. . . .

As he walks on, the poet sees (and the poem contains) a landscape filled with events ("saliences," Ammons would probably call them) of greed, of terror, of death, of chaos: the "black shoals of mussels exposed to the risk / of air / and, earlier, of sun"; the "young mottled gull" which "stood free of the shoals / and ate / to vomiting"; that other gull, "squawking possession," which "cracked a crab, / picked out the entrails; swallowed the soft-shelled legs"; the "small white blacklegged egret," which, no matter how beautiful, "quietly stalks and spears / the shallows, darts to shore / to stab—what? I couldn't / see against the black mudflats—a frighted / fiddler crab?"

Chaos, particularly, is the terror:

> pulsations of order
> in the bellies of minnows: orders swallowed,
> broken down, transferred through membranes
> to strengthen larger orders: but in the large view, no
> lines or changeless shapes: the working in and out, together
> and against, of millions of events: this
> so that I make
> no form of
> formlessness. . . .

And rigidity, closing in, is the corresponding temptation, resisted: resisted it may be with a deep reluctance, but once resisted leading on to that remarkable sense of a visionary freedom, a radical if bounded openness, with which the poem concludes:

> I see narrow orders, limited tightness, but will
> not run to that easy victory:
> still around the looser, wider forces work:
> I will try
> to fasten into order enlarging grasps of disorder, widening
> scope, but enjoying the freedom that
> Scope eludes my grasp, that there is no finality of vision,
> that I have perceived nothing completely,
> that tomorrow a new walk is a new walk.

After reading through—walking through—"Corsons Inlet," there was little choice: next day, I wrote W. W. Norton and Company to order the *Collected Poems* of A. R. Ammons.

III

> Change the glacier's loneliness and the ice melts,
> streams going off into sundry identity systems,
> bog floats, lakes, clouds, seas, drinking water:

flux heightens us into knots of staid tension:
we live and go about containing various swirls:
too much swirling improves loneliness poorly:

we take advantage of separateness to unite sensible
differences, the tube in the fineness of its coupling
nearly a merging: well, nothing's perfect: fall

away, of course—we have other things to do alone,
go to the bathroom, brush our teeth, reel:
how can we give ourselves away if we're not separate

enough to be received: and, given away, we know
no desire but the other's desire: and given each
to each, we're both both, indistinguishably, sort of.
                (A. R. Ammons, "Late Romantic")

To read in the poems of A. R. Ammons is to see at once that he is well acquainted with that "anthology" of world literature which, as he observes in *Sphere*, is "the generations and becomings of our minds." I myself hear most frequently in his poems echoes, allusions, half-quotes, reverberations of the great English Romantic poets (Lord Byron especially, I think, would have enjoyed "Late Romantic," and perhaps even have heard himself echoed in it, but all the Romantics would have seen clearly what Ammons was there about); and of such American predecessors as Emerson, Stevens, Frost, and Williams. Other readers, different readers with different angles of movement to his work, doubtless find other poets, other traditions, other modes of perception in those complicated lines which converge to Ammons's poems. But I have no desire in these pages to collect allusions, nor to tally up "sources" or "influences": the point I wish to make, in passing, is that Ammons is very much aware of the long heritage of writings from past decades and past centuries, and that he explicitly sees himself and his work as a part of "the whole body of the anthology."

He has read all the books, that is to say; he knows what has come before him; and he continues to pose those large, returning questions which seem somehow to be embedded within the human situation: such questions as the nature and conditions of reality, of how to achieve some deep sense of personal identity, of how to live with dignity and meaning and even sometimes with joy in a universe which seems always ready to fade toward chaos, or past. And, like the long line of poets and prophets before him, he continues the search for a language answerable to the large task.

The questions are large, and the language therefore sometimes difficult; complex perceptions lead on to complex metaphors and stretch-ings of the ordinary boundaries of vocabulary and sentence structure. For that reason, it strikes me that it may be useful at this point to attempt some generalizations about some themes, some perceptions, some move-ments which help to shape the body of Ammons's poetry.

At the live and moving center of his poems, there lies one large and shaping theme: a theme which recurs, shifts, moves from form to form and from metaphor to metaphor. In first one language then another, he tells us that between ocean and hard ground, between cynicism and fanaticism, between old tradition and future shock, between blinding dark and blinding radiance, there is room—lots of room, a bounded infinity of room—for life, for movement, for love, for joy.

Room, most centrally, for a real and living present: a made form of the present, created by incorporating both past and future into an ex-tended body of the present moment. That dimensionless present of the solipsist, "this point in time," must enlarge, gain shape and scope and dimension: become a sphere, with space.

The earliest metaphor, and a recurring one, which Ammons uses to embody this theme is that of the dunes of sand at ocean's shore. (Ammons does not see—he insists on not seeing—the universe in a dune of sand; in a way which at least at the peripheries resembles Robert Frost's superb little poem "Sand Dunes," he does see infinitely variable possibili-ties in the small events and movements of common human experience.) Between the ocean and the hard ground, he tells us in "Dunes," there is the windy sand: "not an easy way," as he observes, "to go about finding / a place to stay": it has only the advantage of being possible. The hard ground won't take the seed, the ocean will merely swallow it.

His theme is large, inclusive, protean: any prose attempt at its statement inevitably distorts. Any single occurrence of the theme even in his poems perhaps distorts it; quite certainly provides only an entry into his central understanding of it; that fact is doubtless one reason that he returns to it, almost obsessively, over and over again. But prose too may try again, may try to surround that understanding, to lead toward it, fully accepting the impossibility of capturing it. Try this approach: imagine a pole, a polar concept, one end pure white, the other end pure black. Both ends will blind: only toward the middle are there possibilities of vision, or color: the "sober colouring" of Wordsworth's great Intimations Ode, per-haps; or perhaps that many-coloured dome of life which Shelley sees as staining the white radiance of eternity. Or: to stay alive (that recurring theme of contemporary poetry in America), one must be skeptical without being cynical, visionary without becoming Eric Hoffer's "true believer";

must inhabit the plains and hills between mire and mountaintop. Both mire and the mountaintop, to be sure, may be visited, explored; but one may not stay, and stay alive.

Or perhaps we may steal a metaphor from those students of linguistic structure who teach us that meaning, all meaning, is outgrowth from partial predictability. Given a linguistic structure, with a blank: for the structure to predict with certainty what will fill the blank is to allow no possibility for a gain of meaning. But if the blank filler is totally unpredictable, the structure is meaningless. (For example: "The . . . . is on the table." The reader can partially predict, within limits imposed by the linguistic structure of the sentence, the possibilities of what will fill the blank—"Ma tante," for example, will not fit—but the reader cannot predict with certainty how the blank will indeed be filled. Therefore when I say "The *Collected Poems of A. R. Ammons* is on the table," the reader gains an increment of meaning.) In his poem called "Identity," Ammons uses the spider web, which "identifies a species," as metaphor:

> if the web were perfectly pre-set
>   the spider could
> never find
> a perfect place to set it in: and
>
>   if the web were
> perfectly adaptable,
> if freedom and possibility were without limit,
>   the web would
> lose its special identity. . . .

All meaning is grey. All life is color. All growth is on the shifting dunes of time and space, between the unknown past and the forgotten future, between chaos and chaos.

For still another approach: assume peripheries at both edges of the vital center, the lively present; have the peripheries move, and fade, and surge. Then move from pole to sphere, from polar concept to spherical concept. The pole moves, as it must; it spins round its midriff. Both ends appear to shine; in the dark it makes full circle then full sphere (as Ammons says, in *Sphere*, "a single dot of light, travelling, will memorize the sphere"). The ends, the peripheries, become light; the center then grows dark, underground, unconscious: the light edges extensive, the dark center intensive. The peripheries of light lead one on, with compelling magnetism, in search of radiance, of total understanding, of that immortality which comes like very death ("he perished, / swilling purity," reads the conclusion of "Separations," in Ammons's most recent volume). Or sometimes one retreats, to deep and dark center of self, to that deepness of sleep, that fullness of isolation, which carries the odor of final unity and absoluteness of perfection.

Between peripheries, fade and surge as they will, elude as they finally must, there is life and meaning and color and presence. Beyond the peripheries lies chaos and death and no human understanding.

A shaping force in Ammons's central theme, in his ideas of order at Corsons Inlet and thereabouts, is the pervasiveness of motion. All measures of time are motion: sundials, heavenly bodies of all varieties, all clocks and watches—wound-spring, fifty- or sixty-cycle electric currents, tuning fork, vibrating crystals of quartz, carbon-14. "This point in time" (that tag phrase of Watergate) is mathematical abstraction with no experiential reality, like the spectre of Blake's Urizen, blindly cogitating on selfhood. Words themselves have meaning only in the moving flow of mindful process: pin a word on a wall to stare at, it wriggles and dies; pin a spectral point of time on the dark bones inside the skull and life loses all space.

"So I said I am Ezra," reads the first line, and the title, of the first poem in the *Collected Poems*; the line is thrice repeated, and the poem concludes:

> I am Ezra
> As a word too much repeated
> falls out of being
> so I Ezra went out into the night
> like a drift of sand
> and splashed among the windy oats
> that clutch the dunes
> of unremembered seas

Words isolated from flow, stopped by repetition or too much staring, lose all sense. No electronic instrument of analysis, most highly refined, can pinpoint and capture that meaningful difference of human sound which is the phoneme, that smallest aural unit of human sense, flowing. The gestalt of human perception, integrating the atomistic into shaped contour of sound, is necessary for meaning.

Meaning of word, or meaning of self, Ammons tells us: human identity must ultimately be participial, must involve search and flow and movement: "to be," he writes, "you have to stop not-being and break off from *is* to *flowing*." If "present only toucheth thee," like Burns's terror-stricken fieldmouse, with neither backward cast of eye nor forward guess of fear or hope, then present doth not touch thee either, then life does not flow, does not be; life is a moving experience, and must be. All search for identity, all questings for *who am I* (as Oedipus and Sophocles learned long centuries past) must end in destruction; the only final solution is the final solution, the universal solvent, entropy fulfilled. Until that end, or some other—solitary death or universal cataclysm (however we go, we will all go together, and all all alone)—the present is infinite, or can be; and life can be *open*, as Ammons says in the poem with that word standing as title:

> Exuberance: joy to the last
> pained loss
>   and hunger of air:
> life open, not decided on,
> though decided in death:
>
> the sun will burst: death
> is certain: the future limited
>   nevertheless is
> limitless. . . .

This all being so, and integral to the condition of life, the poem suggests, one must make the most of it, and "lust forward, rushing."

IV

On my desk before me are Ammons's *Collected Poems*, together with the three volumes not therein collected: *Tape for the Turn of the Year, Sphere: the Form of a Motion,* and *Diversifications*. Together, they come to almost eight hundred pages. Leafing through those pages, in some moods, one sometimes wishes to find things not there to be found. There are few people in these pages, and little explicit concern with the crevices and outcroppings of the human comedy. Those great social, moral, and political issues and events of our own time are rarely present save by implication, deep under the surface. Despite the frequent close descriptions of external nature, the strong sense of place which may be found in a David Wagoner or a James Dickey or a Gary Snyder is not here; neither are the compelling explorations of the individual psyche which are to be found in a Denise Levertov or a W. D. Snodgrass. The characteristic poem of Ammons gives us man exploring the universe of human possibility, testing human potential against the peripheries; when his poem is flawed, at the edges or at the center, the characteristic flaw is an excess of abstraction, much as the characteristic flaw of a Wordsworth is an excess of unassimilated detail. Ammons is explicitly aware of that charge of "abstraction"; he both reacts to it and jokes about it in *Sphere*, and it doubtless is at least a partial stimulus for "He Held Radical Light," perhaps the most nearly "confessional" poem in his body of work:

> . . . he
> had trouble keeping
> his feet on the ground, was
> terrified by that
> and liked himself, and others, mostly
> under roofs:
> nevertheless, when the
> light churned and changed
>
> his head to music, nothing could keep him
> off the mountains, his
> head back, mouth working,
> wrestling to say, to cut loose
> from the high, unimaginable hook:
> released, hidden from stars, he ate,
> burped, said he was like any one
> of us: demanded he
> was like any one of us.

But we read our poets for what they offer us, not for what lies by the way, outside the angle of focus; and the achieved vision contained in those eight hundred pages is a large one. Every page, I think, repays its reading, and almost every page even its rereading; if his ear on occasion fails him, or nearly so, his grace and ease of seeing do not, and a genial sense of humor always lurks near by, on or under the surface. His "minor poems" (if I may use that awkward and misleading phrase) are almost always of value in and of themselves; they also serve to illuminate the "major" poems, by enlarging the contextual center of his body of work.

Trying to decide which poems to examine in the remaining pages of this essay, I turned to the volumes on my desk and began to check off titles in the tables of contents, titles of poems which simply could not be omitted. When I reached thirty checkmarks long before I had reached the end of the table of contents of the Collected Poems, I began to understand the kind of frustration which all conscientious makers of anthologies must feel (and hereby promise to stop swearing at them in class, at least for the remainder of the semester). What follows, then, must be taken as the expression of a kind of personal choice, shaped by my own angle of movement toward the poems in these volumes, limited by time and space and peripheries of enlightenment and ignorance, fuzzy at the edges.

Immediately following "Corsons Inlet" in the Collected Poems (which is arranged in chronological order of composition) is the poem entitled "Saliences." These two poems are closely related by theme, by metaphor, by time and flow of mind; "Saliences" may be read both as an extension of "Corsons Inlet" and as parallel to it in motion. The language and the flow of thought in "Saliences" is perhaps somewhat more abstracted (or perhaps the more accurate word, here, is "internalized"): the workings of its imagery bring to mind Shelley's statement in the Preface to *Prometheus Unbound* that his imagery "will be found, in many instances, to have been drawn from the operations of the human mind, or from those external actions by which they are expressed." Or, to oversimplify their relationship a bit, in "Corsons Inlet" the dunes of sand and their context serve as metaphors for the operations of human thought; in "Saliences" the operations of human thought serve as metaphors for the workings of the natural world.

"Consistencies rise," the poem begins, stating the problem forthrightly,

> and ride
> the mind down
> hard routes
> walled
> with no outlet. . . .

In order to counteract that impulse toward rigidity, toward all which is closed up, hardened, blinded to possibilities of new and different, Ammons offers a few lines later "this dune fest"—by which phrase, one surmises, we are intended to understand the experience of "Corsons Inlet" itself, both as a poem and, literally, as the walk described in the poem. And thus we are invited to incorporate the earlier poem into the latter, joining the internal and the external into a wholeness of understanding:

> and so
> to open a variable geography,
> proliferate
> possibility, here
> is this dune fest
> releasing
> mind feeding out,
> gathering clusters,
> fields of order in disorder. . . .

Within the space—within the experience—of these dunes of Corsons Inlet, opposing forces of rigidity and of chaos can meet—

> straight line
> and air-hard thought

(what William Blake might well have called "petrific chaos")

>   can meet
>   unarranged disorder

—and destroy each other, momentarily; and from that destruction, that dissolution—that clash of movement—can grow a spacious and moving reality, a "present time" with "multivariable scope," a felt reality like that of the dunes themselves, with no two moments ever precisely the same but having a variably predictable direction and position and sound and shape, holding meaning by never grasping it tightly.

If the patterns of order are always shifting, they are still still patterns (in "Hibernaculum," Ammons writes: "A cud's a locus in time, a staying change, moving / but holding through motions timeless relations, / as of center to periphery, core-thought to consideration"), and therefore may be held lightly in the palm of the still mind, moving in concert. The final lines of "Saliences" need no comment save that the doubling of the word "single" is not to be read as a misprint: they speak directly, and must be quoted:

>   where not a single single thing endures,
>   the overall reassures,
>   deaths and flights,
>   shifts and sudden assaults claiming
>   limited orders,
>   the separate particles:
>   earth brings to grief
>   much in an hour that sang, leaped, swirled,
>   yet keeps a round
>   quiet turning,
>   beyond loss or gain,
>   beyond concern for the separate reach.

A third poem which groups itself with "Corsons Inlet" and "Saliences" is "Expressions of Sea Level," the title poem of Ammons's second volume of poems as "Corsons Inlet" is the title poem of his fourth. ("Saliences" appears in *Northfield Poems*, his fifth volume: the date of composition of his poems appears to have little relationship to which volume they were published in; one may infer from the ordering of the *Collected Poems* that "Expressions of Sea Level" is earlier but not much earlier than the other two poems.) The title is to be taken literally, or nearly so: the subject is language, and therefore conversation, and communication, and elastic ideas of shifting order.

Even though the word itself does not appear in this poem, the dunes of "Corsons Inlet" and "Saliences" here too have a commanding presence, a central import: the "sand turbulence changed, / new sand left smooth" is precisely the "expression" of sea level, of ocean's edge. The sounds of the sea, the moans of the deep, the ocean's roar and splash of spray, are all of them beyond the peripheries of coherent sound:

> it is a dream the sea makes,
>
> an inner problem, a self-deep
> dark and private anguish
>   revealed in small,
> by hints, to
> keen watchers on the shore. . . .

As for the "sky sealed unbroken to sea," as for those rocks lying on the beach,

> it is hard to name
> the changeless:
> speech without words,
>   silence renders it. . . .

Only in between, only in the reverberating clash of contraries,

> only with the staid land
> is the level conversation really held:
> only in the meeting of rock and
>   sea is
> hard relevance shattered into light. . . .

The staid land, that sandy and turbulent level space between ocean and rock, joining the two but different from either,

> that is the
> expression of sea level.
> the talk of giants,
> of ocean, moon, sun, of everything,
> spoken in a dampened grain of sand.

As that other deep skeptic Shelley has his Demogorgon say, "a voice / Is wanting, the deep truth is imageless": gods and oceans don't talk. Speech, and therefore meaning, is only human.

Taken together, these three poems, totaling some three hundred and fifty lines (about ten pages of the *Collected Poems*), serve well, I think, to shape the outlines, to delineate the peripheries, of Ammons's central perception of the world we live in. I might easily enough have selected from the volumes of his work other poems, different poems which also serve this essential task, but I like these better; and I learned long ago—specifically in trying to decide how best to begin a presentation of William Blake's poems to classes of advanced students who knew a great deal about poetry but who knew Blake's poems not at all—that it appeared to make little difference where the entry was made into the body of work by any true poet: what was essential, it seemed finally clear, was to make the entry, and yield to the spiral of movement demanded, and repaid, by the poems.

There are also many other poems by Ammons which do not so much present the large perception as take their places within it: expanding it sometimes, and working at its edges; but always, I think, both gaining from the large context of the entire body of published work and also, in some not clearly explicable way, containing the whole body.

Such a brief lyric as "Winter Scene," for example—short, hard, imaginative, finally transfixed to joy—would doubtless stand well, even superbly, alone:

> There is now not a single
> leaf on the cherry tree:
>
> except when the jay
> plummets in, lights, and,
>
> in pure clarity, squalls:
> then every branch
>
> quivers and
> breaks out in blue leaves.

But when these lines are read in the context of the other poems, when the extensions and precisions of language in those poems are here incorporated, the lines connect up, and move to spiral.

The same comment might well be made, I think, for "Facing," a late poem, and one of Ammons's rare love poems:

> I take your hand:
> I touch your
> hair, as if
>
> you were going away
> to be a long time
> away, as
>
> you must someday go
> forever away:
> lust burns out high
>
> into light: I walk
> away and back: I
> touch your hair.

The achieved simplicity of these lines, these words, which makes the poem sound almost as if it were a late addition to the *Greek Anthology*, is surely grounded in that complex perception of human experience which Ammons has presented in such other poems as "Corsons Inlet" and "Saliences," and explored most fully in "Sphere"; the reader who knows those poems can see them lying here, just under the surface.

Or, for another example: that delicately elegiac poem called "Discoverer" (one imagines it—though Ammons may have had something quite different in mind—as being addressed to someone like Theodore Roethke, perhaps, off on one of his periodic voyages to the interior depths). "If you must leave the shores of mind," it begins,

> scramble down the walls
> of dome-locked underwater caves
> into the breathless, held
> clarity of dark, where no waves break,
> a grainy, colloidal grist
> and quiet, carry a light. . . .

In order to survive, the poem instructs, take something hard, to hold on to; take a line to lead the way back: "the words of / the golden rule," perhaps, or "Kepler's equal areas in / equal times," or "Baudelaire's *L'Albatros*." And, to stay alive, take nourishment: "feed the / night of your seeking with clusters / of ancient light." The poem concludes with the same precarious balance of yearning and admonishment, the same delicate precision of tone, with which it began:

> if to gather darkness
> into light, evil into good,
> you must leave the shores of mind,
> remember us, return and rediscover us.

Ammons's volumes contain still dozens of other examples of his ability to make superb short poems with deeply spiralling centers. Were I making my own personal anthology of his work, among the poems I would quite certainly include would be "Bonus" (with the beginning of new snow, "the hemlocks, muffled, / deepen to the grim / taking of a further beauty on"); and "Event" ("time is allowed / in an instant's event"); and "King of Ice" ("I'll take the cold when it comes, / but I will never believe in ice"); and "Locus":

> . . . the small oak
> down in
> the
> hollow is

> lit up (winter-burned, ice-gold
> leaves on)
> at sundown,
> ruin transfigured to
> stillest shining. . . .

Somewhere near the center of that anthology would be "This Bright Day," with its enlargement of Ammons's vocabulary of light and color and radiance:

> Earth, earth!
> day, this bright day
> again—once more
> showers of dry spruce gold. . . .
> I've had many
> days here with these stones and leaves:
> like the sky, I've taken on a color
> and am still. . . .
> none of the grief
> cuts less now than ever—only I
> have learned the
> sky, the day sky, the blue
> obliteration of radiance:
> the night sky,
> pregnant, lively,
> tumultuous, vast—the grief
> again in a higher scale
> of leaves and poppies:
> space, space—
> and a grief of things.

Also at the center, or close by, would have to be the poem entitled "The City Limits." This poem is quite certainly one of his most powerful lyrics; that it is the ultimate poem in his 1971 volume *Briefings: Poems Small and Easy* also perhaps suggests Ammons's sense of humor, for this poem, at least for me, is one of his most difficult:

> When you consider the radiance, that it does not withhold
> itself but pours its abundance without selection into every
> nook and cranny not overhung or hidden; when you consider
>
> that birds' bones make no awful noise against the light but
> lie low in the light as in a high testimony; when you consider
> the radiance, that it will look into the guiltiest
>
> swervings of the weaving heart and bear itself upon them,
> not flinching into disguise or darkening; when you consider
> the abundance of such resource as illuminates the glow-blue

bodies and gold-skeined wings of flies swarming the dumped
guts of a natural slaughter or the coil of shit and in no
way winces from its storms of generosity; when you consider

that air or vacuum, snow or shale, squid or wolf, rose or lichen,
each is accepted into as much light as it will take, then
the heart moves roomier, the man stands and looks about, the

leaf does not increase itself above the grass, and the dark
work of the deepest cells is of a tune with May bushes
and fear lit by the breadth of such calmly turns to praise.

When I read this poem through aloud in class last spring, there followed—first and only time all semester, if memory serves me right, the class being an exceptionally articulate one, and the instructor also liking to talk—there followed that rare experience of absolutely total silence. The silence hung on, hovering over the room, for a long moment; and I remember a temptation to say nothing whatsoever about the poem. I did, of course, finally resist that temptation, and broke the silence with a sentence, or something; what I said I do not at all remember, and have no wish to do so; I am certain enough that I uttered nothing of substance.

I do, however, remember learning as I listened to myself reading the poem aloud that first time that its formal appearance on the page (six stanzas of three lines each) had little discernible relationship to the rhythms of sound and of sense which were shaped by the flow of its language. (This observation holds for a number of Ammons's poems, and perhaps also for a significant portion of contemporary American poetry: whatever the poet may have had in mind when deciding to end one line and begin another, the tradition of the poetic line may by now have come so close to vanishing that the reader can make little or no meaning of it, cannot perceive pattern enough in the line as unit of poetic structure to allow for that partial predictability out of which meaning grows. What we are left with, it may be, is a kind of vestigial unevenness of right-hand margin, an unevenness—a difference—which carries with it a single message, but that a message of high importance: perhaps it says, if quietly, "This is a poem. Read with all the skill, intelligence, understanding, all the resiliency of thought and imagination and expectation, all the willing flow of mind which you are capable of bringing to the act of poetry.")

Perhaps I also noticed then, as I have since, that the rhythms (those long flowing parallel structures, carefully varied and artfully balanced) and much of the diction, though certainly not all of it, somehow reminded me of the sounds which emanated from the pulpits in those religious camp meetings my parents were always taking me to during summer vacations when I was a little boy, down south. ("Birds' bones make no awful noise against the light," for example, sounds very like the King James Bible, even though my concordance reveals nothing closer than "make a joyful noise unto the Lord.")

For that reason, perhaps, as well as for others, the title of the poem seemed at first to suggest "The Heavenly City," or "the City of God," or perhaps William Blake's Eternal City of Jerusalem. But then I found (there it was, some thirty pages later on in the *Collected Poems*) that Ammons had written a poem with the title of "Eternal City." And the city of that poem turned out to be not Jerusalem, nor the City of God, at all (or perhaps it was), but rather Hiroshima—or, at any rate, some city, past present or future, "after the explosion or cataclysm, that big / display that does its work but then fails / out with destruction." The latter poem is another (and impressive) poem of survival, giving instructions on how to stay alive: "ruinage is hardly ever a / pretty sight but it must when splendor goes / accept into itself piece by piece all the old / perfect human visions, all the old perfect human loves."

And all other references to the city, and to city life, which I have found in Ammons's writings reveal some degree of distaste: "cities, societies / are exclusive," he says in "Looking over the Acreage," and, in *Sphere*, "most of our writers live in New York City densely: there in the abstractions of squares and glassy / floors they cut up and parcel out the nothingness they think / America is: I wish they would venture the rural and / see that the woods are undisturbed by their bothering / reputations and that the brooks have taken to flowing / the way they always have and that the redwing pauses / to consider his perch before he lights in a cedar . . . ." And in the interview published in *Diacritics* (Winter, 1973) Ammons says: "I identify civilization (the city) with *definition*, as against the kind of center-and-periphery, closed-openness that I identify with nature. The city represents to me the artificial, the limited, the defined, the stalled, though obviously the city changes. I often think the city represents the confrontation of the artificial in man with the natural process and I tend to think the natural process produced everything— including the city." There can be little doubt, I think, that the pun lurking within the title of this poem is intentional, and functional: the City does, in some way, limit.

"The City Limits," I believe, stands close to the peripheries of Ammons's poetry, so close that it pushes those peripheries yet further off into the distance. The radiance emanating from that Eternal City, that transcendental city, is finally neither pure nor blinding, for the speaker of the poem stands outside the City Limits; there he may see, as in another context Ammons is able to see, in *Sphere*, "all / the greens, a company of differences, radiant, the source / sunk, the mellowing left-over light suffusing." The lines of the poem are filled with color; there, close to the source but still outside the limits of the city, the world is formed with bright blues and brilliant golds. And if even the deepest cells, there, are open to some possibility of penetration by light, there are still admissions of dark.

The peripheries of my own understanding of the poem begin at this point (perhaps before this point) to close in, to become fuzzy. But I will risk ("the unassimilable fact leads us on," as Ammons writes in "The Misfit") one further comment. "The City Limits" is a hymn of praise to the processes of life itself, and to the varieties of human possibility; it is a hymn addressed to that Promethean light which penetrates deeply toward all which is open to receive it, to that radiance which flows over the stain of human sense (to steal the phrase from William Carlos Williams), permeates it, differentiates it, gives it bright and lively color, makes it luminous. And the poem does all these things in part through its complex reverberations of the Eternal City of radiant destruction and death and therefore its deep implications of the necessary (and continuous) rebuildings, and recapturings and reorderings, and movings on, and (still) on.

V

> The brine-sea coupling
> of the original
> glutinous molecules
> preserves itself all
> the way up into our
> immediate breaths:
> we are the past
> alive in its
> truest telling:
> while we carry it,
> we're the whole
> reading out of consequence:
> history is a blank.
> (A. R. Ammons, "History")

During the time that I spent preparing myself for that course in Contemporary American Poetry, reading and rereading poems and books of poems by a wide variety of poets and then presenting what I had read and learned to a bright and lively group of students who greatly enlarged my understanding of those poets and those poems, I gradually became aware of a sensation, a feeling, off somewhere at the edges of my mind. At first I was unable to put a name to that sensation, for it was different in kind from those earlier feelings of excitement and pleasure which I had found in exploring areas of writing, spaces of imagination, new to me. As the sensation grew stronger, though, its name finally came to me: it was the feeling of coming home.

I was somewhat startled, not having known that I had been away. The vocabulary of William Blake's poems, after all, has entered the vernacular of contemporary American thought and feeling; and Keats's Nightingale, I would have been prepared to argue, still sings from time to time in my own back yard. But the name of homecoming carried with it the shock of recognition. The poets I had been reading are poets of my own generation, of my own country and my own time, of my own innocence and my own experience; and in their voices I hear my own idiom and my own patterns of intonation, transformed.

One of the most illuminating readers of Ammons (as he was earlier one of the most illuminating readers of William Blake) is Harold Bloom, the literary critic and theorist whose most recent work has been the tetralogy he began in 1973 with *The Anxiety of Influence: A Theory of Poetry*. The principal argument of this set of volumes (which may be taken as an extension—perhaps finally to the point of absurdity—of Walter Jackson Bate's earlier study *The Burden of the Past and the English Poet*) is a complex one, closely reasoned and founded on immense learning. But it may be described, over-simply and somewhat loosely, as concerning itself with that feeling of dreadful certainty, largely repressed by the poet, that everything worth saying was said, and said better, long before the "belated" poet was even struck by the possibility of saying it. In order to cope with that anxiety, Bloom argues, "strong" poets inevitably and necessarily "misread" and "misinterpret" their predecessors, "so as to clear imaginative space for themselves." The unavoidable implication of this theory, Bloom finds, is that "poetry in our tradition, when it dies"—and the question is not whether, but when—"will be self-slain, murdered by its own past strength."

Several of Ammons's more recent poems, I think, may be read at least on one level as direct and explicit responses to Bloom, written in defense of the contemporary, or "belated," poet; these would include "The Arc Inside and Out" and *Sphere*, both of which are dedicated to Bloom (as the final volume of Bloom's tetralogy, *Poetry and Repression: Revisionism from Blake to Stevens*, is dedicated to Archie Randolph Ammons). Another is "History" (given in full above), which Ammons talks about in the interview in *Diacritics* (Winter, 1973), where the poem itself was also first printed. "Whatever you see when you look out of the window at any particular moment is history—is the truest history surviving into the immediate moment," Ammons says. "The whole history of the planet earth is in your body at this moment, and so on. So that I don't have to structure it into time periods. Perhaps this is another reason why I do not have problems with the anxiety of influence, because I believe that what is here now, at this moment, is the truest version of history that we will ever know. Consequently, I have as much right to enter into it with all the innocence of immediacy as anyone else possibly ever could."

But his best response to Bloom, I should wish to argue, is the whole body of his work. There can be little doubt, I think, in the mind of anyone who reads these poems closely, that they have been shaped in important ways—even central ways—by the poems of Blake and Shelley and Pound and Wordsworth and Emerson and Whitman and Frost and Williams and no doubt dozens, even hundreds, of other poets in verse or prose. But these poems may not be taken as mere readings or misreadings or reduplications, for they are just as certainly—and just as importantly (not more, not less)—shaped by the fact that Ammons was born in a farm house four miles southwest of Whiteville, North Carolina, on February 18, 1926, and that he has a wife Phyllis and a son John, and that he has lived through the great depression and a world war and the death of god and droppings of atomic bombs and television and jet planes and My Lai and radical chic and the pill and civic turmoil and Buchenwald, and that he moved from industry to the academy and has hemlock trees in his back yard, and has lived with mountains, and has suffered and pleasured in thousands of other kinds of ways large and small and different from the ways and events of Stevens and Frost and Shelley and Blake and Milton.

Like the great poets who came before him—modern American, English Romantic, or Classical Greek—Ammons understands that if the large questions are old unto agelessness the answers are never quite the same—that (to modify his own lines from "Saliences") if the overall endures, the new and different reassures. And that is why he must continue the search for a language answerable to the large task: for a new language, different at the edges, which may be answerable to our own community of fact and of experience, to our own changing perceptions, our own permutations' of that tenuous network of human possibility and human desire.

The Burden of the Past—past centuries, and past months and days and years—is a real burden, and actual; and the Anxiety of Influence is also real, and true, and carries with it the possibilities of devastating force.

But to see that one might be "the past / alive in its / truest telling," as Ammons suggests—to see that one might make "history . . . a blank," by incorporating a living past into an extended body of the present moment and projecting both imaginatively into the future, rushing—to see all of this is to move toward that state of mind which William Blake almost calls "organized innocence": a state of mind neither innocent of the past, nor overwhelmed or jaded by its experience; an ideal state much like that described by the contemporary British philosopher John Wisdom, who tells us that "we need to be at once like someone who has seen much and has forgotten nothing; and also like someone who sees things for the first time." To yield to that anxiety of influence, to collapse under the burden of the past, is to give up to darkness; to remain blindly ignorant of the past is to be the eternal freshman, roasted on a point in time. But to live in a world which is alive and human, which remains wisely innocent in its organization, is to act on the possibility, as Ammons suggests in his *Tape for the Turn of the Year,* that we may "make a world / we need out of the reality / that is / and is indifferent."

All of which is to say that the new poets of each new generation can newly teach us, as Ammons says in *Sphere,* that "to live in / the shifts of facts, unorganized and dark, is to know only / generation, mindless, fallen senselessly repeating," can show us that "tomorrow a new walk is a new walk," can move us toward ways of reconciling our lives to a human world filled with both risks and possibilities; can do this, even, with a single short lyric, once more, as he does in the opening poem ("Transcendence") of his newest book, *Diversifications:*

> Just because the transcendental,
> having digested all change into
> a staying, promises foreverness,
> it's still no place to go, nothing
> having survived there into life:
> and here, this lost way, these
> illusory hollyhocks and garages,
> this is no place to settle: but
> here is the grief, at least,
> constant, that things and loves
> go, and here the love that
> never comes except as permanence.

DAVID LEHMAN

Where Motion and
Shape Coincide

"Continuous present is one thing
and beginning again and again is another thing. These are both things.
And then there is using everything." Had Gertrude Stein set about to
characterize the long poems of A. R. Ammons, she could not have proved
her prescience better than with these words from "Composition as Explanation." It is as if she were listing the primary ingredients of the recipe
with which Ammons has cooked up quite a storm, tossing "everything"
into his tempestuous teapot or oversized cauldron:

> one thing poetry could be resembled to is
> soup: the high moving into clarity of quintessential
> consommé: then broth, the homogeneous cast of substance's
>
> shadow: then the falling out of diversity into specific
> identity, carrot cube, pea, rice grain: then the chunky
> predominance of beef hunk, long bean, in heavy gravy:
> ("Hibernaculum," #20)

The metaphor serves a purpose beyond its charm and humor. By Ammons'
reckoning, the humblest phenomena, closely observed, will be seen to
participate in "a united, capable poem, a united, capable mind"; the
workings of each disclose the logic of all. Poetry is the supreme hierarchy,
madame—or so Ammons would revise Wallace Stevens to read. Ammons'
project is as much prophetic as imaginative in character: he aspires to
apprehend "a unity / approach divided"; to give the sense of a turbulent

From *Parnassus* 9 (Fall/Winter 1981). Copyright © 1982 by Poetry in Review Foundation.

but harmonious whole, "homogeneous" yet thriving on "diversity" and on the "specific identity" of each component, ever in motion whether the soup is stirred or not, and blessed with the capacity for spontaneous change.

It is very much as a dizzying downpour of language that one experiences "Essay on Poetics" and "Hibernaculum" (both included in the *Selected Longer Poems*) and the yet more magnificently torrential poem for which "Hibernaculum" seems, in retrospect, to have served as a study, *Sphere: The Form of a Motion* (published separately in 1974). For these works Ammons contrived a form that would enact the motion of a spiral, twisting and coiling incessantly like a snake, and as apt to shed the skin of its defunct selves in order to begin anew. The poems' relentlessly self-renewing energy gives the effect of a continuous present, a grand pageant of simultaneous "events" (in the sense that, because their shape and motion coincide, beach dunes are "events of sand"). Above all, the long poems are monuments to inclusiveness and possibility as twin ideals. Cheerfully "not a whit manic" about Whitman's influence, Ammons is indisputably large, multitudinous, and democratic, given to the making of lists and to the use of the widest possible focus for his lens; everything from etymological investigations (*true* goes back to *tree*) to weather reports (variations on a theme of snow) to car repair receipts (quoted verbatim!) can enter the picture of poetic possibility. As a nominal subject of the poetry, and as a statement of the formal principle it bodies forth, "motion as a summary of time and space" enables the poet to "Pray Without Ceasing" in the uplands, and at sea level to "talk fairly tirelessly without going astray or / asunder," while he works to extend the Orphic tradition of praise to particulars of Einstein's cosmos, once thought inimical to the spirit of poetry. In this manner, and with the casual, friendly air of a Sunday stroller, Ammons has dedicated his formal innovations, his poetry in motion, to the task of achieving what Emerson called "an original relation to the universe."

"A poem in becoming generates the laws of its / own becoming," Ammons observes in "Essay on Poetics." The statement occurs within the context of a theory of organic form: "we are not only ourselves—i.e., / the history of our organism—but also every process that went into / our making." Accordingly, like verbal equivalents of action paintings, Ammons' long poems aim to chronicle the career of their making, and they do so with remarkable knowingness; few poets seem so well informed about what they're up to as the Ammons of "Essay on Poetics." As if to illustrate "the laws of its / own becoming," the poem interrupts itself to accommodate several self-contained short poems; in the process we meet with various of

Ammons' stylistic signatures, tried on for size. Apparently, when Ammons starts to write a poem he has his choice of three weapons. One, derived from William Carlos Williams, relies on short lines, quick jabs and feints; the perfect example is "Reflective":

> I found a
> weed
> that had a
>
> mirror in it
> and that
> mirror
>
> looked in at
> a mirror
> in
>
> me that
> had a
> weed in it

Such poems as the frequently anthologized "Corsons Inlet" feature a more rambling gait, uneven lines with jagged edges that suggest a grammar of space; the poet constantly shifts his margins in an effort to set up antiphonal patterns apposite for "a walk over the dunes" beside "the inlet's cutting edge." The measure that predominates in "Essay on Poetics," making room for the others, is a long line curving dramatically at its close in a serpentine gesture. This last, I would argue, is a distinguishing trait of Ammons at his very best—in short poems like "The City Limits," "Triphammer Bridge," "Cut the Grass," and "The Unifying Principle," as well as in *Sphere* and "Hibernaculum," each of which consists of a series of three-line stanzas. This is the stanza of "Ode to the West Wind" and "The Triumph of Life," and indeed, in his handling of it, it almost seems as though Ammons—equally enamored of the wind—had undertaken to translate Shelley across an ocean and a century.

In these poems, Ammons' "hard" enjambments, winding syntax, and Shelleyan stamina all work to produce a bend-and-swerve motion; the reader participates in the poem as a skier on a slalom slope. The effect is rather like that of *terza rima* without the *rima*. Every trick up the poet's sleeve impels the reader to turn and turn about, whirling like a dervish from line to long line, stanza to stanza. The sense is variously drawn out from one verse into another, as Milton prescribed, in (for example) these lines from "The Unifying Principle":

> what then can lift the people
> and only when they choose to rise or what can make
> them want to rise, though business prevents: the
>
> unifying principle will be a
> phrase shared, an old cedar long known, general
> wind-shapes in a usual sand: those objects single,
>
> single enough to be uninterfering, multiple by
> the piling on of shared sight, touch, saying:
> when it's found the people live the small wraths of ease.

Notice how the two "what" clauses stretch across lines; to complete the thought, the reader must turn his head. By enjambing both the definite and indefinite articles in subsequent lines, Ammons issues an even more forcible reminder that *versus*, the Latin root of "verse," literally means "turning" or "turning toward." The repetition of "single," at the end of the poem's penultimate stanza and at the start of the finale, adds insistence and reinforces the sense of continuity, continuation, extension; and both "general" and "multiple by," set off between commas on their left and blank space on their right, beckon the reader to spin around to the following line. Only with "saying" in the next-to-last verse do end-of-line and end-of-thought coincide; only at the very end is there the sense of an ending, of resolution and rest, and even here a fine semantic explosion ("small wraths of ease") goes off in counterpoint to the syntactical resolution toward which the lines' downward pull has guided us.

Characteristically, it is through the language of landscape that Ammons discloses the principles of his prosody. I refer to "A Note on Prosody," which Ammons published in *Poetry* in June 1963; he is discussing the verse line:

> The center of gravity is an imaginary point
> existing between the two points of beginning
> and end, so that a downward pull is created
> that gives a certain downward rush to the movement,
> something like a waterfall glancing in turn off
> opposite sides of the canyon, something like the
> right and left turns of a river.

Again with an appeal to landscape Ammons accounts for the dialectic between his lyric "briefings" and his epic (or mock-epic) extensions of the self:

> I would call the lyric high and hard, a rocky loft, the slow
>
> snowline melt of individual crystalline drops, three or four to
> the lyric: requires precision and nerve, is almost always badly
> accomplished, but when not mean, minor: then there is the rush,
>
> rattle and flash of brooks, pyrotechnics that turn water white:

In one sense the suasion (to use a word the poet favors) that led in the direction of the longer poems betokens a shift from the "minor" key of "individual crystalline drops" to the grand, symphonic boom of the sea, a perpetual motion machine:

> genius, and
> the greatest poetry, is the sea, settled, contained before the first
> current stirs but implying in its every motion adjustments
> throughout the measure: one recognizes an ocean even from a dune and
>
> the very first actions of contact with an ocean say ocean over and
> over: read a few lines along the periphery of any of the truly
> great and the knowledge delineates an open shore:
>
> what is to be gained from the immortal person except the experience
> of ocean:
>
> ("Essays on Poetics")

Cause of celebration becomes cause of lament, however, when the terms of discussion are drawn from the topographical paradigm that holds an evident attraction for this poet. Ammons always has loved a neighborly chat with a mountain—in A Coast of Trees, "Continuing" takes the form of such a dialogue—and for this predilection I can think of several compelling reasons. The shape of an average mountain, to one who sets store by the shapes of things, cannot fail to fuel some abiding philosophical interests: in its pyramidal aspect, a mountain signifies hierarchy; peak corresponds to "the one," base to "the many." Moreover, mountains figure as emblems of religious experience; they loom large as stern figures of authority—excellent to question or talk back to—though it is usually they who have the last word:

> and the mountain that
> was around,
>
> scraggly with brush &
> rock
> said
> I see you're scribbling again:
>
> accustomed to mountains,
> their cumbersome intrusions,
> I said
>
> well, yes, but in a fashion very
> like the water here
> uncapturable and vanishing:
>
> but that
> said the mountain does not
> excuse the stance
> or diction
>
> ("Classic")

To move from uplands to sea level is to describe a downward arc; "it's surprising to me / that my image of the orders of greatness comes in terms of descent," Ammons muses.

That mountains should give rise to a myth of decline is indeed a subtle irony, but the logic is unassailable. Ammons associates the lyric impulse with the "summit" of a mountain; to embrace the epic world of "differences"—"enriching, though / unassimilable as a whole / into art" —requires that the poet slide to the prosaic base, to a place "comfortable on the lowerarchy." Something like Harold Bloom's parable of the poet as "spent seer" emerges; with the wind as guide, the wind which has "given up everything to eternal being but / direction," the poet has ascended the heights of soul-making where, in the "changeless prospect," he cannot find "an image for *longing*" but suddenly draws a blank in nature; he has no choice now but to come back down, having like Moses communed with the Lord, whose tablets he must shatter upon his return to the riotous tribe. The wonder is that, as Bloom argues, the smashing of vessels occurs not as an imaginative defeat but as a necessary prelude to the achievement of restitution, the gathering of dispersed light.

Unlike his lyrics, Ammons' long poems have encountered resistance from critics who discern in them a falling off in intensity from the controlled outbursts found over and over in *The Collected Poems* (1972)—and now again in the fiercely elegiac poems of *A Coast of Trees*. It seems to me remarkable that poems such as "Hibernaculum" and *Sphere*, which give about as much word-for-word pleasure as one could ask for, should want defending. Not merely do they complement the lyrics but they round them into a completed vision. Without denying "the bitterest thing I can think of that seems like / reality," and without surrendering to it, they assert the priorities of the creative imagination, the "radiance" that never "winces from its storms of generosity," however provoking the circumstances. The particular quandary that has nourished Ammons from the start is at once resolved and renewed in these lengthy meditations on, and in, motion, as if increase of appetite had grown by what it fed on. Wedding Williams' love of minute particulars with Stevens' "metaphysicals . . . sprawling in majors of the August heat," Ammons finds the mechanism

> by which many, kept
> discrete as many, expresses itself into the
> manageable rafters of salience, lofts to comprehension . . .
> ("Essay on Poetics")

The mechanism is the poem itself, an ordered but not too orderly cosmos. Within its flexible borders all things are seen, by an assertion of Romantic will, as destined to end up in "the form of a motion," a phrase the poet has liberated from the language of the faculty meeting. All things exist in patterns of correspondence, having a design in common. Mountain peak "equals" vertex of isosceles triangle "equals" mound of Venus; if nothing else, lust links subject and object:

> if one can get far enough this way where imagination
> and flesh strive together in shocking splendors, one can
> forget that sensibility is sometimes dissociated and come . . .
> *(Sphere, #5)*

"Fluted trashcan" and "fluted Roman column" likewise enjoy separate but equal status since, Ammons writes in "Hibernaculum," "matter is a mere substance design takes / its shape in."

Not surprisingly, the formal choices Ammons makes—choices of design and shape—are decisive to his meaning. Form he conceives as waterfall, not container: he favors a cascade of words rather than a tidy English garden of them; the *sine qua non* of his prosody is a "downward rush," like that exhibited vividly in *Tape for the Turn of the Year* (1965), Ammons' most "vertical" poem. In another sense, form provides the hidden unity that can suffer the many to cohabit peaceably on its vast expanse. One distinctive quirk of form deserves special notice in this connection: I refer to what several critics punningly call Ammons' "colonization" of the universe. Ammons has invested the humble colon with poetic potency; he has made it his own, as Byron and Emily Dickinson may be said to share a patent on the dash. No first reader of these volumes can fail to register surprise at encountering colons where commas, periods, or semicolons usually go. To some extent the colons in *Sphere* and in the other long poems act like the word "so" in the early "Ezra" poems: like shrugs of the shoulder, implying consequentiality but leaving the causality unclear. Frequently they seem determined to establish linkage between seemingly unrelated phenomena, as between essence and fashion, center and periphery, the "radiant" and the "lowly"; the sublime and the quotidian link hands by dint of these elliptical transitions. And yet the transitions differ from what Elizabeth Bishop described when she wrote of "Everything only connected by 'and' and 'and.' " Both writers wish to give new meaning to E. M. Forster's "only connect," but where Bishop's "and" does the work of an inspired ampersand, Ammons' colons act now as "equal" signs, now as miniature arrows pointing in opposite directions. Acts of closure that double as re-beginnings, they advance the tape without erasing it.

Consider the multiple functions entrusted to the colons in the following section of "Hibernaculum":

work's never done: the difficult work of dying
remains, remains, and remains: a brain lobe squdging
against the skull, a soggy kidney, a little vessel

smartly plugged: wrestling with one—or those—until
the far-feared quietus comes bulby, floating, glimmer-wobbling
to pop: so much more mechanical, physical than

spiritual-seeming grief: than survivors' nights filled
without touch or word, than any dignity true for a state
of being: I won't work today: love, be my leisure:

The first colon indicates that an explanation will follow; the second introduces specific, concrete examples in illustration of the abstract explanation; splicing together the run-on thoughts, the next three permit the meditation to spill over the bounds of ordinary syntactical limitations—they eliminate the usual need for verbs; and the final two precede lyrical leaps forward, taking the place of periods. The unity of the section is clear; the movement from "work's never done" to "I won't work today" has, in effect, been annotated in the lines. But the last two clauses are kept from appearing conclusive by the colons around them and by the absence of capital letters. Think how different the effect would be were the lines printed this way:

I won't work today.
Love, be my leisure.

By insisting that all utterances renew or extend those that precede them, the colons reduce the pause between one and the next and in so doing they imply that each is a mere fragment of some larger, cohesive structure. A unifying principle rolls through them all.

If the *Selected Longer Poems* makes a valuable companion volume to *The Selected Poems 1951–1977, A Coast of Trees* is that yet more precious thing: fresh poems bearing witness to the powers that make Ammons one of the indispensable poets of his generation. Were new evidence needed to counteract the charge that Ammons is too abstract, that he doesn't plant enough people in his poetry, the prosecuting attorney might be pacified by this volume. Some of the most moving poems are populated not only by the backyard elm, the local brook, the lofty "saliences" of the terrain, and like presences, but by the infant brother who died when Ammons was a child, by the elderly in "homes" but not at home, and by other denizens of "the bleak land of foreverness," burger-eaters magnetized by the twin golden arches on yellow brick roads. "Parting" and "Sweetened Change," for example, are no less kindly and warmhearted for their terrifying vision of ultimate aloneness. An aged husband wheels his sickly wife

> through the hospital doors; soon the quick
> man is out again, squeals away to parking
> spaces allotted longer stalls of time:
> he jogs back by and back through the doors
> he goes: one mate gives out and the other
> buzzes fast to sing he's not alone and idle.
> ("Sweetened Change")

A unique moment of lucidity permits the victim of a stroke almost to recognize her spouse of fifty years:

> her mind
> flashed clear through, she was
> sure of it, she had seen
> that one before: her husband
>
> longed to say goodbye or else
> hello, but the room stiffened
> as if two lovers had just caught
> on sight, every move rigid
> misfire in that perilous fire.
> ("Parting")

That, for Ammons, is one half of the truth; the other is that "being here to be here / with others is for others," as he writes, somewhat anxiously, in "Poverty." But the knowledge brings ample compensation in its train:

> alone, I'm not alone:
> a standoffishness and reasonableness
> in things finds
> me or I find that
> in them: sand, falls,
> furrow, bluff—
> things one, speaking things
> not words, would
> have found to say.
> ("Strolls")

The world consents to our poetic experience of it; its "things" have been spoken into existence. It is, of course, the God of *Genesis* who enjoys this "original relation to the universe" that Ammons holds up as an unattainable ideal. He would seem to subscribe unabashedly to Coleridge's conception of the primary imagination as "a repetition in the finite mind of the eternal act of creation in the infinite I AM." Therein lies the problem: repetition implies lateness, and the discrepancy between the primal word and its most recent echo measures the extent of the poet's alienation from the natural world. "I looked into space and into the sun,"

Ammons writes in one of his great moments, "and nothing answered my word *longing.*" It is this consciousness of the imagination's constraints and limits that tempers the sweetness of the lonely urge to celebrate, always strong in Ammons. But precisely because it is problematic, the rift between nature and human nature acts as a sort of stimulant to this exemplar of what Quentin Anderson calls "the imperial self."

In the tone of an Old Testament prophet, Ammons starts off his new volume with a lyric statement of the problem of naming, the inadequacy of language for the task Adam mythically performed:

> if the name nearest the name
> names least or names
> only a verge before the void takes naming in,
> how are we to find holiness,
> our engines of declaration put aside,
> helplessness our first offer and sacrifice . . .
>
> ("Coast of Trees")

The question gets, in lieu of either a question mark or a definitive answer, the resolve to "know a unity / approach divided," to trust "to the cleared particular." Ammons puts enormous pressure on his capacity for such trust, his ability to suspend the disbelief that gnaws away in his mind. Like W. C. Williams, Ammons goes out on fact-finding missions, looking for the raw materials of a renewed belief. But where the author of *Paterson* prized the concrete particular for its concreteness, Ammons would grasp—if you will—the zen of the thing "emptied full." Harold Bloom has a word for this puzzling trope: *kenosis.* It puts in several appearances in *A Coast of Trees.*

The ways Ammons departs from Williams' example are instructive. While the two poets have certain prosodic habits in common, and while both bet heavily on the American idiom, Ammons breaks fundamentally with Williams on the latter's central dogma, that there can be "no ideas but in things." Here is the final word on that subject:

> the symbol carries exactly the syrup of many distillations and
> hard endurance, soft inquiry and turning: the symbol apple and the
> real apple are different apples, though resembled: "no ideas but in
>
> things" can then be read into alternatives—"no things but in ideas,"
> "no ideas but in ideas," and "no things but in things": one thing
> always to keep in mind is that there are a number of possibilities:
>
> ("Essay on Poetics")

If, following Williams' lead, Ammons writes a poetry of reportage, it differs in giving equal time to the metaphysical news, broadcasting landscapes made into metaphors, not morals, as the poet sees (and sees through) them. These are crucial distinctions. Much will also have been ascertained about the differences between an English and an American sensibility once we compare Auden's moralized landscapes (in the *Bucolics*, for example) with the landscapes and country matters that Ammons favors although (or because) they exist seemingly without reference to human passions, love, and grief. Where Auden preferred a "region / Of short distances and definite places" to the "reckless" sea, Ammons espouses "a region without definite boundaries" ("Terrain"); where Auden, distrustful of the high and mighty and dangerous mountain, sought the reassurance of a limestone landscape, Ammons depicts himself as an inveterate mountain climber; where Auden opposed the artist's mirror to life's sea, Ammons would wish *his* mirror to have the sea's choppy surface and unrelenting motion. Ammons adopts the scientist's neutrality in the presence of his landscapes; it is their sublime otherness that fascinates him. Significantly, one of the elegies in the new volume has the refrain, "this is just a place."

Nature's neglect of us is, one feels Ammons would aver, benign, because? although? it implies an aesthetic rather than an ethical universe. The elements refuse to "mean" anything, yet they cohere; they form "patterns and routes," and apprehension of these casual (as opposed to causal) designs comes as the sublime afterglow to a bout with terror and awe. With "majesty and integrity" nature can be counted on, finally, to calm if it cannot quite placate the unappeasable heart. Accordingly, the most transcendent image in *A Coast of Trees* exemplifies a type of "natural supernaturalism," to borrow M. H. Abrams' useful term: it comes in an Easter ode that makes no reference to Christianity, and it heralds an entirely secularized resurrection. "Easter Morning," whose crisis of mourning and mortality marks the vital center of the book, concludes with the image of "two great birds, / maybe eagles," flying in circles. As if endowed with the Teiresian ability to interpret the secret messages of birds, Ammons watches them perform

> a dance sacred as the sap in
> the trees, permanent in its descriptions
> as the ripples round the brook's
> ripplestones: fresh as this particular
> flood of burn breaking across us now
> from the sun.

The divine adjectives ("sacred" and "permanent" and "fresh") attach themselves to natural particulars. The point is made partially by enjambment: the "particular" hanging at the edge of space, three lines before the conclusion, does duty as a noun before taking its place as a modifier. And partially by trope: notice that the similes all emerge from the same rural picture, the identical scene, as that of the things they illustrate. Nature refers only to herself, not to any wished-for presence off stage. And if the emphatic, somewhat abrupt ending makes it difficult to ignore the old sun / son pun, the metaphysicals sprawl, if at all, in majors of the physical morning.

Students of the sublime may wish to relate the workings of this ambitious, sure-to-be-anthologized poem with those of Stevens' "Sunday Morning." By his title alone Ammons takes the risk of making such a comparative reading inevitable. Some broad strokes link the two poems. Most visibly, the swooping eagles at the end of "Easter Morning" recall Stevens' "casual flocks of pigeons" which "make / Ambiguous undulations as they sink / Downward to darkness, on extended wings." Both poems revive a Romantic formula; they make the sort of appeal to the sensually real that Helen Vendler associates with Keats' ode "To Autumn." But the value of any such comparative reading would derive not from what "Easter Morning" shares with its antecedent but from how it veers off into a space of its own. Ammons' poem is personal, autobiographical, intimate, idiomatic, as by temperament Stevens never was or wanted to be. As an elegy, "Easter Morning" leads ineluctably from the death of another to the realization that time and change mean death for the self. And it is as such that the poem would seem to indicate a new phase in Ammons' career: he pictures himself now as "an old man having / gotten by on what was left."

Impelled by a Wordsworthian visit "to my home country" (North Carolina), "Easter Morning" begins as a meditation on the death of a younger brother, "a life that did not become, / that turned aside and stopped" in infancy. The memory of that death aches like a miscarriage. To see the event "by / the light of a different necessity" promises some relief "but the grave will not heal" and the grief widens to include the friends and relatives who populated the poet's childhood—and that childhood itself—irrevocably "gone." "The grave will not heal": this, the poem's dominant chord, chimes throughout A Coast of Trees, as though it were a carol of death. Death is conceived variously as the still point in a turning world ("Where"), as an ontological issue ("In Memoriam: Mae Noblitt"), as an "immediate threat" ("Swells"), as the fatigue that announces imaginative loss—

> sometimes
> a whole green sunset
> will wash dark
> as if it could go
> right by without me
>   ("Distractions")

—and as the lonely cry that cleaves the graveyard air:

> I stand on the stump
> of a child, whether myself
> or my little brother who died, and
> yell as far as I can, I cannot leave this place, for
> for me it is the dearest and the worst,
> it is life nearest to life which is
> life lost.
>
> ("Easter Morning")

Of all contemporary poets, Ammons employs the most idiosyncratic vocabulary, and strewn like markers throughout the volume are the *multiplicities* and *radiances* and *motion* that serve as counterpoise to this weary weight of mortality. The last two lines of the last poem in the book gesture wonderfully to the whole:

> in debris we make a holding as
> insubstantial and permanent as mirage.
>
> ("Persistences")

A *Coast of Trees* is a spare volume. Like *Briefings* and *Uplands*, it omits the inventories, statistics, elephant jokes, folksy ruminations, and assorted time-killers with which the poet liberally spices his longer poems. This is the stuff that drives sober critics to take a powder. I rather miss it, however, and—in a digression that will, I hope, find the true direction out—I want to put in a good word for the noble eccentricity responsible for *Tape for the Turn of the Year* and *Sphere* and *The Snow Poems* (1977). Like other practicing poets I tend to read hedonistically. As Auden put it, you can count on a poet to read a poem as "a verbal contraption," to keep an eye out for what makes it tick; as Eliot might have put it, the poet in the act of reading prepares for the larcenies of composition. From this point of view, which prizes technical innovation and audacity, one must give a high valuation to Ammons' most extreme performances. Take *Sphere.* Its prosody enacts the spinning of the planet; its logic is that of metonymy, a single common characteristic—the speed of gravitational pull, for example—sufficing to connect everything. The only thing at all like it is William Gass's marvelous *On Being Blue,* in whose ravishing prose blue laws and dahlias and blazers and Mondays all have their place—and in whose "blues" we find confirmation of the truth of *Sphere*'s opening proposition, "The sexual basis of all things rare is really apparent." Like Gass's philosophic meditation-by-way-of-revery, *Sphere* has high, orgasmic moments—"ecstatic as mating, the transforming's pleasing"—and its comments about itself similarly manage a textured textuality that should even make it popular among those of the "diacritical" persuasion. The poem's "low" moments seem equally vital, however, and not only because they are "true to life" and because it would be impossible to imagine the lyric flights without also imagining an authenticating, quotidian context for them to lift off from. All points along the periphery are potential centers, Ammons is saying, and it is precisely their potentiality, their curve of possibility, the whole doppler shift of their existence that the poet praises in *Sphere*. Generosity is a critical aspect of the radiance he continues to aspire to in *A Coast of Trees*, albeit in terse accents edged with sorrow. The force of lamentation can meet but not vanquish the power of praise, the impulse of objects as they approach to "praise themselves seen in / my praising sight" ("Vehicle"). The tug between elegy and praise defines, I think, the special quality of Ammons' latest volume. And if it lacks the ecstasy and creative abandon of *Sphere* or *The Snow Poems*, the lack is also its own poignant compensation.

One of poetry's great walkers, who composes while walking and whose poems keep to a peripatetic pace, Ammons continues on his "unappeasable, peregrine" way to explore the states of mind as landscape, of landscape as mind, that in his aloneness he experiences. In his poems he makes palpable his willed apprehension of *abundances*—"an abundant tranquillity," "the abundance of clarity." And it is *clarity*, in its oldest sense of "brilliancy, glory, and divine lustre," that we find in satisfying abundance in all of Ammons' work. It is too bad that, for the new collection's cover, its publisher used a photograph of a bank of trees, since, in the terms proposed in "Essay on Poetics," Ammons' poetry fronts the ocean, not a mere river:

> read a few lines along the periphery of any of the truly
> great and the knowledge delineates an open shore:

> what is to be gained from the immortal person except the experience
> of ocean.

JOHN HOLLANDER

"*I Went to the Summit*"

Ⅰn an astonishing little one-line poem,
Emerson once implied that poetry associates the extra-urban scene with
the broadcasting of knowledge which in the city is kept pent: "A man tells
a secret for the same reason that he loves the country." Emerson's image is
the exultant yell of openness here, but it must not be mistaken for an
echo of the country's own voice, which broadcasts nothing in the way of
truth. Like the urban scene, it presents emblems to be read, and it
presents the general enigma of emblem—of making sense out of what we
know we are amidst. Whether for Whitman's post-initiate consulting the
oracle of the sea after hearing the great Ode of the mockingbird's loss, or
for the guarded Frost, not even inquiring of his long scythe (in "Mowing")
whether it knew the relevant text in Deutero-Isaiah, the voice of nature
could only come in a whisper. Straining to hear that whisper has been a
major American poetic act always, just as squinting at our scenes for the
shadows cast upon them by our lives has been one of the major visions of
"that wilder image" (as Bryant called it) of our painting. In one sense, the
poet should not want to have nature's voice, for no matter how mighty in
decibels the roaring wind, it is a philosopher with laryngitis; the truth of
audibly moving water can only be hearsay. And yet the poet's longing for
nature's way of making things, and of making things happen (beyond
breed to brave Time when he takes you hence), reflects so many of our
general longings for authenticity in the manufacture of our lives.

A. R. Ammons is a poet who strains for whispers and squints, not
so much for the shadows as for what hides in them and how they appear to
lengthen and deepen apart from the time of day. As a poet of nature he

From *The Yale Review* (Winter 1981). Copyright © 1981 by Yale University Press.

walks in the country accompanied by the moving shadow cast by the light of his own consciousness. More than a reader of emblems, more than an epigrammatizing biologist or even a chanting thanatologist, he engages the countryside with the powerful hands of awareness in a working of the land that is also a playing with it. Santayana warned that "if we do not know our environment, we shall mistake our dreams for a part of it, and so spoil our science by making it fantastic, and our dreams by making them obligatory." He was talking of a culture which has gone well on its way toward doing just that; but there is the internalized civilization of the individual imagination which provides us with exemplary states of consciousness, and in Ammons's poetry, the mythology of structure and function in plant and animal flowers all year long.

The last of the poems with which we shall now confront ourselves is perhaps atypical of Ammons's meditations on a site or sample, but representative of the American poem of longing for natural power. It is a text of the 1970s, marked by a somewhat deceptive rhetorical ease and, unlike both "Mirror" and "Soonest Mended," standing clear of the shifting track of memory. It is the set of dedicatory verses to Ammons's long poem, "Sphere." More than some of his rightly best-known meditations on radiance and clarity such as "Gravelly Run" or "The City Limits," it points to the question of our naturalness. The poet starts out from a familiar point: the mountain top from which both classical and biblical visions are vouchsafed:

> I went to the summit and stood in the high nakedness:
> the wind tore about this
> way and that in confusion and its speech could not
> get through to me nor could I address it:

The first *modern* summit is probably that of Mont Ventoux, which Petrarch attained in April of 1336, partially on the original grounds that "it was there and so I had to climb it," partially because of the injunctions of biblical and classical story. He ascended to the very windy summit, accompanied by a beloved brother, ignoring the aged shepherd "in the folds of the mountain" who tried to dissuade him from the climb and, most important of all, carrying with him a pocket-sized manuscript of Augustine's *Confessions*. At the summit, by a kind of *sortes*, he opened his codex to a text which indicated that men go to admire high mountains, the sea, the great rivers, the stars, and thereby desert themselves. What Petrarch discovered on the windy mountain was about the height and scope of consciousness; never again would summits be the same.

Ammons's unnamed, general summit does not afford him the

opportunity for discourse, much less communion, that Whitman might
have felt there, and having been brought to where he stands by personal
history, and by the history of poetic art, he can only examine nature's
inability to reflect, or to echo:

> still I said as if to the alien in myself
>> I do not speak to the wind now:
> for having been brought this far by nature I have been
> brought out of nature
> and nothing here shows me the image of myself:
> for the word *tree* I have been shown a tree
> and for the word *rock* I have been shown a rock,
> for stream, for cloud, for star
> this place has provided firm implication and answering
>> but where here is the image for *longing*:

What Ammons, what we all, have inherited from our meditative tradition
is a way of reading parts of a world for the whole; his summit-climber finds
at the top of contemplation the signatures of the divine words in the
things that embody, or image, them. But what had led him to try for
heights remains unrepresented in the vision those very heights afford.
Neither would natural philosophy afford him that, nor would the most
profound caressing of the phenomena themselves, rather than an unpeeling
of them in quest of the structures which produce those appearances.
Ammons continues, in the next lines, to maintain this, starting with an
important echo of Whitman's syntax:

> so I touched the rocks, their interesting crusts:
> I flaked the bark of stunt-fir:
> I looked into the space and into the sun
> and nothing answered my word *longing*:

—And again, his final exhortation to an unlistening nature sings a tune
sadly playful in a Whitmanian way at first—

> goodbye, I said, goodbye, nature so grand and
> reticent, your tongues are healed up into their own
> element
> and as you have shut up you have shut me out: I am
> as foreign here as if I had landed, a visitor:

As if the tongues by which nature could speak to Wordsworth, or to
Emerson, had been wounds of some sort? The single word "element" is
isolated in its verse, free of local syntax, as if thereby to represent its
silence. The art which must speak for nature, as, indeed, for all of the rest
of our silence, must come from some other, unsublime "element," and

Ammons's climber descends to baser ground, to muck around in the Adamic mud and shape a new piece of natural history. It will not be a mere filling of a void, no fantastic substitution for the longed-*for*, but, of necessity, a human image of another sort.

> I took the image to the summit: first
> I set it here, on the top rock, but it completed
> nothing: then I set it there among the tiny firs
> but it would not fit:

Unlike Wallace Stevens's jar that "did not give of bird nor bush / Like nothing else in Tennessee," Ammons's image completes nothing because it answers to no longing of the hilltops, to nothing in rock, tree, stream, cloud, or star that has ever quested after a greater naturalness, or hearkened after a prior voice. This is not the complaint of the First Shaper that His human creation would not fit in Paradise, nor that of some human simulator of forms that his golem would not play properly and quietly in the back yard. I suppose that it is possible to imagine the "image for longing" as a woman, or a beautiful youth—an image *of* (but not, in Ammons's richer sense, "for") a longed-for object of desire. But in this case, it would be the image of an image, and the longing of the poet-climber for the intercourse with mute nature would be troped by the absence of a beautiful body. Nor would a reflexive emblem satisfy the conditions of the poem—a modelled image of a man modelling an image of what—or of whom—he desires. One need only think of the Creator, contemplating his garden with a sense of his distance from his own creation, and setting amid its rocks and trees an image of himself, in order to decide what sort of figure Ammons's image for longing makes.

But its appearance is not in fact the problem. It is a question of the ecology of significance, of what in this poem is spoken of as a setting. Even the poem that would complete the silences of nature must seek out the city of understanding. And "so," says Ammons,

> I returned to the city and built a house to set
> the image in
> and men came to my house and said
> that is an image for *longing*
> and nothing will ever be the same again

—And to do that to everything was why the poet came. Perhaps this ends with the same ambiguity of syntactic closure that makes us wonder, in the absence of canonical punctuation, about who is saying exactly how much at the end of Keats's poem on the urn: despite its present tense, is the last line only what the others say in recognition of the image? Is it not part of the testament of the poem? The time of poetic vocation which lies in the distant past of Merrill's mirror, unremembered or, at any rate, unrecalled, and which Ashbery continually reinvokes, is here memorialized as a bardic anecdote. The image completed nothing in the wild which called forth the need of it; the maker had to return to the ground to gather the element of such an image, and to return to the city to build a house which the image might complete.

In one sense, "I Went to the Summit" is the poem of the First Poem, both in the poet's history and in that of the world. A parody of Creation, it reminds us of the Original Trope (and, perhaps, causes us to linger for a moment over the identity of that trope: is the relation of Creator to Man one of metaphor? irony? synecdoche? metonymy?). But in its parody, Ammons's tale avoids the confusions of the uninspiring winds that tear about the summit. If at a lower altitude they would whisper of death—that message which is our imagination's overload always—at the privileged, high place which seems to point toward transcendence, there is nothing to be understood. In all our general American longings, our uneasy quest for "firm implication and answering," it is so easy to pretend to understand the wind in the high nakedness, and to descend, ever to echo its roaring. But the poet will not have that, nor will, by extension, the unpublishing poet who fills every wise, passionate consciousness. He must make an image for longing, and then build a house of life for which that image will remain the *lar familiaris*, as the Romans referred to it, the household spirit.

Every stage of life has its losses, and every age of culture its own longings. Not to avow these will probably not lead to the making of poems which command us to change our lives, poems imbued with what D. H. Lawrence called "a passionate, implicit morality, not didactic." Much well-intentioned verse which, as we have seen, can respond too directly and too trivially to the violences from without remains, in Ammons's myth, the equivalent of carefully-worked samplers hung on the walls of a house not even built for them, but inherited. (Were I to have been discussing style here, I might have added that during the last decade it even became fashionable for the samplers to present their ABCs and their pieties not in the careful fancywork of long tradition, but overwrought instead with the *fausse-naïve*, misshapen and tearstained as if by an incapacitated or miserably unwilling child.) But the true poems which embody images for the losses as well as the longing cannot merely *be* homely wisdom. They must reinvent wisdom and even homeliness itself.

To this extent, then—that at the end of every true poem "nothing will ever be the same again"—the problems of American affirmation, of modern heroism, and of the apparent impossibility of wisdom seem part of the same condition. Like the medieval *chansons de geste*, the heroic poems which flowered in times of treasons, stratagems, and spoils, and the *chansons d'amour* which filled in with language the space created by absence, our poems of love and deed at once blossom only in our own late aftertime. After the originations of nature, our images of rocks and trees are not enough, and it is only in our poems of awareness of this insufficiency that we can live our imaginative lives. Such poems fill in the spaces vacated by the ever-vanishing hope of our ever *being* our models, our heroes, our images of the good, original life, and aid us to become them, by, and within, ourselves. In an America past the time of its own youth, promise, and capability, it is not for a major poetry to mourn the time of year, but to provide images for *imagining*. If a man, to be greatly good, must indeed "imagine intensely and comprehensively"—if, the more complex his nature, the more dialectic, the more historical vision, and the more humor he must be able to exercise—then it must be such poems which will nourish the imagination, if only by forcing the reader to cooperate in their creation. We may want verses to touch, to tickle, to caress, to remind, to wound us: the many modes of sermon, editorial, and epigram contrive to do those and more. In the absence of wisdom, the poetry of modernism informed us, there is only the sad knowledge of that absence and a way of putting what we know in "a series of isolated perfections" perhaps. Our epigrams continue in that task. For the larger questions, our late epics, our derived romances, our scriptures and their commentaries, come more and more to be scattered among the leaves of our meditative lyrics.

It is these poems which have come to be our poetry of restitution— for local and for general losses; for the exhausted powers of private and public language (and when the sword avers the pen to be mightier, let us beware, for that will only occur in a police state); for vanished emblems of wisdom, ever needing replacement; for the vacancies left by modernist poetry's view of its own history; and for the continuing American task of self-invention—a burden as cruel as that of the demand for originality which modernism has thrust upon all poor artisans—if not even half-completed in a summer of national power, then perhaps to be continued in a brave autumn of decline.

HELEN REGUEIRO ELAM

Radiances and Dark Consolations

Emerson tells us that the ruin that we see when we look at nature is in our own eye. When the axis of vision is not coincident with the axis of things, objects appear not transparent but opaque, and thus ghostlike we glide through nature, never knowing our place again. Ammons' poetic endeavor is to bring us to know our place again, to achieve that moment of transparence in which vision and object are one. In this sense his poems celebrate a plenitude that most post-Enlightenment poetry finds difficult to achieve, a homecoming into nature that overcomes the mind's otherness. Where so much of post-Enlightenment poetry affirms the isolation and power of the will, Ammons' poetry seems to come to rest on "the victory of stones and trees" ("Gravelly Run").

The opening of the *Collected Poems* ("So I Said I Am Ezra") gives a good indication of the direction this poetry will take. The human voice, even the prophetic voice in this poem, is surrounded and gloriously defeated by the forces of nature. "There were no echoes from the waves / The words were swallowed up / in the voice of the surf." The ocean never forms to mind or voice, but remains unalterably itself, alien to the poet so long as the poet retains his particularity and his otherness. But the poet goes out into the night like a drift of sand, and with his voice "scattered" and "broken" he "build[s] the whole silence back" ("Rack"). That which appears antithetical to poetic voice is also in Ammons part of the sublimity of voice—the poet's ability to break himself over the earth, to recapture the silence of unsaid things:

Turning a moment to say so long
    to the spoken
    and seen
    I stepped into
the implicit pausing sometimes
on the way to listen to unsaid things
At a boundary of mind
    Oh I said brushing up
    against the unseen
    and whirling on my heel
    said
    I have overheard too much
Peeling off my being I plunged into
the well

In a casual, conversational tone, Ammons engages a metaphysics of presence. The movement away from the spoken and seen is a crossing into the presence in which the self no longer knows itself, and no longer knows itself as other. Silence is thus privileged in Ammons over speech, and poetic voice becomes the medium of its own disappearance into the unspeakable richness of nature. At a boundary of mind the mind crosses over into what is no longer mind but earth—an earth luminous with sight, as Ammons will say, and thus a point of Emersonian transparence. Universe and self move through each other ("the universe . . . pours in and out / through me"), and the poetic self reaches a point of stasis, where absence turns to presence and silence to fulfilment: "There is a point, / only itself, / that fills space, / an emptiness / that is plenitude" ("Come Prima"). If the critic is tempted to read Ammons in phenomenological terms, this is because the poetry engages itself in the presence/absence dialectic and appears initially to privilege presence over the fictions of poetic will. In "Joshua Tree," for instance, the poetic self has no liturgy, and thus no way of singing wet news of joy, no way of poematizing a simple and yet splendid event like rain. But the poem proposes a point at which the self will indeed be "let loose" from the form to which it is consigned, a point at which a syllable's rain will anoint the poet's tongue and make it sing to strangers. It is not poetic will, not imaginative knowledge, nor consciousness of poetic history, but a simple syllable's rain that brings the tongue to song. The syllable's rain of course may be natural or poetic—either rain or syllable—but Ammons emphasizes the self's dissolution in nature, and the consequent utterance of nature's voice. In "Schooling," the subject is the poet's "yielding" to "an abundance," yet all the yielding has been to things of magnitude—ranges, glaciers, breadth of plains—and the poem turns to a prayer that the poet may yield to the smallness of things, a "total yielding past shadow and return." The dissolving of the self in the plenitude of nature brings about a moment of oneness and vision, privileged by what the poetic self knows yet cannot name.

> Like a single drop of rain,
>   the wasp strikes
> the windowpane; buzzes rapidly
> away, disguising
>
> error in urgent business:
>   such is the
> invisible, hard as glass,
> unrenderable by the senses,
>
> not known until stricken by:
>   some talk that
> there is safety in the visible,
> the definite, the heard and felt,
>
> pre-stressing the rational and
>   calling out with
> joy, like people far from death:
> how puzzled they will be when
>
> going headlong secure in "things"
>   they strike the
> intangible and break, lost,
> unaccustomed to transparency, to
>
> being without a body, energy
>   without image:
> how they will be dealt
> hard realizations, opaque as death.
>   ("Epiphany")

The poem marks an epiphany or crossing that does not take place but that is potentially there, for our "seeing." The wasp inadvertently comes upon the glass it cannot see, and diverts itself from it. Wasp and drop of rain in the first stanza are proof of the sudden apparition of an invisible "bourn" that makes possible our vision or our blindness. The wasp's "error" constitutes a potential epiphany, for the glass—invisible, hard, unutterable—is that threshold into transparence "not known until stricken by." When in Dickinson's poem the fly interposes itself between her and the light ("I heard a fly buzz when I died"), she tells us that she "could not see to see," and the doubling of the verb suggests precisely this recognition of glass as either transparence or opacity. To "see" in order to "see" one must "see through" what is invisible. "From reality's flowing flurry / take out a glass bead / and steer round & / round / it, an everlasting: / the center's in there, / its invisibility seen through" ("Turning"). In "Epiphany," that invisible center is a "bourn" that the wasp cannot "see," and the poem pointedly suggests that to "see clearly" is to see transparency, to "see" what one "sees through," that is to say, to recognize the invisible, pass over the bourn without transgression.

Yet transgression there is, or at least what Ammons terms the "hard realization" of opacity. To strike the window is to "break" in the presence of transparency, to be imageless, "opaque as death." One cannot, it seems, "see to see," and thus one cannot see to sing. "Bourn" traces this crossing over into the invisible, but there too what the poet sees beyond the "decimal of being" is untranslatable. "What light there / no tongue turns to tell / to willow and calling shore / though willows weep and shores sing always." The poet witnesses in the beginning of the poem the singing shores dancing "willows of grief" and enjoining him to "turn back." But though the poet figures himself a zero (*Sphere*), at the end of this poem he remains with the trope of willows weeping and shores singing, for the tongue cannot "turn to tell" except in tropes that miss the mark. The vision of presence at this bourn is untranslatable, and the threshold thus posited constitutes both a seeing and unseeing—a light that covers itself in the opacity of poetic language.

Ammons' vision of nature entails presence and transparence, but it refuses the absolute or the immutable. What is absolute and unified is aligned with death and thus with the ultimate opacity. "When you arrive / you have gone too far: / at the Source you are in the mouth of Death" ("Guide"). Nature, on the other hand, involves a presence and a transparence that shine forth in the transient and the particular. To see the object as it passes, to be witness to its transparence, to become part of the continuum of presence—this is a major impulse in Ammons' poetry:

> He turned and
> stood
>
> in the moment's
> height.
>
> exhilaration
> sucking him up,
>
> shuddering and
> lifting
>
> him
> jaw and bone

> and he said
> what
>
> destruction am I
> blessed by?
> ("Moment")

The emphasis here is on temporality, on passage, on dissolution. The moment's height is the self's breaking, and this breaking or "destruction" is a "blessing" because it reduces the self to jaw and bone and makes it part of the presence of things. In "Then One" the poet is "addled by the possible closures," for closure implies an encompassing form and defies the notion of continuum. "Then one thinks finally / with tight appreciation / of nothingness / or if not that far of / things that loosen or come apart." The breaking in Ammons incites revelation, and it does so because it turns the permanent into the transient, turns it, as he says, from *is* to *flowing*. In "Eyesight" the poet misses the spring ("It was May before my / attention came / to spring") and the mountain tells him he can still reach for it by climbing the southern slopes. But it also tells him that "it's not that way / with all things, some / that go are gone." The passage of things out of the range of the poet's eyesight makes them thresholds of the very presence he seeks.

> Everything begins at the tip-end, the dying out,
> of mind:
> the dazed eyes set and light
> dissolves actual trees:
>
> the world beyond: tongueless,
> unexampled
> burns dimension out of shape,
> opacity out of stone:
>
> come: though the world ends and cannot
> end,
> the apple falls sharp
> to the heart starved with time.
> ("Peak")

Presence begins here at the threshold where mind dissolves—at the Stevensian end of the mind, the tip-end, the dying-out, where shapes become less diffused, and world and mind seem to blend with the light. The light renders objects shapeless, less distinct in themselves as what they are, and thus less closed within themselves. It thus turns opacity into transparence (burns opacity out of stone), for without dimension, without shape, objects pass into a flowing continuum in which, as Stevens says, nothing is its solid self. Poetry for Ammons never tends toward solid ground ("Dunes") but toward this dissolving in the presence of what appears to be "other"—a world that is at the same time alien and familiar. "Peak" envisages the Emersonian moment of transparence, in which the axis of vision is also the axis of things.

But this transparent world "beyond" is also "tongueless"—a word that repeatedly occurs in the Ammons canon to suggest the bourn where poetry is rendered mute by fullness. The price of transparence is silence, and with this equation the central problematic in Ammons' poetry becomes the poem's attempt to speak at the threshold where voice tends to disappear. The world beyond is "unexampled," but the "come" enjoins reader and poet to see not presence itself but the recollection of a "peak" that has passed. The threshold reappears in the last stanza as a barrier, for the world finally cannot end in the depths of presence. But presence yields a single object in all its particularity and its temporal finiteness. The apple that falls sharp to the heart starved with time comes as a privileged object from the world of presence, but comes by way of a fall into absence. It falls sharp, like an object that must die, and its temporality is itself the "cure" for the heart starved with time. No hunger generated by our mortality can be assuaged except by what is itself finite. The peak is merely a moment of vision in an endless continuum, but to reach that peak is to apprehend the immediacy of the object as it passes from presence into absence, to see the sky acutest at its vanishing. "The exact is a conquest of time that time vanquishes" ("What This Mode of Motion Said") is Ammons' proverbial version of the concept, an exactness which has to do with seeing and with voicing. There can be no utterance of permanence in Ammons' universe, only of things that peak and disappear, and this means that the poet has to be open to what the moment makes available to him, for each moment is a potential threshold into the privileged continuum:

> I look for the forms
> things want to come as
>
> from what black wells of possibility,
> how a thing will
> unfold:
>
> not the shape on paper—though
> that, too—but the
> uninterfering means on paper:
>
> not so much looking for the shape
> as being available

to any shape that may be
summoning itself
through me
from the self not mine but ours.
                    ("Poetics")

The poet holds himself open to the forms he has not named, so that the naming might be an unfolding of both object and language. Poetic language is here the "uninterfering means" which renders itself "available" to the transient shape "reality's flowing flurry" ("Turning") might take—the shape that "summons itself." That this poem should be entitled "Poetics" suggests Ammons' insistence on poetry as a mode of relationship. This is a poetry that wills to believe in language as potential transparence. If we separate "symbol and translucence," our minds can only see blankness in the place of presence, and we "stand around dazed / and separate, sunless and eventful" ("Crevice"). To be "eventful" is to measure the world by the sequences of our time; but there are no "events" in nature, only passages, and the poetic self needs to pass into this other mode of being, to participate in the luminous presence of objects by losing itself to them. Loss and gain are intermingled in Ammons, for self-loss entails loss of our opacity and the gain of a blindness, as Stevens says, in which seeing would be false: "Losing information he / rose gaining / view / till at total / loss gain was / extreme: / extreme & invisible: / the eye / seeing nothing / lost its / separation: / self-song / (that is mere motion) / fanned out / into failing swirls / slowed & / became continuum" ("Offset"). The self is no longer self but nature's song here, a syllable of rain, a song that sings itself beyond the world of the will.

This attitude toward poetic speech accounts in part for the sparseness of Ammons' verse. Though in many ways he is Whitman's heir, he favors in the early part of his career the brief poem, the even briefer title—Three, Off, Circles, Miss, Square, Needs, Celestial, Correction, Mirrorment, Coming To, North Jersey, Exotic, Even, Hosts, Help—as if to speak were somehow tantamount to loss. Even in the longer poems, like *Sphere*, this attitude remains:

when we have made the sufficient mirror will

it have been only to show how things will break: know thyself
and vanish! and the knowledge not for itself or the self
but so the ambience may call itself vacantly expressed,

fully exfoliated, empty! sunrise this morning was not
a fraction: it was self-full, whole in motion: the man
falling asleep in the cave winters of time ago swayed

into the fullness, assumed the measure: we are as in a
cone of ages: each of us stands in the peak and center
of perception.

The breaking and the vanishing are also the transcendence of otherness,
for vanishing in Ammons is a disappearance into unspeakable presence.
Just as the sunrise is self-full, man has the capacity to "sway into" the
fullness, at the center of which he is least and most himself. The difficulty
with this concept is that such fullness must be "vacantly expressed," and
though Ammons treats the problem of poetic language peripherally, that
is, subsuming it in the presence/absence dialectic, poetic utterance nonetheless becomes a central problematic. What to say, how much to say,
how to listen to the language of nature, and what that language has to do
with ours—these are questions central to the American tradition, and
Ammons' ambiguities are part of its vital saying.

"Expressions of Sea Level," in this context, is a poem in the
tradition of Whitman and Stevens, a poem written by the shore, at the
rim of the land, at an edge which Ammons likes to call a clearing.

> Peripherally the ocean
> marks itself
>   against the gauging land
> it erodes and
> builds:
>
> it is hard to name
> the changeless:
> speech without words,
>   silence renders it:
> and mid-ocean,
>
> sky sealed unbroken to sea,
>   there is no way to know
> the ocean's speech,
> intervolved and markless,
> breaking against
>
>   no boulder-held fingerland:
> broken, surf things are expressions:

The ocean for Ammons is the "expression" of the continuum of nature, a
force that builds, erodes, changing yet changeless, a force whose very
speech is silence. In "The Idea of Order at Key West," Stevens recognizes
that the song of the girl by the sea is *her* song, not the ocean's, for what
she sang was uttered word for word. Ammons wills us closer to the word
unsaid here, the unimaginable word that seals us closer to nature as the

sky is sealed unbroken to the sea. The ocean's speech in this poem is "markless," that is to say wordless, reached only by that which is unspoken, and the "expressions" are finally the remnants, the broken remnants, at the ocean's rim—that which at the periphery yields to our sight. Expressions of sea level are thus expressions necessarily broken, segments of an unutterable whole, expressions of the vastness of the unsaid. This vastness is suggested by nature's periphery, but also by poetry's: "Read a few lines along the periphery of any of the truly / great and the knowledge delineates an open shore" ("Essay on Poetics"). What is said is merely a threshold from which to hear the unsaid, a threshold that never becomes the perfect moment, the perfect statement, the perfect and fulfilling place: "Is there a point of rest where / the tide turns: . . . Is there an instant where fullness is, / without loss, complete: is there a / statement perfect in its speech" ("Expressions of Sea Level"). The poem's answer is that there is not—that the expression of sea level is the Emersonian retreating horizon, a phenomenon witnessed only through the broken remains left behind—"spoken in a dampened grain of sand."

Stevens' experience at the periphery of an open shore opens up into a vision of his own alienness, of his ghostlier demarcations. Whitman reads this otherness as death in "As I Ebb'd," and the triumphant voice of nature as the dirge for poetic voice. Both poets attempt to give names to human experience, but the sea, unless transformed, becomes the whisper of death. Ammons reads the sea as essential life, and refuses its implication with death. There is no way to know the ocean's speech in this poem, and to know it, for Whitman, would be to know the whisper of death. But Ammons is reluctant here to read the sea's hostility to poetic voice. No statement is "perfect in its speech," but poetry is an "expression" of the unnamable, the remnant, like the shore's fragments, of a fullness that lies in the deep.

There are in the American tradition two major strategies: the encompassing of nature by sheer accretion, and the retrenchment of the self to its ultimate core. In "The Arc Inside and Out" Ammons sums up these two strategies and equalizes them:

> If, whittler and dumper, gross carver
> into the shadiest curvings, I took branch
> and meat from the stalk of life, threw
>
> away the monies of the treasured,
> treasurable mind, cleaved memory free
> of the instant . . .
>
> would I begin to improve the purity,
> would I essentialize out the distilled
> form . . .

> . . . the face-brilliant core
>
> stone: or if I, amasser, heap shoveler,
> depth pumper, took in all springs and
> oceans, paramoecia and moons . . .
>
> . . . would I finally come on a
> suasion, large, fully informed, restful,
>
> scape, turning back in on itself, its
> periphery enclosing our system with
> its bright dot and allowing in nonparlant
>
> quantities at the edge void, void, and
> void, would I then feel plenitude
> brought to center and extent, a sweet
>
> easing away of all edge, evil and surprise.

To whittle and shave away, as Dickinson does, or to amass, as Whitman does, encompasses the American tradition. One way reaches for the core; the other is what Ammons likes to call a suasion, a gentle and persuasive movement leading outward to an encompassing periphery—a Whitmanian expansion of the self so that the self becomes everything it sees. Ammons' strategy in this poem is to suggest that both traditions come down finally to an arc-line "inside which is nothing / outside which is nothing":

> however big,
> nothing beyond: however small, nothing
>
> within: neither way to go's to stay, stay
> here, the apple an apple with its own hue
> or streak, the drink of water, the drink,
>
> the falling into sleep, restfully ever the
> falling into sleep, dream, dream, and
> every morning the sun comes, the sun.

Ammons seems to have more affinities with Whitman than with Dickinson, but in this poem the circumference or arc-line is the imagined edge of nothingness. The great dream of American poetry ("these two ways to dream!") is to create an arc that encompasses and names—Crane's bridge, Stevens' orb. But Ammons suggests that the arc-line is an edge of nothing, and what remains is the apple—the natural object which again peaks and falls, a nature that passes yet renews itself ("every morning the sun comes, the sun").

"The Arc Inside and Out" can thus be read as an affirmation of nature, of the moment, of self-abandonment—a poem which knows itself to be peripheral, at the sea's rim, a broken voice. Or we may choose to read it as the affirmation of the arc-line, the edge of nothingness which redeems the self from natural repetition ("every morning the sun comes, the sun") and the final drifting into tongueless sleep. Perhaps Ammons might say that either way to go's to stay, but there is a movement in his poetry from the celebration of nature at the expense of voice to the affirmation of poetic voice even when the only possible subject for that voice is loss.

That intimacy with nature should be purchased at the expense of voice is knowledge Ammons resists, yet poems that begin with the celebration of intimacy often close with either the recognition that such intimacy is impossible, that nature resists the poet's advances, or with a lamentation for what such intimacy costs.

> I don't know somehow it seems sufficient
> to see and hear whatever coming and going is,
> losing the self to the victory
>   of stones and trees,
> of bending sandpit lakes, crescent
> round groves of dwarf pine:
>
> for it is not so much to know the self
> as to know it as it is known
>   by galaxy and cedar cone,
> as if birth had never found it
> and death could never end it: . . .
>
> so I look and reflect, but the air's glass
> jail seals each thing in its entity:
>
> no use to make any philosophies here:
>   I see no
> god in the holly, hear no song from
> the snowbroken weeds: Hegel is not the winter
> yellow in the pines: the sunlight has never
> heard of trees: surrendered self among
>   unwelcoming forms: stranger,
> hoist your burdens, get on down the road.
>   ("Gravelly Run")

To lose the self to the victory of stones and trees (reminiscent of Words-worth's "rolled round in earth's diurnal course / with rocks and stones and trees") is Ammons' great trope for oneness and for "sufficiency." The casual tone of the poem ("I don't know somehow it seems sufficient . . .") belies the import of the philosophical issue. Where Stevens' answer to the question of what will suffice is "nothing" ("The mind can never be satisfied, never"), Ammons suggests that this intimacy with nature, indeed this self-loss, is itself what will suffice. The victory of nature over the self is perceived as the self's own victory. In this union, the self comes to know itself as it is known by nature—by galaxy and cedar cone—much like St. Paul wishes to come to be known by God ("Now I see as in a mirror, darkly, but later I shall see face to face; now I know only in part, but later I shall know as I am known"). St. Paul conceives of this moment as revelation, and for Ammons the opposite of "seeing darkly" is a "clearing." At the clearing the self enters the spinning dance of nature, in which there are no beginnings or endings, only ceaseless transformations. Neither birth nor death can find this naturalized self, for the self passes into the universe of things.

Yet the last two stanzas move away from this proposed oneness, and present a self that has been turned back to itself, to its opacity and its homelessness. Nature's silent assimilation of the self becomes here the opposite movement—a movement by which each object in nature closes itself off from poetic scrutiny, seals itself in the air's glass jail. The sense of power and sacrality of nature—the god in the holly—is absent, for what we read into nature is not what nature knows. Nature is constituted here by "unwelcoming forms," and the poet's surrender is translated into estrangement. Amid the richness of nature he is the "stranger" who obtrudes, who must hoist the burden of his isolation and move on.

This sense of estrangement is linked in Ammons to the problematic of naming. In "Two Motions" language is the will to clarity, yet what Ammons demands of poetic language is that it not cast a shadow but uncover the deep radiance of things. To "stir" things into radiance is another version of the poet's assimilation into the continuum of nature, and Ammons' predilection for the colon, which he uses as liberally as Dickinson does her dashes, is the syntactic equivalent of this constant "passage." The colon makes of each phrase an example that opens up into and looks back upon another example, and all together constitute not a strict naming of the object but a mirroring of its flowing movement. Yet there is in "Two Motions" a sense that poetic language entails not flowing but separation—"in naming have we divided what / unnaming will not undivide"— and the poem ends with the will to "disperse the ruin of our gains"— that is to say, the poem—so that we may reach the unspeakable radiance.

> . . . listen for the things I have left out:
>   I am
>   aware
> of them, as you must be, or you will miss
> the non-song

in my singing: it is not that words *cannot* say
what is missing: it is only that what is missing
            cannot
      be missed if
spoken: read the parables of my unmaking.
                                    ("Unsaid")

Poetic language constitutes an absence because it displaces the very thing
it attempts to name, but Ammons' strategy here is to "unname," to "unmake,"
to force upon poetic language the recognition of its limits and thus to
open it up to what is absent within it. The recognition of absence thus
becomes the potential for presence. What is missed and lamented becomes
insistently present by virtue of being missed. Thus for Ammons poetry
comes to be not a celebration of presence but an elegy which takes the
form of a celebration. What is broken turns to radiance: "out of place, /
recalcitrant, the one observed fact / that tears us into questioning: / what
has not / joined dies in order to redeem, with / loss of singleness extends
the form, / or unassimilable, leads us on" ("The Misfit"). The tearing or
breaking of the "fact" ("the unassimilable fact leads us on") is also the
tearing or breaking of the word, the unnaming which miraculously and
circuitously "leads us on." What is out of place, what tears us into
questioning, what remains unassimilable (one is reminded of Stevens'
"that which rejects it saves it in the end") promotes our movement
beyond the space of our estrangement.

To be a misfit, in a poem entitled "Muse," is more pointedly to be
broken, to be at the point where language itself becomes vision.

            From the dark
      fragmentations
            build me up
      into a changed brilliant shape,

            realized order,
         mind singing again
   new song, moving into the slow beat and

            disappearing beat
               of perfect resonance:

         how many
times must I be broken and reassembled! anguish of becoming,
      pain of moulting,
descent! before the unending moment of vision:

   how much disorder must I learn to tolerate
      to find materials
               for the new house of my sight!

        arrange me
        into disorder
   near the breaking of the pattern
   but

          should disorder start to
    tear, the breaking down of possible return,
      oh rise gleaming in recall,

  sing me again towering remade, born into a wider
      order, structures deepening,
           inching rootlike into the dark!

Song for Ammons is the privileged word for poem—a poem that never reaches words, or that transcends them, the "disappearing beat / of perfect resonance." Perfection is aligned here with disappearance, vision with breaking, singing with loss. To be broken is to "see," and the poet prays to the muse to "arrange him into disorder near the breaking of the pattern" so that he may come to the point of vision and of voice, then "recall" him from ultimate fragmentation ("Oh rise gleaming in recall / sing me again towering remade") so that he may speak. The poem utters the danger of scattering and loss (the breaking of the pattern mirrored even in the changing indentations of the lines), the simultaneity of seeing and breaking, and finally becomes a prayer for the reconstitution of language "near the breaking."

    In "The Strait" the poet again recognizes the muse's presence, which leaves "wounds that are invisible," and he is fearful that like her he might go past return. But the poem witnesses a turning back, a passage from song to language, from the visionary to the actual: "step / by step into the / actual, / truth descending / breaks, / reaches us as / fragmentation / hardened / into words." Poetic language, in the measure in which it brings us to "see," leaves an invisible wound or scar—Dickinson's internal difference—but it remains precisely a language, a naming that can never suffice the vision of presence. Song has a power in Ammons which poetic language paradoxically is denied, so that his poems give us both the unspeakable vision and the wounds that are the marks of its passage, the fragmentary language which remains on the page. Stevens' "Is there a poem that never reaches words" is echoed by Ammons' "Is there a statement perfect in its speech," yet both know the woeful interaction between presence and absence. In "Spindle," for example, "song is a violence / of icicles and / windy trees . . . a violence to make / that can destroy," but the song is unnamable vision, and the poem is finally what Ammons terms fragmentation hardened into words. The poem is a song that "takes its blessings to itself / and gets away" ("Medium").

This dialectic of presence and absence runs through the Ammons canon, and it accounts for the double perspective of poetry as vision and poetry as loss. In *The Snow Poems* the poet attempts to make nature "a dance of mind, not words" and the poem reaches for words that transcend themselves and disappear:

> if words
> hurt me, why do I
> come to them to move a saying through:
> am I saying in words how I wish nature
> in fact were, though impersonal: fluent,
> yielding, showy, a dance of mind not
> words (though in words) but things:
> I could get something straight but
> it would stop winding:
>
> with words to make nature sound off
> speak up
> till we find the place where it
> will say nothing further,
> be of no further use, an example to
> no further imposition,
> an illustration of, allegory of, nothing
>
> so that we can achieve the podium of
> inhumanity, the clearing, wherefrom
> we can look back and away to the
> astonishing thing, man's rise and demise,
> and then what, the crazy universe here,
> here, here for thousands, even millions
> of years, going on with purposes, if
> any, not ours: room
> enough for every correction of view,
> where perspective is never sold out, utero,
> utero, the
> commencement before the commencement.
>
> ("Hard Lard")

There is a will in this passage to find the place where nature is so completely itself that it will say nothing—a vision of silence arrived at through the spinning dance of words. Ammons calls this place or this moment "the clearing," and indeed it is a moment of transparence, words that have themselves become part of the "spinning dance" of nature. "A dance of mind not words (though in words) but things" suggests the ultimate connection between mind and nature, a connection that reaches back in Ammons to what he terms "commencement"—the origin which is the clearing, where poetry and nature become dance.

Yet this particular poem has difficulty beginning and ending—"hard lard hard fact . . ." is a rather awkward beginning, and "I have something / to lean against" hardly an adequate ending to a poem that deals with the clearing. Beginning and ending signal the inevitable fragmentation or hardening, the halting of the dance. Poetic language wills relation but brings about disruption; it yearns for origins yet finds itself bound by the temporal world. A promise of presence and a recognition of absence, it is the trace of a song that as Stevens says "never clears."

The desire to clear the Stevensian "edge of song" is very strong in Ammons, and some of his longer poems offer strategies toward this transparence. In "Hibernaculum" Ammons speaks of poetic language as a connection between self and world:

> poems connect the threads between the tuft of his head
> and the true water: that's important to him, like roots
> to a turf: without it, the separation would be awful:
>
> poems deepen his attention till what he is thinking
> catches the energy of a deep rhythm: then he becomes
> essentially one: one in thought and motion: . . .

Like Stevens' "Tattoo," the poem is a web of connections between poet and nature, so that the very process of thinking becomes a process of relation—"one in thought and motion"—taking part, through the mind's projections, in the deep rhythm of being. Similarly in "The Marriage" Ammons speaks of threads and tangles and spools, of binding filaments of sight by which meanings of the mind and the being of being become one: "ah, this caught thing! / it can't get loose from / meanings and the mind / can't pull free of it." Mind and world for Ammons are bound together in this dream of a deep rhythm, and in "Hibernaculum" he views mind as another earth, earth as the origin of mind, earth as its visionary end:

> . . . even before it was
> mind it was mind plausible: it was the earth: when
> it is fully born, it will be another earth, just like
> the earth, but visionary, earth luminous with sight.

Vico speaks of this sensory apprehension of the world among the first human thinkers, and associates sublimity with what he calls a corporeal imagination—an imagination which apprehends through the senses, but which further responds to the unknown by creating its own relations, thus understanding the things which it has made. Ammons affirms the mind-nature relationship, but he recognizes the potential of poetic language to so position itself that its relations with the world are severed, that it dismisses reality: "for language heightens by dismissing reality, . . . / language must / not violate the bit, event, percept, / fact—the concrete—otherwise the separation that means / the death of language shows" ("Essay on Poetics"). What keeps language alive for Ammons is its Vichian contact with the concrete, and the danger of language is that it may transgress its purpose, lose its relation to the real. Yet the severance of language's bonds with nature, which Ammons sees as the death of language and Vico as a fall, is a violation which repeatedly and pointedly occurs in this canon, almost as if the purpose of poetic language were to achieve sublimity by its renewed transgressions.

Part of the reason for this attitude is that, as we have seen, nature has a way of withdrawing from the word's revelation: ". . . to see if I could take on the center of a filled out / world but heard from another fallen tree / a branch-trickle whose small music / from breakage and hindrance brought the world / whole and full again and to itself" ("Three Travelogues"). The breaking of the branch is a revelation of nature unto nature, but one from which the poetic word is shut out. As the poet tries to discover a center, the breaking of the branch makes the world whole, full, and *to itself*. Nature remains radically alien to the poet, and wills, so to speak, an antagonistic relation to the word. The word, then, is not revelation but appropriation—a stealing, a netting, and a plunder:

> I have appropriated the windy twittering of aspen leaves
> into language, stealing something from reality like a
> silverness: drop-scapes of ice from peak sheers:
>
> much of the rise in brooks over slow-rolled glacial stones:
> the loop of reeds over the shallow's edge when birds
> feed on the rafts of algae: I have taken right out of the
>
> air the clear streaks of bird music and held them in my
> head like shifts of sculpture glint: I have sent language
> through the mud roils of a raccoon's paws like a net,
>
> netting the roils: made my own uses of a downwind's
> urgency on a downward stream: held with a large scape
> of numbness the black distance upstream to the mountains
>
> flashing and bursting: meanwhile, everything else, frog,
> fish, bear, gnat has turned in its provinces and made off
> with its uses: my mind's indicted by all I've taken.

The poem is appropriately entitled "Plunder," and is reminiscent of "plunder poems" in the Romantic tradition—the "merciless ravage" of Wordsworth's "nutting" is just one example. Poetic language here takes into itself in acts of stealth and violence the detailed expanse of the landscape. The windy twittering of aspen leaves, the black distance upsteam to the mountains flashing and bursting, the loop of reeds over the shallow's edge—these are Ammons' glimmerings of a continuum which, in speaking, he necessarily brings to a halt. If presence is to be arrived at through language, language paradoxically spells out the impossibility of presence. In some sense the verbs in this poem tell the story of language's necessary relation to the external world—the story of a will to power, the will, as Ammons says in "Cut the Grass," "to take on the roundness and withdrawal of the deep dark." The poet's desire is for clear vision ("between life and me obtrude / no symbolic forms"—"This Black Rich Country"), yet poetic language is this ambiguous obtrusion, that which makes us "see" and that which keeps us from seeing. In "Plunder" it "takes" from reality, and takes possession of reality, but the possession is tainted because finally language closes over an absence. It makes its "own uses" of nature, and holds it "with numbness." The numbness is a trope for blankness here, for to hold and not to feel what one is holding is to arrive precisely at a point of detachment and opacity, the point of disjunction between the axis of vision and the axis of things. The poet has willed nature into submission, but nature at the end "[makes] off with its uses"—the uses of nature itself, which means that nature as in the preceding poem closes itself off from the poet, and the uses of poetic language, which is rendered silent by the disappearance of its subject. Poetic language in this poem takes what is not proper to it, and is left at the end with the burden of its ravage.

This ravage is more than once resisted by nature in the Ammons canon. In "Salt Flats" the poet runs across the sand informing it with glyph and figure (themselves the figures of writing), yet nature refuses to be textualized or marked, and the wind comes in a strange personalization ("set down its many hands") to "make him out." To make him out suggests nature's recognition of the self, but a recognition that again as in the preceding poem entails an indictment of his actions. Nature in Ammons holds to its inviolability, does not wish to exceed itself, and the poet's movements are always a violation of its state of being. At the end of "The City Limits," the "leaf does not increase itself above the grass, and the dark / work of the deepest cells is of a tune with May bushes / and fear lit by the breadth of such calmly turns to praise." Ammons once again in this poem sums up a powerful mode of the American tradition—the Whitmanian leaf of grass which democratizes radiance, the Stevensian cry of leaves that do not transcend themselves. For Stevens the absence of fantasia is a mournful cry—leaves that do not transcend themselves can say nothing, he nothing more than what they are. In Ammons' poem such absence of fantasia is to be cherished, for the imagination's silence is in some sense the apprehension of nature's radiance. Yet the last line tellingly suggests that fear turned to praise is in some measure already fantasia, that the radiance pours its abundance without selection, but its fountains are always within.

Ammons is uneasy at the power the mind can exert over nature, and he stresses the problematic elements of locating the source of radiance within. In "The Unmirroring Peak" the mind has a will to fullness, to completion, but that will imprisons it within itself and blocks any relationship with nature. "A land, the mind's, / where nothing comes / to pass, / lies, abides, untouchable / and unyielding: / down the slopes / changeable forms and colors / assume their fictions, / dread, joy, / despair but lie, press against / the rise whose angle / is invariant and whose / completion is final." The fictions here—fantasia—are nature's; they are part of nature's ability to change forms and colors. The mind, on the other hand, reaches a deadly point of completion, a fullness that is unyielding, invariant, final. In rejecting its complex relationship to temporality, to "what changes: the changeable which / everything . . . is," the mind renders itself homeless. Though changes may themselves be the fictions of continuum, what is eternal and unyielding has no place in the world we know. Completion becomes the opposite movement of "Peak," and leads to opacity and alienation.

In *Tape for the Turn of the Year* Ammons suggests that there is no imaginable center except the one the lichen makes, yet the little volume *Diversifications* suggests that the victory of stones and trees does not take place. The self no longer simply yields here to the outside world: it has to be "translated" into it, and that translation—in symbol and in space—does not occur. There is a resistance of mind in *Diversifications* which places a different emphasis on the poetic enterprise, even when such resistance is considered a defeat and not a victory.

> After the complex reductions come
> the simple reductions, the apple
> firm in the hand, weightless in the mind,
>
> the elms drifted out of their roots, strung
> into a green-wind wear, a sense of
> seeing through never ending
>
> in the endings, a piling into the sun
> of the mind's sun returned: and then,
> high with reductions, the chill that

> we live where we can't live but
> live there if we live, a house of mind
> we never quite get the door open to.
> ("Mind")

This little poem sums up one of the strains of *Diversifications:* the mind's power, and its homelessness. After the complex reductions of abstract thinking come the simple reductions to an apple that is held but not felt, not apprehended well—an apple weightless in the mind. Vico mourns the passage from the corporeal imagination to abstract thought, and locates sublimity in the imagination's ability to respond to its fear of the unimagined and alien environment by imagining it and thus rendering it knowable. The poetic mind in Vico apprehends the world through the senses, responds in fear, creates sublimely, and comes to know centrally the world which it has made. The center for Vico is not the lichen but the mind. For Ammons, this movement is itself transgression, a violation which reduces to the disparity between mind and nature—the apple held but not felt or understood imaginatively, the mind which renders nature weightless. There is a sense of the inefficacy of nature, since the apple cannot make its weight felt any more than in "The Unmirroring Peak" the changeable forms and colors can penetrate the invariable angle of the mind. But the inefficacy of nature is translated here, albeit gloomily, into the mind's power, into its potential to "make." The elms drift, and the mind sees through things—a sense of seeing through never ending in the endings— without ever coming to the lichen as center, without ever finding a point of rest. But its alienness stems too from its inability to create a place—a place of mind—that is, as Stevens says, fully made, fully apparent, fully found. The mind's sun piles up into the sun, and the outside world is always there to remind us, alien and unapproachable as it is, of our homelessness. We live where we can't live, this poem tells us, because we cannot fully belong to nature, or to ourselves. We inhabit a house of mind which remains in some sense as "other" as the world of nature, a house we never quite get the door open to but which offers us at least the potential for such exploration. The poem thus witnesses a turn from nature to the mind's centrality, from the privileged place of the lichen to the mind's potential to create. "Given mind, we became / stranger here: / with mind, we convert / strangeness / to humanness: / we unnaturalize" (*Tape*). The mind renders the world strange and "unfamiliar" so that it may more properly inhabit it. The lichen is finally "unnaturalized" in *Tape for the Turn of the Year,* and the mind's estrangement from nature becomes an index of its potential to make the world anew, to convert "strangeness" to imaginative humanity.

This movement from the privileging of nature to the privileging of the mind is most movingly set forth in the dedicatory poem to *Sphere*.

> I went to the summit and stood in the high nakedness:
> the wind tore about this
> way and that in confusion and its speech could not
> get through to me nor could I address it:
> still I said as if to the alien in myself
>   I do not speak to the wind now:
> for having been brought this far by nature I have been
> brought out of nature
> and nothing here shows me the image of myself:
> for the word *tree* I have been shown a tree
> and for the word *rock* I have been shown a rock,
> for stream, for cloud, for star
> this place has provided firm implication and answering
>   but where here is the image for *longing*:
> so I touched the rocks, their interesting crusts:
> I flaked the bark of stunt-fir:
> I looked into space and into the sun
> and nothing answered my word *longing*:
>   goodbye, I said, goodbye, nature so grand and
> reticent, your tongues are healed up into their own
> element
> and as you have shut up you have shut me out: I am
> as foreign here as if I had landed, a visitor:
> so I went back down and gathered mud
> and with my hands made an image for *longing*:
>   I took the image to the summit: first
> I set it here, on the top rock, but it completed
> nothing: then I set it there among the tiny firs
> but it would not fit:
> so I returned to the city and built a house to set
> the image in
> and men came into my house and said
>   that is an image for *longing*
> and nothing will ever be the same again
>   ("For Harold Bloom")

The poem begins in a rather typical way, with the poet facing the enormity of nature, at the summit, and in the midst of a blowing wind. Yet nature is here high nakedness which turns to speechlessness and which thus will not suffice. Ammons' conversations with wind and mountains are scattered through the canon, but in this poem communication between speaker and nature breaks down, and the fault seems to lie not with the poet but with the wind. The wind tears about in confusion, and the human voice takes over and addresses not the wind—"I do not speak to the wind now"—but the self. Pointedly departing from the opening of the *Collected Poems*, where the wind whips Ezra's throat and his voice goes out into the night like a drift of sand, the speaker here addresses his own self, and the turning is significant, because the self appears the only proper subject for the poem. In "So I Said I Am Ezra" the prophetic voice is scattered by the wind, and the poet is unable or unwilling to commit the act of appropriation by which Shelley's wind becomes assimilated into the poetic consciousness ("Be thou me"). In "For Harold Bloom," the second stanza expands on the priority of self over nature, for nature has brought him "this far"—to its summit (Ammons usually speaks to a mountain from the valley), but not to the self's summit or its depths. The alien in the self commands the scene now, and estrangement becomes voicing as the poem addresses the longing for wholeness that arises out of the recognition of one's otherness. The self is brought so far by nature and finally is brought out (brings itself out) of nature, because nature cannot respond to human language, cannot render back to him the image which he seeks. The poet in so much of Ammons' poetry wills to come to rest in the unknowing beneficence of nature. But nature in this poem is a condition of estrangement, for its vocabulary of objects is limited—tree, rock, stream, cloud, star—and it excludes precisely the poetic self, the reason for poetic voice. Nothing in nature can speak the self or respond to its demands, the most important of which is the longing for itself that it might know the completion of homecoming.

Thus the poet turns away from a world that is self-fulfilling, silent, and impenetrable ("as you have shut up you have shut me out") to make the missing image of the self's longing. The notion of sufficiency, welcome, and homecoming undergoes a significant transformation in Ammons: we see him move from "Gravelly Run," where "it seems sufficient / to see and hear whatever coming and going is / losing the self to the victory of stones and trees," to the affirmation of the self's own making in this poem as the only possibility to stand complete in a completed scene. The tongues of nature are "healed up" here, as if their silence were the healing / sealing of the wound made by the poet's presence, and in response the poet creates an image of the wound itself—an image of his voice. From the sufficiency of nature we pass into the metaphysics of desire, a desire that is antithetical to the notion of homecoming and yet propels the poet to reconstruct the scene, to make an image of his otherness that will yield itself to him in response. The poet turns away from nature and like a god makes from nothing—from mud, from language. His making does not transform nature, for nature remains to the end alien and forbidding, and the poet's image neither alters nor completes it. But for the poet nothing will ever be the same again, for the poem turns to itself for its own subject, creates for itself an image of its own movement through itself. The longing *is* the poem, and the poem comes to itself to discover that its homecoming is synonymous with its loss. To come home for the poem is to come to itself as longing, to find within itself the unfulfilled desire that constitutes poetic voice. Just as insistently in *The Snow Poems* Ammons reads the poem as a will to transparence born of blindness, a will to fullness that, thwarted, turns into its own dark consolation.

Chronology

1926	Born February 18, near Whiteville, N.C., the third child of W. M. Ammons and Lucy Della McKee Ammons.
1939	Graduated New Hope Elementary School.
1943	Graduated Whiteville High School.
1944–46	U.S. Navy; active service in South Pacific.
1946–50	Attended Wake Forest College.
1949	Married Phyllis Plumbo of Northfield, N.J.
1951–52	Graduate work at Berkeley.
1952–64	Managed glass factory in southern New Jersey.
1955	First book of poems, *Ommateum*, published.
1963	*Expressions of Sea Level.*
1964	Begins to teach at Cornell University, where he is now Goldwin Smith Professor of Poetry.
1965	*Corsons Inlet: A Book of Poems* and *Tape for the Turn of the Year.*
1966	*Northfield Poems* published; birth of son, John Randolph Ammons.
1968	*Selected Poems.*
1970	*Uplands: New Poems.*
1971	*Briefings: Poem's Small and Easy.*
1972	*Collected Poems: 1951–71.*
1973	National Book Award for *Collected Poems.*
1974	*Sphere: The Form of Motion*; Bollingen Prize in Poetry.
1975	*Diversifications: Poems.*
1977	*The Snow Poems.*
1978	*The Selected Poems: 1951–77*; *Highgate Road*, privately printed.
1980	*Selected Longer Poems.*
1981	*A Coast of Trees: Poems*; National Book Critics Circle Award.
1982	*Worldly Hopes: Poems.*
1983	*Lake Effect Country: Poems.*

Contributors

HAROLD BLOOM, Sterling Professor of Humanities at Yale University, is the author of *The Anxiety of Influence, Poetry and Repression* and many other volumes of literary criticism. His forthcoming study, *Freud: Transference and Authority,* attempts a full-scale reading of all of Freud's major writings. He is the general editor of *The Chelsea House Library of Literary Criticism.*

RICHARD HOWARD is equally renowned as poet, critic and translator. *Alone with America* gathers his essays on contemporary American poetry. His own poetry includes *Untitled Subjects* and *Findings.*

JOHN ASHBERY is recognized as one of the crucial living poets. His books include *The Double Dream of Spring, Houseboat Days, Self-Portrait in a Convex Mirror* and *A Wave.*

HYATT H. WAGGONER is Professor Emeritus of English at Brown University. He has published widely on American poetry and Emerson.

HELEN VENDLER is Professor of English at Boston University and at Harvard. Her books include studies of Yeats, Stevens, George Herbert and Keats.

PATRICIA A. PARKER is Associate Professor of English at the University of Toronto, and the author of *Inescapable Romance.*

DAVID KALSTONE is Professor of English at Rutgers University. His books include *Sidney's Poetry* and *Five Temperaments.*

JEROME MAZZARO is Professor of English at the State University of New York, Buffalo. He has written extensively on contemporary and modern poetry.

LINDA ORR, Professor of Romance Languages at Duke University, is the author of a book on Jules Michelet.

DENIS DONOGHUE is Henry James Professor of English and American Literature at New York University. His books include *Thieves of Fire* and *Ferocious Alphabets.*

R. W. FLINT, critic and translator, edited *The Selected Writings of Marinetti.*

ROBERT PINSKY is Professor of English at the University of California, Berkeley. His criticism includes *Landor's Poetry* and *The Situation of Poetry*; his poetry includes *An Explanation of America* and *History of My Heart*.

FREDERICK BUELL, Professor of English at Queens College, is the author of a study of W. H. Auden.

HUGH LUKE, Professor of English at the University of Nebraska, has published many articles on Romantic and modern poetry.

DAVID LEHMAN, critic and poet, is book reviewer for *Newsweek*. He has edited critical anthologies on the poetry of Ashbery and Merrill.

JOHN HOLLANDER is Professor of English at Yale University. His most recent books are *Powers of Thirteen*, a long poem, and *The Figure of Echo*, a critical study of allusion in poetry.

HELEN REGUEIRO ELAM is Professor of English at the State University of New York, Albany, and the author of *The Limits of Imagination*.

Bibliography

Ammons, A. R. *Ommateum*. Philadelphia: Dorrance, 1955.

————. *Expressions of Sea Level*. Athens: Ohio State University Press, 1963.

————. *Corsons Inlet: A Book of Poems*. Ithaca: Cornell University Press, 1965.

————. *Uplands: New Poems*. New York: Norton, 1970.

————. *Briefings, Poems Small and Easy.* New York: Norton, 1971.

————. *Collected Poems, 1951–1971*. New York: Norton, 1972.

————. *Sphere: The Form of Motion*. New York: Norton, 1974.

————. *Diversifications: Poems*. New York: Norton, 1975.

————. *The Selected Poems, 1951–1977*. New York: Norton, 1977.

————. *The Snow Poems*. New York: Norton, 1977.

————. *A Coast of Trees: Poems*. New York: Norton, 1981.

————. *Worldly Hopes: Poems*. New York: Norton, 1982.

————. *Lake Effect Country: Poems*. New York: Norton, 1983.

Bedient, Calvin. "Sphere." *The New York Times Book Review* (Dec. 22, 1974): 12–13.

Bloom, Harold. "Emerson and Ammons: A Coda." *Diacritics* 3 (Winter 1973): 45–46.

————. "In the Shadow of Shadows: For Now." In *The Map of Misreading*. New York: Oxford University Press, 1975.

————. "Dark and Radiant Peripheries" and "The New Transcendentalism." In *Figures of Capable Imagination*. New York: The Seabury Press, 1976.

Davie, Donald. "Cards of Identity." *New York Review of Books* 6 (March 1975): 10–11.

Fink, Thomas A. "The Problem of Freedom and Restriction in the Poetry of A. R. Ammons." *Modern Poetry Studies* 11: 138–48.

Fishman, Charles. "A. R. Ammons: The One Place to Dwell." *The Hollins Critic* 19 (Dec. 1982): 2–11.

Fogel, Daniel. "Toward an Ideal Raggedness: The Design of A. R. Ammons's *Hibernaculum*." *Contemporary Poetry* 3: 25–37.

Hartman, Geoffrey H. "Collected Poems 1951–1971." *The New York Times Book Review* (Nov. 19, 1972): 39–40.

Holder, Allen. *A. R. Ammons*. Boston: Twayne, 1978.

Hollander, John. "Briefings." *The New York Times Book Review* (May 9, 1971).

Howard, Richard. "A New Beginning." *Nation* (Jan, 18, 1971): 90–92.

Jacobson, Josephine. "The Talk of the Giants." *Diacritics* 3 (Winter 1973): 34–39.

Kalstone, David. "Uplands." *The New York Times Book Review* (May 9, 1971).

Kirby, David. "The Measure of Man." *Times Literary Supplement* (April 24, 1981).

Lehman, David. "Perplexities Embraced." *Times Literary Supplement* (May 25, 1984): 523.

McClatchey, J. D. "New Books in Review." *Yale Review* (Spring 1975): 430–32.

Meredith, William. "I Will Tell You About It Because It Is Interesting." *Parnassus* 2 (Fall/Winter 1973).

Perloff, Marjorie. "Tangled Versions of the Truth: Ammons and Ashbery at 50." *American Poetry Review* 7, (1978).

Reid, Alfred S. "The Poetry of A. R. Ammons." *The South Carolina Review* 12, (Fall 1979).

Rosenfeld, Alvin. "A. R. Ammons: The Poems of a Solitary." *American Poetry Review* 5, (1976).

Rotella, Guy. "Ghostlier Demarcations, Keener Sounds: A. R. Ammons's *Corson's Inlet.*" *Concerning Poetry* 10 (Fall 1977).

Vendler, Helen. "Spheres and Ragged Edges." *Poetry* (Oct. 1980): 26–33.

Wilson, Matthew. "Homecoming in A. R. Ammons's *Tape for the Turn of the Year.*" *Contemporary Poetry* 4, (1981): 60–76.

Wolf, Thomas J. "A. R. Ammons and William Carlos Williams: A Study in Style and Meaning." *Contemporary Poetry* (1977) 3: 1–16.

Zweig, Paul. "The Raw and the Cooked." *Partisan Review* (Fall 1974): 608–12.

Acknowledgments

"The Natural Man" by R. W. Flint from *Parnassus* 4 (Spring/Summer 1976), copyright © 1976 by Poetry in Review Foundation. Reprinted by permission.

"Ammons" by Robert Pinsky from *The Situation of Poetry*, copyright © 1976 by Princeton University Press. Reprinted by permission.

" 'To Be Quiet in the Hands of the Marvelous' " by Frederick Buell from *The Iowa Review* 8 (Winter 1977), copyright © 1977 by the University of Iowa. Reprinted by permission.

"Event: Corrective: Cure" by A. R. Ammons from *Acts of Mind: Conversations with Contemporary Poets*, copyright © 1983 by The University of Alabama Press. Reprinted by permission.

"Gestures of Shape, Motions of Form" by Hugh Luke from *Pebble* 18, 19, 20, copyright © 1979 by Greg Kuzma. Reprinted by permission.

"Where Motion and Shape Coincide" by David Lehman from *Parnassus* 9 (Fall/Winter 1981), copyright © 1982 by Poetry in Review Foundation. Reprinted by permission.

" 'I Went to the Summit' " by John Hollander from *The Yale Review* (Winter 1981), copyright © 1981 by Yale University Press. Reprinted by permission.

"Radiances and Dark Consolations" by Helen Reguerio Elam, copyright © 1985 by Helen Regueiro Elam. Published for the first time in this volume.

Index